Mazda MX-5 Miata

Roadster

Design & development: the inside story told by Mazda's designers & engineers

Written by Toshihiko Hirai and others
Edited by Takaharu 'Koby' Kobayakawa
Translated by Daisuke Koujiya

VELOCE PUBLISHING
THE PUBLISHER OF FINE AUTOMOTIVE BOOKS

This edition first published in 2004 by Veloce Publishing Limited, 33 Trinity Street, Dorchester DT1 1TT, England. Fax 01305 268864/e-mail info@veloce.co.uk/web www.veloce.co.uk or www.velocebooks.com. Original Japanese-language edition published by Miki Press under the title *Roadster*.
ISBN: 1-904788-29-7/UPC 36847-00329-6
Readers with ideas for automotive books, or books on other transport or related hobby subjects, are invited to write to the editorial director of Veloce Publishing at the above address.
British Library Cataloguing in Publication Data - A catalogue record for this book is available from the British Library.
Typesetting, design and page make-up all by Veloce Publishing Ltd on Apple Mac. Printed in Italy

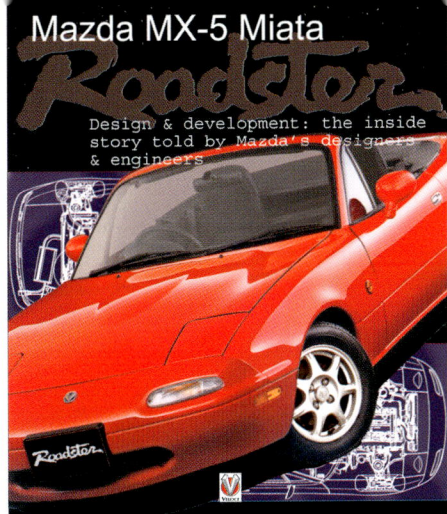

Contents

Jacket of the original Japanese-language edition published by Miki Press.

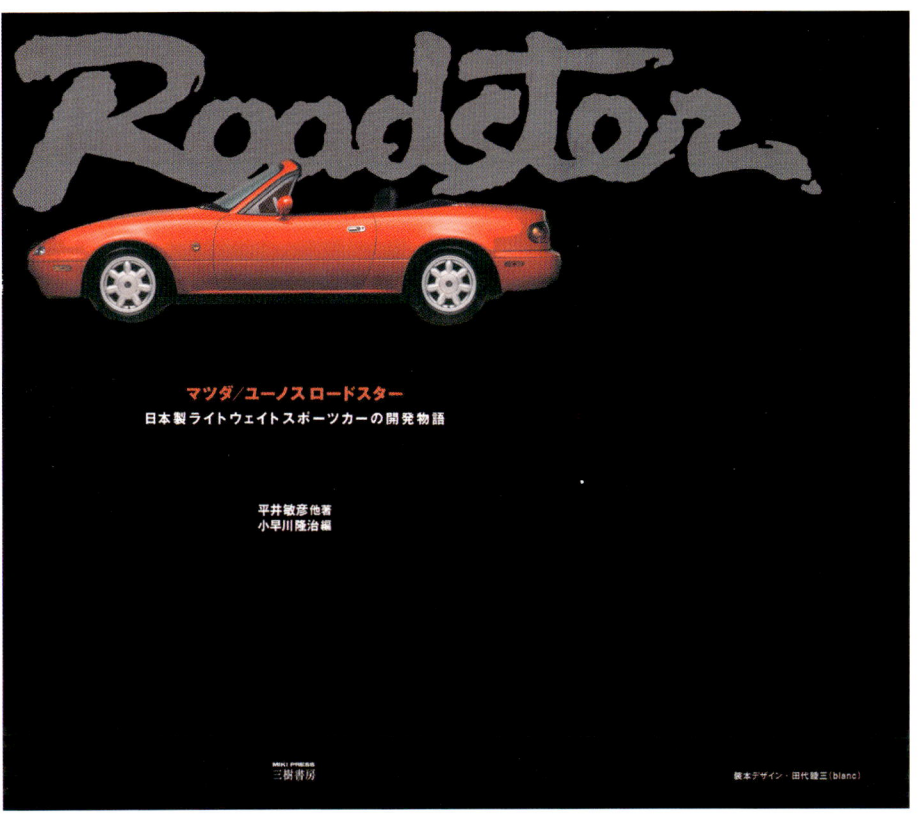

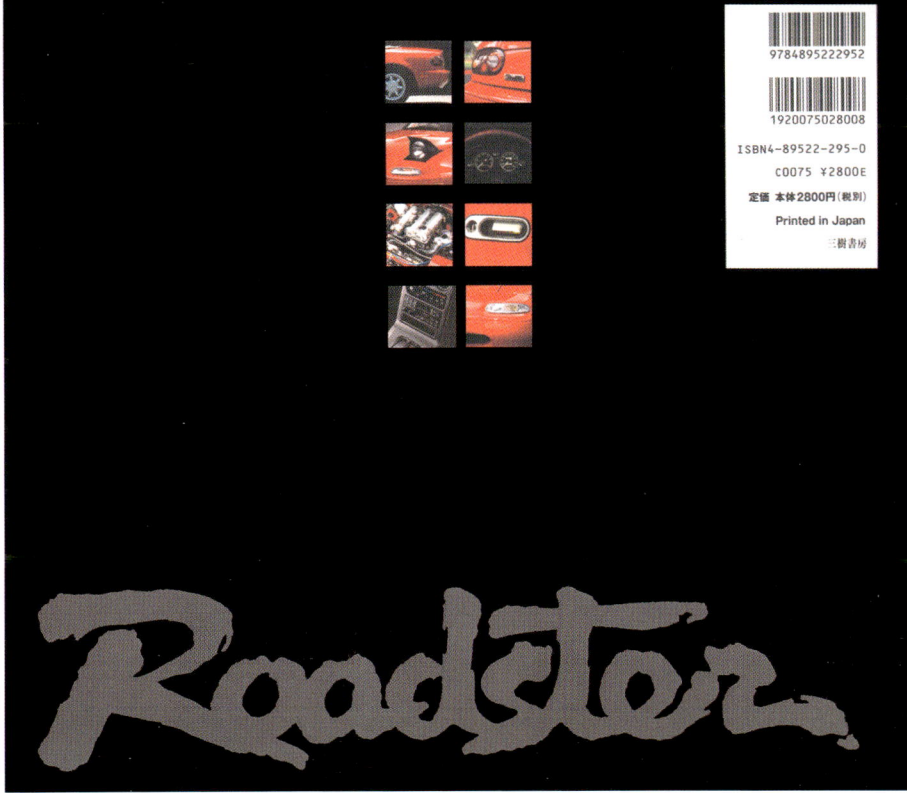

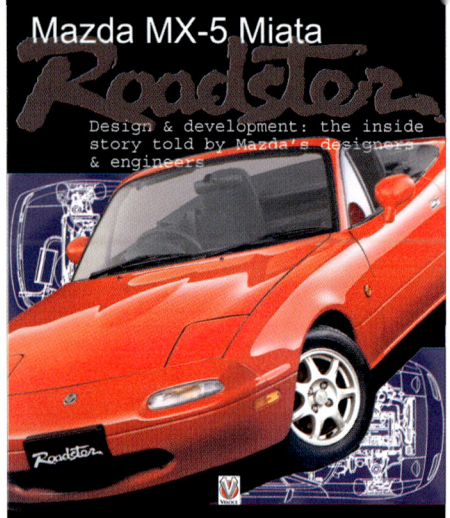

Preface

The Mazda MX-5/Miata is a two-seater, lightweight roadster of traditional layout, with front engine and rear-wheel drive. Since its debut, the car has been exceptionally well received by the global market, selling far beyond Mazda's original expectations, and has become the company's image-leading product. At a time when the sports car market was diminishing worldwide, the efforts of Mazda's engineers, grasping the attention of the public with this little, classic-looking sports car, should be highly regarded.

This book, unlike any other on Mazda's roadster, is a compilation of memoirs of the individual engineers who participated in the car's development, bringing to life the process of how this endearing little automobile was developed and brought to market. This book relates many true stories that were not previously available to the public. It should be noted and accepted, however, that because each chapter is written by an individual, there are unavoidable repetitions over some design issues which involved several parties: however, the different perspectives are fascinating.

The editors and writers are happy to see this book published, first in Japanese and now in English, so that the story of this delightful Japanese roadster - welcomed and accepted by sports car enthusiasts all over the world - is recorded and made available for posterity.

Brian Long, Tokyo

Publisher's note: Many of the technical illustrations in this book are original, historical documents rarely seen by 'outsiders.' For the sake of authenticity, these documents and other illustrations have been reproduced in their original Japanese format, complete with pictograms: the relevant captions and text should explain their content.

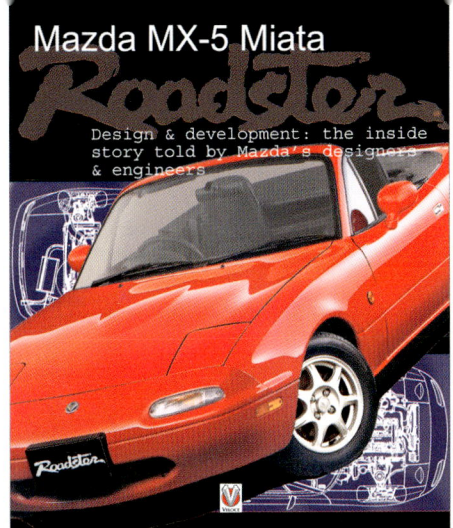

Mazda MX-5 Miata

Roadster

Design & development: the inside
story told by Mazda's designers
& engineers

1

Development of the MX-5/Miata
by **Toshihiko Hirai**

From the outset of development, Hirai volunteered to lead this difficult task. Since joining Mazda in 1961, Hirai worked on the layout design of all Mazda cars and firmly established a sense of total balance for a car design. Although the success of the MX-5/Miata has been widely recognized today, in the beginning Hirai had to endure many difficulties and half-hearted support from within the company. It is very questionable that the car would look the way it does today - even that it would have reached the production stage at all - without his involvement.

Hirai, looking back, has said that during his temporary transfer to a subsidiary dealership he heard many customers say: "We don't want a car from Mazda that's similar to a Toyota or a Nissan." Although this was not a happy time for him, these remarks really hit home, and without this unhappy experience the roadster project would probably not have come to fruition.

Soon after the roadster went

into production, Hirai encountered another challenge: he was coerced to become involved in developing the AZ-1 (a mini sports car) for Mazda, which was a market failure. Hirai left the company before the compulsory retirement age and became a professor of engineering at Oita University. Subsequently, in 1999, Hirai retired from the university and now works as a visiting lecturer.

Hirai recently commented: "The experience you get when you are young may change your later life. It is, therefore, worth challenging something while you are young, even though you may not really like to do it. I was fortunate to have had a career full of enjoyable adventures and tension and, as my curiosity will never cease, my adventure will never end ..."

T. Kobayakawa

The Mazda MX-5/Miata is a lightweight sports car (LWS), developed by Mazda as a strategic addition to its product line for the then forthcoming 1990s and then the new millennium. At the start of its development, we wanted to provide an answer to the long-term quest for the ideal LWS, which could later become a major part of Mazda's sports tradition. We wanted to create a back-to-basics car that would provide pure and simple driving pleasure for consumers in an age of high technology.

To achieve this goal, we chose a two-seater model with an open top, featuring a traditional front engine/rear wheel-drive layout. We put Mazda's state-of-the-art technology into this simple concept, enabling the owner to achieve the ultimate unity of car and driver.

There was only one body design and a single powerplant

choice. The clear-cut design concept required no more than that, but, in reality, there were no extra resources available from the company for the development of this car: we had to fight for them throughout the development of the MX-5/Miata.

By way of an introduction - and as the Product Program Manager responsible for the MX-5/Miata - I would first like to state the key targets of the project and its product outline, as well as our philosophical background relating to development. In the latter part of this book, engineers and designers who were directly involved in the project will tell their own stories of the MX-5/Miata as it was developed.

The birth of a project
To be asked to design a sports car must be the dream of any automotive engineer. To achieve the goal, however, engineers must

negotiate many hurdles and difficulties. It was no exception at Mazda and, until the MX-5/Miata was officially on track for mass production, many problems were encountered and overcome.

In the Executive Committee meeting of February 1986, an LWS, as originally proposed by the Technical Center (TC), was approved (along with many other potential projects): I was appointed as its Product Program Manager. The role of a Product Program Manager at Mazda at that time was to function as a pivot for the entire project, from basic layout design to mass production, with authority to control all aspects. Despite the heavy responsibilities of this project, very few staff were assigned to help with it.

Mazda was very busy meeting the market demand for multiple sales channels, and there was a chronic shortage of human resources, with many new projects waiting in line. In order to cover this shortage in manpower, the company tried to outsource some of its development work to outside consultants.

Upon reviewing the pre-prototype design, which was provided by a consultant company, it was difficult for me to imagine that the proposed vehicle was fit for Mazda's mass production system. Whilst I understood how difficult it must be to come up with a suitable design outside of the

company, I quickly came to the conclusion that the project had to be handled in Japan to have any hope of success. It was a hard lesson ...

My first task, then, was to gear-up to do the job within Mazda, and terminate the existing contract we had with the British consulting firm (which had previously achieved some great results in plastic body development). After some hard negotiation, the outsourcing agreement for the roadster was terminated in March 1986. My next objective was to secure the necessary manpower for the vehicle's development.

The first task in the design of an automobile is to prepare the basic layout drawing (also called the whole layout drawing), which will show the location of all components in the new car. I was told by the head of the R&D Administration Department that its engineers, who were supposed to prepare this drawing, were not available, as they were too busy with the many other projects in-hand. My first few days as the Product Program Manager were spent idle as far as basic design work was concerned. I had to beg to get a few engineers for this project through negotiation with Masataka Matsui (then head of the TC), who originally proposed the idea of a roadster. The newly assigned engineers were newcomers to this part of the

design process, with the exception of a Section Chief, Masaaki Watanabe. At the beginning of the design work, I had no choice but to start with a small group of mostly untrained engineers.

The Product Planning Division, charged with the commercial planning of the product, had serious reservations regarding the entire project. It maintained that there was no longer a market for a LWS anywhere in the world, and didn't agree with the detailed specification of the MX-5/Miata concept: after all, this project was not of its origin and, therefore, could not expect any support. I soon abandoned the idea of any help from this quarter.

Instead, I sought the support of the Planning Group at Mazda TC, which had originally proposed the LWS concept. The Planning Group there, headed by Masakatsu Kato and Kazuyuki Mitate, had provided minimal support so far, because it was most unusual for the TC to provide direct support for a project that would later go into mass production. I requested further support from this group, and had Hideaki Tanaka, a young planning engineer, relocated to my team for more direct control. Without this sort of flexible support and back-up from the TC, I could not have formed a project organization, or realized the important design basis of an LWS, and the whole project would have

disintegrated at an early stage in the proceedings.

In the preparation of the basic layout design, I concluded that support, other than that from the TC, could not be expected. In order to make up for the lack of human resources, I decided to introduce a computer aided design technique (it was called GNC II within Mazda) to create the basic layout design drawings. This was the company's first application of a comprehensive CAD system in project work.

Until then, major components, such as engine and suspension system layout, human engineering design, and body structure design, were all performed via two-dimensional drawings, drafted by hand. This was the first attempt to conduct such vital basic design work on a three-dimensional CAD system, and it was full of adventure, and trial and error.

The first layout design work done by the novice project engineers had one advantage: because of their relative lack of experience, they readily accepted the CAD system, which resulted in very accurate basic layout drawings, something not previously achievable with only very limited manpower. I am very grateful to those members of the TC who faced up to this difficult task, and feel proud that their work laid the foundations for the use of 3-D CAD systems in subsequent basic layout designs at Mazda.

Another objective was to find a proper location at which to conduct our work. In the beginning, a small conference room, big enough for four or five engineers, was all that was available. Situated on the 6th floor of the Development Division building, the project officially started in this conference room in March 1986. As time passed, and rumors spread that something interesting was going on in the small room, many engineers came to see the work, and volunteered to join us in the sports car project. It became obvious that a much bigger space was needed and, two months later, the project office was relocated to a bigger space within a 3-D measurement room of the Design Department.

In order to fully utilize the limited manpower available for this project, I had the basic layout design group (with Masaaki Watanabe as its leader), and vehicle engineering design group (with Noayuki Ikemizu as its leader) proceed almost concurrently in order to achieve a continuous flow of project work, even though this was quite unusual. In order to bring the project smoothly to mass production, I requested that the basic layout and vehicle engineering design teams work side-by-side. This was also an unusual step at the time and was limited to this project.

It was advantageous to accommodate all project members in one place, in order to conduct our work consistently, concurrently, and efficiently. Finally, I managed to secure one whole floor of a parking building at the Design Center. As the building was intended for parking, the floor and ceiling had no covering, and the walls had bumper-guards all around! There was also a car lift in my new, dedicated project room. It seemed a very poor environment for a creative project HQ, but we named the room the "Riverside Hotel" as it overlooked a small river. We moved into the Riverside Hotel with five CAD terminals and desks. This was the third relocation of the project office in less than a year.

The first task at the Riverside Hotel was to draft a Product Proposal to obtain corporate approval for the project, and complete all of the associated groundwork to get it on the agenda of the Executive Committee. It was July 1986, and summer was just beginning.

It soon became evident that the Riverside Hotel was an ideal location for gathering the necessary information, and conducting our work in an efficient manner, eliminating unnecessary disturbance from outsiders. Ironically, we were ultimately very thankful for such a nice working space.

Within less than a year, the project organization had become

A dream! The roadster running through the countryside with the top down. The main aim of the project was to let the driver feel at one with nature, and at one with the vehicle.

clearly defined, with support from many volunteers within the company. The concern I had at the beginning that the project would not survive to the mass production stage had melted away ...

Doubting the LWS project

Once the project got underway, and as more people learned about it, many questions were asked within the company. The main questions were: why front engine/rear wheel-drive (FR) at a time when front engine/front-wheel drive (FF) layout was more popular? Why a two-seater, with space for only two passengers? And why go for an open body? Could it be made weatherproof, and meet safety standards?

In other words, there was concern that an LWS had no place in the market with only two seats, a leaky soft-top, an unsafe open body, and an FR configuration in a period just prior to the advent of the 21st century. "You must be out of your mind!," was the usual reaction.

From the US marketing group a common question was: "Most cars now have gone to front engine/front wheel-drive configuration to reduce cost and weight, and to improve productivity. Why go back to FR now?" The opinion was that the Americans wanted an early introduction of a sporty car with the FF configuration on those grounds.

Another criticism was: "Who wants to buy an open roadster just for two people in this day when efficiency is considered ecological?" And: "Who buys a car that needs an umbrella? No chance!" The Mazda R&D arm in Germany, from whom we requested research on convertibles, reported back that to consider a soft-top in a modern automobile was a big mistake. Such a product concept was wrong and outdated.

My only response was: "I'm the guy in charge of deciding on the concept of the car. Do the work you were requested to do."

Among the opposing views, there were some that were tough to rebuff. One critic said: "From past experience of Mazda, it is evident that a convertible weighs more and costs more than a conventional coupé design." This argument was based on two previous experiences, the Familia and RX-7 Convertible, and was quite convincing, although production volume and quality requirements were quite different. I really felt no malice towards those who expressed opposing views to mine; they simply did not understand the undercurrent of LWS culture and its marketing potential. The time needed to convince these people was lengthy, however, and it really got me down.

In the end, I gave the ultimatum that if any one of three elements was ommitted - the FR layout, the two-seater configuration, or the convertible body with a soft-top - the project would end immediately. This worked in part, and the internal wrangling subsided.

The strongest support for this project came from an unexpected source; the Executive Vice-President, Yoshihiro Wada, who had a background in banking, and no technical experience.

Is this car really necessary for Mazda?

Whilst project work started, and the initial engineering drawings were prepared for release in October 1987, internal doubts persisted because of a lack of appreciation of the LWS culture. The necessity of such a concept was questioned by some at Mazda, and misgivings about the legitimacy of the design work were blamed on the designers for pursuing personal interests. I felt that the situation had reached the point where matters had to be brought to a head.

With the help of Tanaka (who had recently transferred from the TC) and Mazda North America (MANA), I decided to conduct a serious market survey in the US for the first and last time. A full-size plastic model of the concept car was made, and 245 people - chosen at random - were invited to assess the mock-up and express their views. (This was done whilst keeping the company name completely hidden from the participants.) They were shown an approximate market price and some technical details, as well as the expected performance of the car.

The participants were divided into small focus groups of seven to ten people, and interviewed by a professional interviewer. The questions we put to them at this clinic were as follows:

Is a convertible attractive, despite its potential safety concerns?
Is this design attractive?
Would you want to buy this car if it was on the market?

We gathered and analyzed the responses from the participants; every result indicated an extremely positive reaction to the concept and the design. A US importer who attended the session made a strong plea that such a car should be introduced as soon as possible, even at the cost of slowing the development of models already in the pipeline. This was a small victory for the project, as we had made this trip with a feeling of desperation.

With this result in hand, I hurried back to Japan and reported to the Executive Committee that the US market was looking forward to having a car like this once again. Executive Vice-President Wada immediately responded: "If the market is there and wants the car as soon as possible, then, as the Product Program Manager, it is your duty to make the car materialize." This comment had an immediate effect and I was no longer subject to internal criticism. Although this was another small victory, getting the car onto the market earlier than declared in the original schedule was a heavy responsibility ...

The starting date of mass production is dictated by many factors, and not easily altered unless drastic measures are taken. By taking steps to speed up the process, we were able to establish a start date of July 1989, four months earlier than the original target. The most effective way we achieved this schedule revision was to call a "design freeze," to avoid design changes after the engineering drawing release (previously the biggest threat to the development schedule). Since the detailed engineering design of the dies and tools starts after the final design changes, I, and Shigenori Fukuda (then General Manager of the Design Division), declared the design freeze in September 1987, prior to the release of the final engineering drawings.

We clearly indicated that no design changes would be accepted after this date: I was confident that, by this time, the design of the car had progressed to such a stage that no further design change would be necessary, thanks to the dedicated work of our project members. This was the first instance in the history of Mazda of enforcing an early design freeze, and it resulted in excellent results, with reduced production and tooling costs, as well as an earlier mass production start date.

An LWS - the creation of unity between man and horse

The LWS I wanted to build was not

Yabusame: the traditional Japanese art of shooting arrows at targets whilst riding on horseback. The horse and rider come together to realize the full potential of both. This is the image we had for the LWS.

a car that would possess high speed at all costs. The concept I had in mind was to enhance the basic fun that derives from sitting in the car and steering; the unity created between the car and its driver for the ultimate pleasure of driving was my target. The key phrase I chose was "Unity of man and horse."

In order to achieve this unity, and appeal to human senses in the manner established by traditional European sports cars of the 1960s, three elements came to the fore as the basis of a fun-to-drive car:

Front engine/rear-wheel drive configuration.
A two-seater cockpit.
Convertible body.

I firmly believed that these elements should be incorporated in our design. My aim was to design and produce an LWS that would meet and exceed the requirements of the 21st century by utilizing Mazda's state-of-the-art technology.

In a lightweight sports car, one of the key elements in making the driver feel the "fun-to-drive" and "unity between horse and rider" sensations is the FR configuration. The biggest advantage of this layout is that, in addition to the steering wheel, the gas pedal shares part of the steering function. The greatest pleasure for a driver of a car with that built-in "unity" is to experience the behavior of the vehicle through both vision, and the seat of his

pants, skilfully steering it through the co-ordination of hands and feet, whilst controlling the car on the road.

To achieve this unity, one option was to choose a mid-engine and rear wheel-drive (MR) configuration, but I did not want this as I thought it would sacrifice the car's utility, however minimal it may be. And, if I may put forward another reason, I felt that an LWS should not only be light in weight, but also light in price. It was very fortunate that Mazda, the third Japanese manufacturer stepping into the LWS market, still had the important FR components. Toyota adopted an MR layout for the MR2, and Honda chose an FF design for the CR-X, largely due to the availability of components.

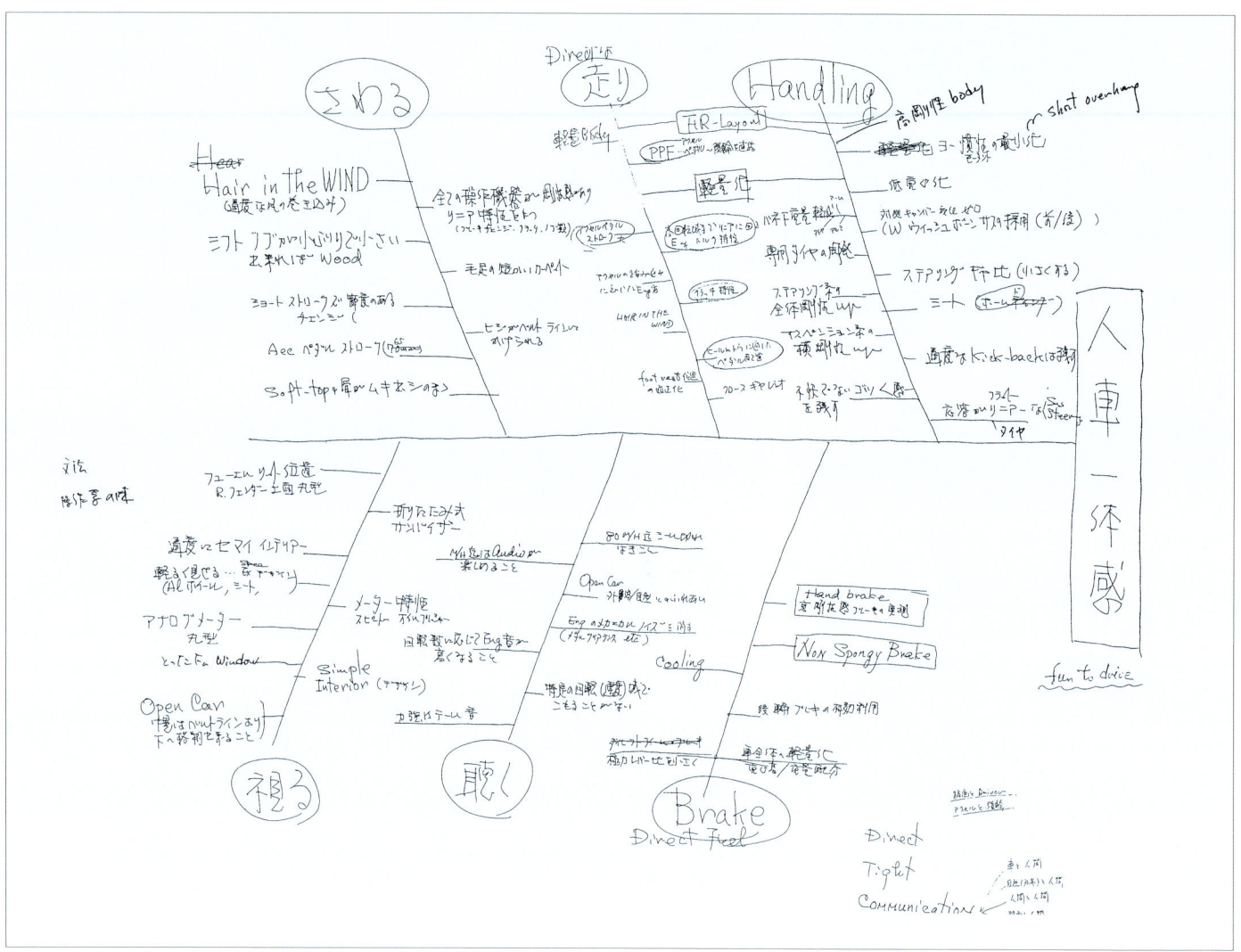

There must be a good dialogue between the driver and the automobile whilst driving. I wanted the driver to feel not only unity with his vehicle, sporty tension, a sense of performance, and a feeling of directness, but also the warmth of an actual life, and not just a machine. I wanted the driver to be aware - directly through the structural design of the vehicle - of every move the components made and every reaction of the car enabling the driver to 'feel' the road through the sensations.

Unity: A feeling of unity enables the driver to communicate with the car to get the maximum performance from it. The car must have a structure and design to allow this communication, allowing the driver to feel and enjoy the driving sensations with his whole body.

Tension: In the cockpit the driver must feel the sense of focus and tension, similar to that experienced by an athlete in competition, through his five senses: this thanks to a tight space, sound, and suitable vibration levels.

Performance: Rather than absolute maximum speed, the feeling of performance is more important.

Directness: The car must have a structure that will give quick and direct responses to driver input.

The "unity between horse and rider" can only be achieved through the combination of all of the above factors, each of which is an important part of *Kansei* (human sensibility). It is not easy to design and build a machine that possesses such sensual capabilities, but we believed we could do it and worked toward this goal.

In order to achieve the unity we hoped for, we employed a herringbone diagram (element analysis) that is commonly used in quality control. This analysis helped us to check the balance of each sensual quality we wanted the car to have. It is, however, absolutely essential that everything is explicitly expressed in the engineering drawing in order for a product to have the required sensual qualities. For instance, directness of a shift lever must be expressed in numerical terms; a gearstick should move X number of millemetres back and forth, and Y millemetres sideways to give the required feel. How much force should be necessary to change gear, and whether it should snap into a gear or have some mechanical resistance, were some of the questions that had to be answered. Compilation of these fine details established the character and feeling of a vehicle, and if we could give each element a specific character, we felt we'd be able to build a car with every aspect of the unity that we intended it to have.

A sports car is not just about speed!

The powerplant for the MX-5/Miata was chosen early in the car's development. A 1600cc B6 type engine used in the Mazda 323 (FF) was to be installed in the car with minimum modification. The Powertrain Design Department had firmly indicated it would modify the design only as much as was necessary to convert the unit for the FR configuration, but nothing more. There were no other suitable powerplants available within the company, so we had no choice.

As expected, opinions were voiced that such a small engine was not powerful enough to propel an LWS which weighed nearly a ton. There were those sports car buffs within Mazda who believed that a sports car should go fast; faster than the next car. We had to fight these people, saying that a sports car is not just about absolute speed, but also the ultimate fun of driving, derived from riding in, controlling, and experiencing the car and the road beneath it. Their criticism continued for a long time until we had a prototype ready to prove our point.

Rationale of an LWS

For an engineer with the passion to design a sports car, it would be more pleasing to have a powerful engine, but the faster you want the car to go, the bigger the engine and chassis gets, so up goes the weight of the vehicle. The concept is then far removed from the original LWS plan, and as the specification of an LWS gets closer to that of the RX-7, the big brother in the Mazda family, the reason for having an LWS in the line-up becomes increasingly weaker. I strongly felt that the key to success in designing an LWS was to stick with the motto, "simple is best." I believed that an LWS must not only be light, but also affordable for younger drivers, otherwise it has no place in the market.

In order to achieve an affordable price, a clear principle had to be implemented throughout development, from the product planning and layout design stages, all the way through to production. In order to save costs, we chose to borrow some components from existing Mazda products rather than design them anew. For instance, the air conditioning system, ashtray, and many other interior parts, were taken from current or past models wherever possible.

At that time there was no internal test code, quality standard, or any other benchmark applicable to an LWS within Mazda. In the past when such standards were missing for a particular product, or the product failed to meet existing standards, the Experimental Testing and Research Division and Quality Assurance Division usually waved a black flag, indicating that mass production of the product should be negated. In the development of the MX-5/Miata, I often encountered a similar situation, and had to resolve many issues by giving my personal assurance (often in writing) that the buck rested with me, thereby relieving others of extra concern and responsibility. As for exterior quality inspection, we made special

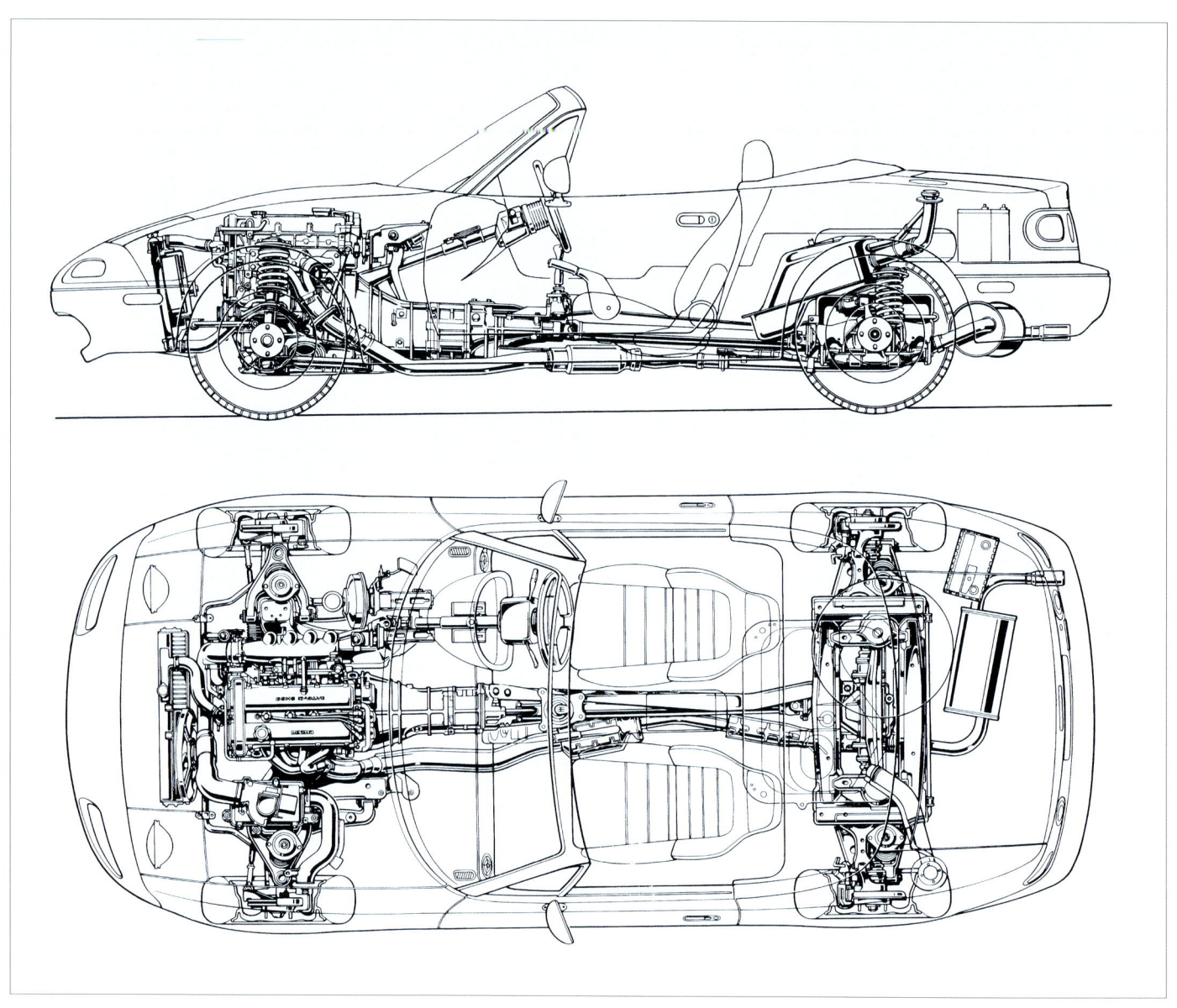

A basic layout drawing - elevation and plan.

visual inspection samples to establish a new set of criteria. The project reached the production stage, thanks to this unusual internal activity, which ultimately had the effect of increasing the project's supporters.

Basic layout design

The basic layout design of an automobile is a drawing that describes the fundamental skeleton structure, and all of the components, reflecting the product concept and all other decisions made in the planning stage. The quality of this drawing has a decisive affect on the basic performance, weight, character, and aesthetic design of the finished product.

From the beginning, I declared that this car was not going to be for big guys and, based on this policy, we allocated the minimum space for two passengers and luggage. Because of this, seats were made smaller, the seat adjusting mechanism was reduced, and there was no provision for steering wheel tilt adjustment. In the back of my mind was the conviction that human beings are capable of adjusting the body to a given condition within a certain range.

16

Main specifications	
Body type	Two-door convertible
Name	MX-5/Miata (E-NA6CE)
Engine	B6-ZE [RS]
Transmission	Five-speed manual
Length	3970mm
Width	1675mm
Height	1235mm
Interior length	935mm
Interior width	1320mm
Interior height	1025mm (1015mm)
Wheelbase	2265mm
Track (front)	1405mm
Track (rear)	1420mm
Ground clearance	140mm
Vehicle weight	940kg (970kg)
Passengers	Two

Dimensions (car with DHT in brackets).

At Mazda, upon completion of the basic layout and exterior design, a full-size plastic model is built to confirm cockpit ergonomics, check its seating position, steering wheel location, and so on. When this plastic model was being built, two tall gentlemen from the Australian distributor were visiting Hiroshima, and came to see the model. Their reaction to the design was very favorable, but we knew they would not fit into the car. As expected, they commented that there should be more room. My answer was: "We do not cater for big people. You can either squeeze yourself in or please forget it." For a moment, they seemed perplexed, but then said: "We'll squeeze in all right. Please get the car to our market soon." They shook our hands warmly and left.

After the market debut of the car, I met many tall users, who showed me how they modified the seat in order to fit into the car; they all seemed very proud to be the owner of an MX-5/Miata. However, it took me some time to get over the feeling of guilt for sticking to my policy so fiercely.

To design and develop a car based around one's own set of strict policies was not easy to do at Mazda, and in order to achieve the LWS we wanted, we had to neglect some internal design standards and test codes. This was unprecedented at Mazda, and we had to fight with the Testing and Research Division, and the Quality Assurance Division, which both normally test and qualify the product for sale to the public.

	Roadster	RX-7
Legroom	1085	1110
Headroom	942	945
Shoulder room	1280	1346

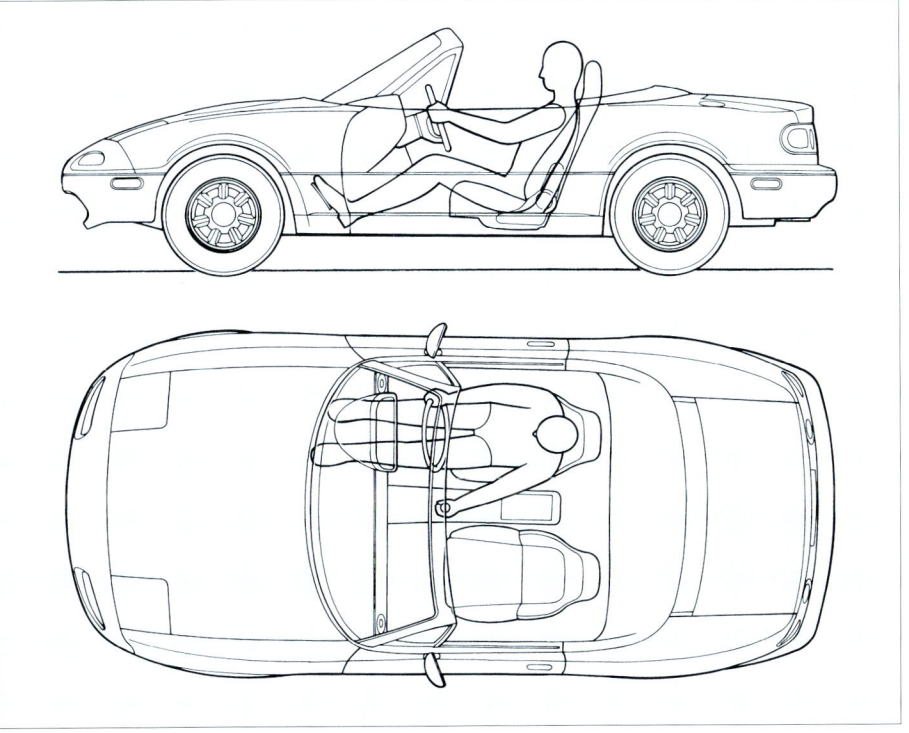

During the basic layout design stage, I laid out the following policy in order to achieve the "unity between horse and rider" and associated performance goals:

50/50 weight distribution with FR layout.
Body structure with high collision impact absorption capability.
Minimize yaw moment of inertia which dictates handling characteristics.
No unnecessary body overhang front and rear for the sake of exterior design.
Lowest possible center of gravity for the car and all components.
Absolute minimum weight and cost.

In order to achieve these targets, we had to properly reflect these policies in the basic layout drawing. As previously mentioned, this project was the first within Mazda to employ a CAD system in the basic layout design stage, and that helped us immensely later, as we were able to carry out a major design change - such as relocation of the powerplant - very easily. Changing complicated drawings was a breeze, requiring minimum manpower.

Car design

In the exterior design an attempt was made to incorporate an element of traditional Japanese culture, together with lines that reflected a combination of state-of-the-art-technology and a fun-to-drive machine. Delicate lines and curving surfaces successfully captured the radiance, simplicity, and tension of a *Noh* mask (a traditional wooden mask employed in Japanese plays, which uses subtle curves and angle changes to create shadows and thus gives the wearer different expressions), whilst strength, agility, and LWS cuteness were nicely integrated, I believe. Lettering in the emblem was done with brush stroke-like lines to emphasize the Japanese flavor.

The body, with long nose and slightly hopped-up rear deck, gave the car a sense of power, even though it had only a rather mild 1600cc engine. A new engine rocker cover was specially designed for this car to evoke memories of earlier LWS models when the bonnet was opened.

The front windshield and rearview mirrors were designed to minimise wind buffeting whilst keeping the driver and passenger in direct contact with nature; the tonneau cover was also designed to blend in nicely with body lines. As an option, we developed a

detachable hardtop concurrently with the start of mass production, under numerous difficult constraints, including structure and vehicle homologation rules. It was an option we very much wanted, as it was the only addition that would give a fashionable twist to the LWS.

In the interior design of the car, all decorative elements were deleted, and we stuck with the "simple is best" principle, even though it meant neglecting some engineering standards and test codes. This was to create some tension in the tight-fitting interior. In fact, the philosophy of interior design in a sports car has much in common with that of tearoom design in the traditional Japanese tea ceremony. Priority is given to functionality, the key ingredient in both designs.

Necessary for a convertible, special theft-prevention features were added to the glovebox and the lockable console box, and the trunk and fuel lid openers were hidden inside the latter item.

As with the engineering, hardware that provided the feeling of "unity between horse and rider," I believe that, through intimate communication with the driver, the aesthetic design of the MX-5/Miata also has the ability to quicken the pulse.

Powertrain

The powertrain of an LWS is normally derived from a model already in production, and the MX-5/Miata was no exception.

Engine

We developed the MX-5/Miata engine from the B6 type used in the Mazda 323 production model, with the minimum of modification.

The level of resources we could apply to engine development was quite limited, although we had two aims in mind. One was to realize a performance 'feel' that would stimulate the driver's mind; the other was to create an engine design with functional beauty in keeping with the LWS it powered. Our task may be summarized into the following:

Modify the engine from its original FF configuration to FR.
Change its torque curve to give good acceleration to the redline, and a sensuous performance feel for the driver.
Develop a new silencer system that gives a feeling of power through low frequency sound.
Invest in a newly designed rocker cover that will assert the LWS image.
Develop a new exhaust manifold

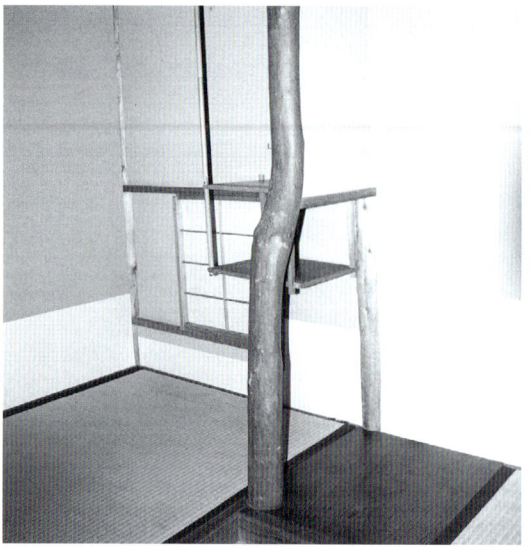

A typical entrance to a traditional Japanese tearoom. A certain amount of tension and excitement is created in the subconscious by the small door, and this design concept was carried over to the MX-5/Miata.

Simplicity is the key element in a traditional Japanese tearoom - function comes first, as in a pure sports car.

View of the cockpit.

The B6-ZE engine and transmission. Designed for the front wheel-drive Mazda 323, it had to be converted to sit longitudinally (it was located in the transverse position in the 323); the distributor drive was also changed, and the exhaust manifold was made up using stainless steel pipe. The transmission (gearbox) was based on that of the Mazda 929.

using stainless steel piping for reduced weight.

From the very beginning of the project, the Engine Development Division clearly indicated that it would only help us in converting the unit from FF configuration to FR. While this was indeed true, our team, including Ohira (who was in charge of the program in the Engine Development Division), wanted to produce an engine that would not only propel the MX-5/Miata in a suitable manner, but also one that could be proudly presented to the customers as a true LWS unit: this wish created much turmoil within the organization.

Transmission and clutch

As with the engine, the transmission was also derived from a production model. It would have been ideal to design a lightweight unit exclusively for this car, but lack of time and resources were the deciding factors. Since the transmission came from the Mazda 929 (a luxury sedan), we had to give it new, more sporting gear

ratios, as well as create a nice shift feel.

In order to achieve the sports car shift feel, the weight of the flywheel and synchronizer rings were reduced to a minimum. Shift strokes were reduced to enhance the direct feeling of the transmission, and the shift lever gate was extended to fall directly under the driver's left hand. These measures helped considerably in achieving the "unity between horse and rider" we were striving for.

Differential gear

An element that enables power sliding is a limited-slip mechanism in the differential gear. As a standard feature, we chose a viscous-type limited-slip differential for the MX-5/Miata. For enhanced safety, the differential gearcase was also modified to absorb energy from a crash impact.

Powerplant frame (PPF)

For the first time in Mazda's history, we chose to use a Power Plant Frame (PPF) in the sports car. This would reduce the time

lag between application of the throttle and car reaction, thereby giving the driver a more responsive, direct feeling of power. Worldwide, only a very few automobiles have this feature, which marks it out as a pure sports car.

Chassis

A lot of effort went into the suspension system in the MX-5/Miata, and it even has the luxury of double-wishbones and coil springs on all four wheels. As engineers, we were convinced - and felt it obligatory - that the car should have the best possible features in this area of the design, as it is one of the most important elements in achieving the "fun-to-drive" quality we desired. We had the following points laid down to form a basis for the design:

Give the car responsive handling in all situations, creating an appropriate level of tension for the driver.
Enable the driver to control the car with his driving technique, such as a controlled power slide, for pure driving pleasure.

An illustration showing the location of the PPF (power plant frame) - an aluminum frame connecting the powerplant and differential casing.

Enable the driver to feel direct contact with the road (road dialogue), whilst reducing jolts and harshness to a minimum.

With a minimum yaw moment of inertia, low center of gravity, and the most desirable suspension on all four wheels, I believe that the resulting LWS has the most predictable, straightforward,

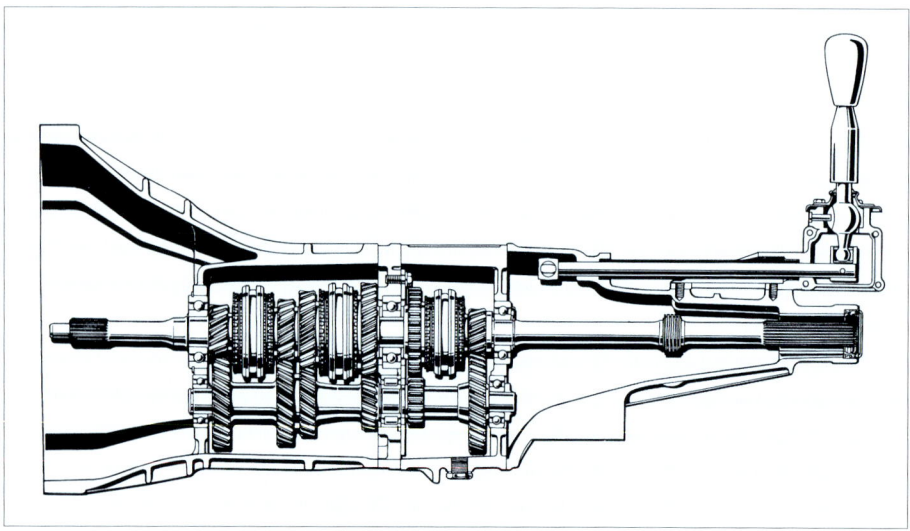

The transmission was based on the Mazda 929 unit, although the gearshift linkage was extended to bring the lever closer to the driver, and then thoroughly developed to impart a direct feel when changing gears.

and controllable handling characteristics possible, all the way to the limit of adhesion.

Steering system

We chose a rack-and-pinion steering system for the MX-5/Miata for its directness. The diameter of the rack was increased to achieve more stiffness in the steering system. The MX-5/Miata

had the option of power steering, along with a manual rack, but both systems applied the utmost emphasis to achieving a feel of directness for the driver.

Since the unity we sought can only be achieved with the vital components - suspension, steering, and rigidly installed brakes - the highest design priority was achieving a very rigid chassis structure. The US export model was to be equipped with the airbag system, whilst all other models had an Italian Momo steering wheel.

Braking system

All four wheels employed disc brakes, with ventilated items at the front. In order to achieve stable braking performance under all conditions, we did not spare any effort in providing good braking for the MX-5/Miata. Whilst rigidity of the braking system components was vital in achieving the unity we desired, the vacuum servo setting was kept at a low level to transmit the braking response to the driver to the greatest possible extent.

Tyres and wheels

We chose 185/60 R14 as the standard tyre size, but wanted a

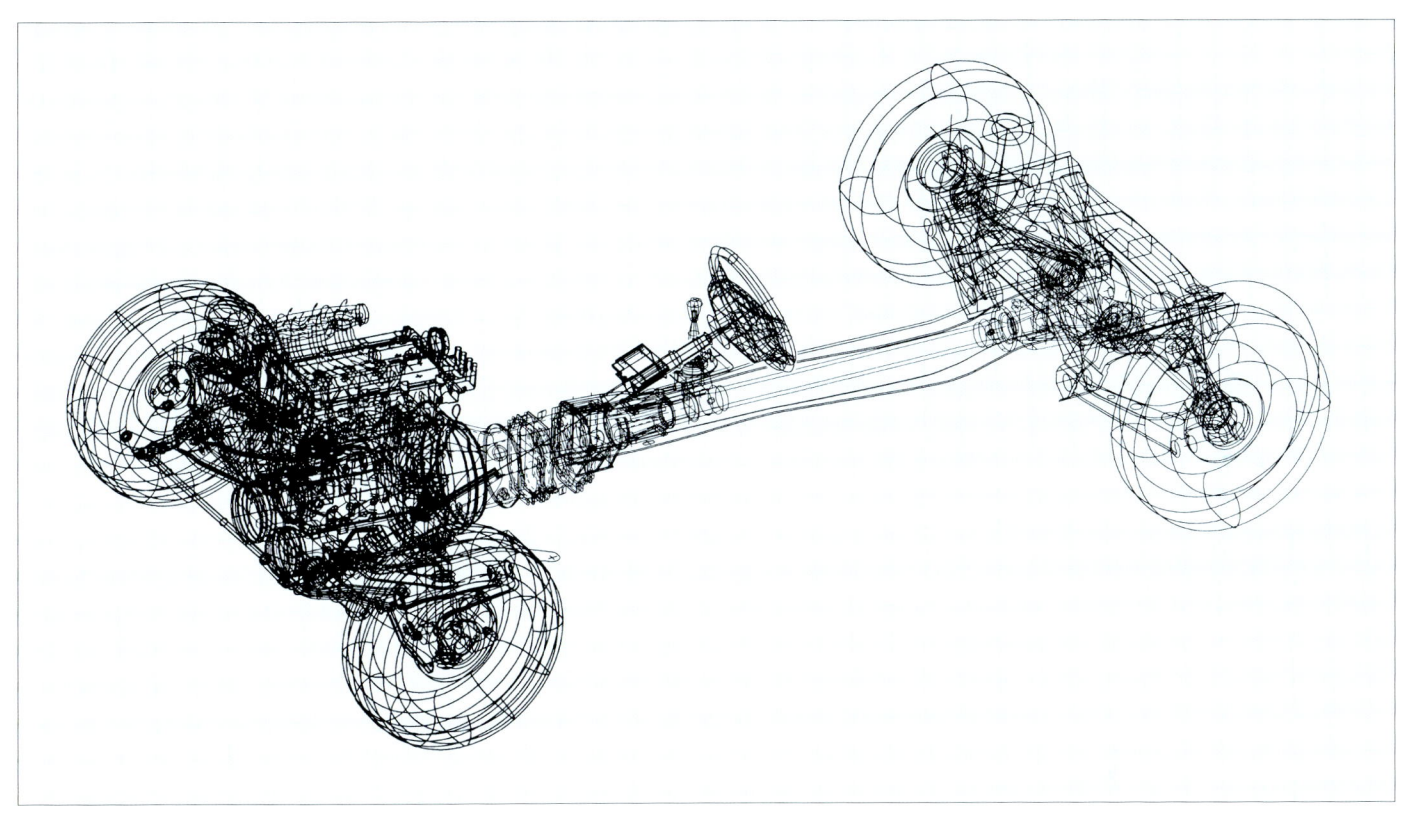

A CAD (computer aided design) drawing showing the powertrain and chassis of the MX-5/Miata. CAD allows engineers to remove and replace virtual components at will, and see the design from various angles.

10 per cent weight reduction. We requested tyre makers to design a special tread pattern for the LWS in conjunction with the new body design. We set a 10 per cent weight reduction target for the aluminum wheels, too, and to achieve this, changed an eight-spoke design to a seven-spoke one based upon the supplier's recommendation. Luckily, the seven-spoke alloy wheels were well received by our American importer, who'd always complained about our wheel designs in the past.

Body design

From the outset we recognized the importance of the body structure in this project. In the body's structural design there are conflicting objectives, such as rigidity, strength, crash safety, and lightness; rigidity and lightness were the key requirements in order to achieve unity with the driver. The frame design was carried out with the following in mind:

Maximize the frame cross-sections in the front and rear, and make them straight. Avoid making any narrow waists in the frame: in the case of a serious accident, the frame should collapse like an accordion.
Maximize the cross-section of the center tunnel, using it as a structural member.
The input load through the suspension system should be evenly distributed through the entire frame, to achieve a rigid body structure that will also be effective in damping vibration and noise.

In the development of the MX-5/Miata body/frame system, the finite element method was used with a computer system. This allowed for extensive trial and error calculations and design improvements, resulting in a very rigid but lightweight body, that still met the various safety regulations with ample margin. While design analysis using a computer system has proven very effective, the time taken to process a large amount of data became excessive, and accelerated the introduction of a Supercomputer system at Mazda.

Soft-top and detachable hardtop

The soft-top for a roadster should be a simple and light device that can be operated with ease; it soon became clear, however, that such a system was very hard to create. Since the soft-top is located at the

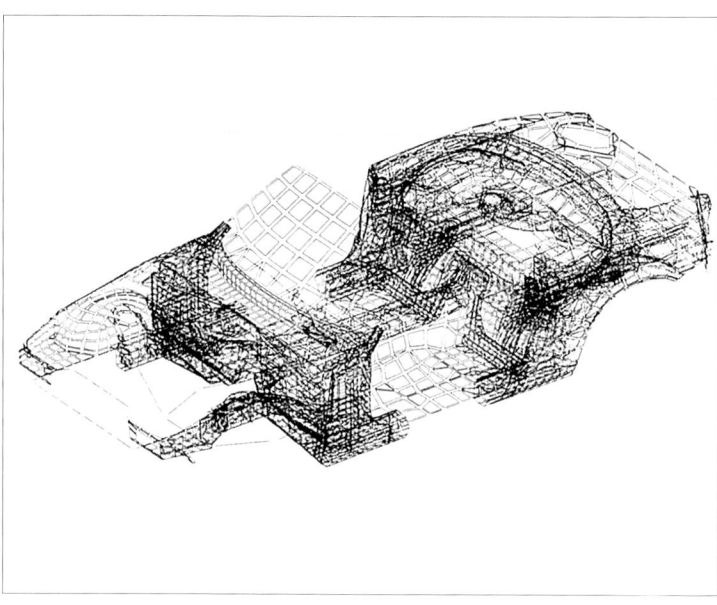

The seven-spoke aluminum alloy wheel. The original proposal had eight spokes, but using seven reduced weight and added a dynamic quality to the design.

A computer generated body built up using FEM (finite element measurement) analysis. This was used to determine body strength; the finer the mesh, the more realistic the results.

highest point in the car, special effort was required to make it as light as possible, to avoid detrimentally affecting handling. The rear window was made from vinyl with fasteners around it, and a single layer top was chosen for lightness. Its skeleton mechanism was a six-pivot linkage system, designed to blend into the body lines when folded. I specifically asked the designers not to design the shape of the soft-top, as this should automatically evolve from the head clearance that was necessary, and the linkage mechanism.

In a single engine and a single body configuration, the detachable hardtop was the only luxury option we gave the MX-5/Miata buyer. The plastic detachable hardtop (DHT) added weather protection, better rear visibility, and more security to the MX-5/Miata design.

Three body colours for production
Mass production for the American market began four months ahead of that for other destinations, and with only three color choices: red, blue, and white. Since there was not much else in the way of options to choose from, I wanted to add more color variations for the American market, but that meant more cost. Contrary to my concern, these color choices were readily accepted by the market. The three colors were, after all, those of the American flag.

Integrated development process
In a situation where human resources, funds and space were all inadequate, and internal support was often missing, we were still somehow able to bring the project to the mass production stage. Integrated development carried out by a limited number of group members is one reason for this success. We knew at the beginning that full support was not available, and a limited number of project members had to struggle

through the process, often going far beyond what their professional discipline dictated. It should be noted also that each project member was not necessarily working hard for the sake of the company: I believe it's true to say that they all worked so hard in order to realize a car of *their own* through participation in this project - to develop a car that *they* wanted to buy.

Masaaki Watanabe (Basic Design leader) and Toshiteru Yoshimura (Interior Design engineer), who participated in this project almost as volunteers, insisted on their own preference in the layout of a number of components and design options. I considered their subjective passion to be more important than their objective judgement, and accepted their choices in order to meld the team into one which shared a common goal: I was most fortunate that the team performed superbly in this quest.

When the yen became so

The MX-5/Miata with the soft-top erected, and with the DHT fitted. The optional hardtop widened the car's appeal by offering better weatherproofing and increased rear visibility.

strong that the exchange rate was 120 yen to the dollar, an executive decision was taken to slow development because of lack of profitability under such an unfavorable exchange rate. As a result, team activity became even more intense in an effort to achieve greater price competitiveness for the car.

Rooter spirit that activated the project

In the early stages of development, when the shortage of manpower became obvious and Basic Design activity (led by Watanabe) was in difficulties, Abe (Manager of Body Design Department) dispatched Naoyuki Ikemizu as a Vehicle Design leader very early in the game to help the situation. Imura and Yoshimura of Body Design and Outer Body Design volunteered to join this project by abandoning their then current assignments. Takao Kijima (Section Chief of the Chassis Design Department), and Fumitaka Ando came to the Riverside Hotel every morning before their routine work to carry out the chassis design, while their managers (Takiguchi and Ito) let them indulge in this extra work.

This, and other outside help, boosted our morale tremendously, but there was still a definite manpower shortage. To supplement our ten engineers, I succeeded in getting the help of five European engineers for six months from a British consulting firm. The European team consisted of English, French, and Polish engineers, none of whom understood a word of Japanese ... Although there were the inevitable difficulties in communication, the experience taught us that a language barrier is not necessarily a problem when a group of people shares a common target.

Sadamu Nishiguchi worked with a French engineer on the soft-top design with no knowledge at all of the French language, but they did a marvelous job in the end. Through the process of solving detailed technical issues, and meeting casually during drinking sessions and on trips, our engineers were able to learn a lot about European culture and bypassing the language barrier.

At about the same time, Watanabe and Ikemizu were busy asking designers and engineers in the company to present ideas for the last time. Because of their hard work, the Riverside Hotel was kept

人馬一体

busy with visiting engineers and other visitors curious to witness a unique international project in progress. Three-dimensional layout drawings utilizing the CAD system were under continuous review by the various branches of engineering, jointly and concurrently. This activity resulted in the latest set of data always being available from the CAD system, and the various traditional steps usually required to hand over the tasks to the next stage (between the basic layout design stages to production engineering) became quite unnecessary. As a result, highly-efficient design work was possible, whilst keeping the original design concept clearly in focus.

The greatest event in this integrated development process was a design review prior to the release of the first production drawing, scheduled for 1 October 1987. Traditionally, this was more of a ceremonial event than a real review, usually drawing attention to sales points rather than discussing real issues. In the case of the MX-5/Miata, though, the points raised were mostly negative issues, and I commented that if no-one had a better idea than ours, then this was the car that would go into production. This was an awkward way to conduct a design review, but it had the effect of raising potential issues earlier, rather than in the prototype stages and putting them aside for later resolution.

Merit of the integrated development process

Traditionally, the development of a new car was carried out in various stages. For example, the Planning Division establishes the objectives for a new car in terms of corporate strategies and market information. Then the Design and Engineering Divisions take over the project and struggle with the task of how to realize the concept and design. The objectives established in the preceding stage were often too idealistic and unachievable in the next process, and the project often ended with a mediocre result.

In order to avoid the shortcomings often encountered in this traditional process, the team worked to establish concurrent targets in cost, weight, and performance, whilst also struggling to develop ways to achieve some of these targets. We also set targets - and trade-offs to reach such targets. For instance, I gave allowable cost increase figures in the development of a lighter battery, exhaust manifold, exhaust silencer and bonnet. To achieve a lighter body, we used the minimum amount of insulation material attached to the bodyshell based on the allowable noise level set as a target.

It was fortunate also that we could retain the key members of the project team from the planning stages until market introduction. Watanabe, Ikemizu, and a few others stayed with the project as per my request, and this helped tremendously with keeping the development work integrated. Following the release of engineering drawings, prototype production began and the Riverside Hotel had regular visitors all day from the Production Engineering group, including Setsuo Nakagaki.

Nakagaki, together with Ikemizu and Watanabe, summoned production engineers whenever necessary, and gave a spontaneous reaction to those issues raised. When prototype testing began, Hiroyoshi Moriyama of the Testing Department joined the group. The Riverside Hotel was no longer a quiet project room, but more like a command center in a battlefield, with discussions, and the necessary feedback regarding the engineering drawings continuing night and day. This integrated project process gradually spread to the Public Relations Department and the Sales Department, and our communication with related internal organizations worked extremely well, with engineers directly conveying their thoughts to sales and PR personnel. This, in turn, was reflected in Mazda's communication with potential clients in the marketplace.

Mazda Cosmo Sport.

Prelude to market introduction

At Mazda, it's usual to send a prototype into the market under strict secrecy, and gather reaction from responsible sales organizations, and a limited number of outsiders. For the MX-5/Miata, we conducted such an evaluation in secret with a limited number of European experts after

Mazda RX-7.

the internal evaluation. One prominent Austrian journalist, invited for this session, was reported to have questioned Mazda's qualification to produce such an LWS (he was a member of the European 'Car of the Year' selection committee). Upon hearing the comment, I was furious and requested that Mazda invite the journalist to Hiroshima, as it was at the height of the project and I could not go to Europe. A meeting with the journalist materialized in a very short time and he came over to Hiroshima. My points to him were as follows:

Mazda has been producing automobiles since 1931, starting with three-wheelers.
A Mazda racer claimed second place in the Grand Prix of Osaka in 1934.
We started production of motorcycles in 1939.
In 1946 after the war, we resumed the production of three-wheelers.
Soon after the introduction of

passenger cars, Mazda engaged in the development of rotary engines, developing the Cosmo Sports and the RX-7. The RX-7s achieved great success in the world market, as well as in various types of motorsport, including IMSA and the World Rally Championship.
Mazda has entered the Le Mans 24-hour race with rotary-engined sports cars with good results (indeed, a little while later, Mazda won at Le Mans in 1991).
While cars produced by Mazda are certainly different to those from Jaguar, its length of automobile production history is comparable, and Mazda has made a great contribution to the automobile industry.
It has been ten years since the last production of a new LWS and the market does not seem certain, but Mazda is taking the risk and challenging the world.

In addition, I conveyed my thoughts about how Japanese industrial products, although high

The press launch in Hawaii, where the MX-5/Miata received a lot of praise.

in quality, were becoming increasingly bland, characterless, and a far from accurate reflection of the Japanese culture. I explained that, with the MX-5/Miata, we wanted to present to the world our own automobile culture. Whilst the marketplace would be the final judge of whether or not our automobile culture was acceptable, we firmly believed that we had the capability and qualifications to produce a fine LWS.

The journalist listened to me and went back to Austria, and since that time has become a very close friend of Mazda. Although the MX-5/Miata could not claim the European 'Car of the Year'

accolade the following year, we were at least able to learn a lot about European automobile culture from the journalist, for which we are very appreciative.

Learning about automobile insurance

During the 1980s in the US, auto insurance premiums increased to such an extent that it became prohibitive to own a sports car. There was even a rumor that Porsche would end sales in the US because of this insurance hike. This could have been a fatal blow to our project, so I had to find out more about the situation.

On inquiry to Mazda's R&D

arm in Irvine, California, it became clear that an insurance corporation in Chicago might have some clue about the situation, and I flew to Chicago with Jiro Maebayashi. The person I visited at Tech-Col, an insurance research organization, gave me a sharp look when I quizzed him - reminding me that this city was once famous for gangsters - but my question was very simple: what should we do to keep the insurance premiums reasonable on the MX-5/Miata?

At first, the person in charge seemed a little confused about the purpose of my visit, but as I explained to him the development of the MX-5/Miata, he became

28

more interested in the car itself and made several valuable comments and suggestions. Based on the information obtained, I learned that if we were to reduce the repair cost of an automobile, particularly of front body parts, this would have a significant positive impact on the insurance premium calculation.

As soon as I got back to Mazda, I went to our Parts Department to negotiate a market price reduction for selected front body parts, including bumpers, fenders, the radiator grille, etc. This proposal met with strong opposition, because the department has to make a profit via parts sales, and cannot simply reduce prices for such a political reason. I finally met with Miyaji, General Manager of the Parts Division, and pleaded with him. Within two weeks, I got the reply that the department would co-operate with me, and the revised price list complied closely with my suggestions.

After the market debut of the MX-5/Miata, I was able to confirm that the insurance premium set for the car was much lower than that of other sports cars, warranting all the effort we had put in. This was another reason why the MX-5/Miata enjoyed market success in the US.

Japanese sales

In the autumn of 1988, Mazda as a whole was preparing to put the car into production. The Export Division was the primary department responsible, of course, although Domestic Sales had its own challenge to face. Okabe, who was responsible for this section, was planning to establish a new "Eunos" sales channel for Mazda in Japan, and christened our car the "Eunos Roadster" for the home market. I had previously asked Okabe to increase his average monthly sales target from 150 to 300, but it finally became 500 in order to clear the Executive Committee! Whilst the domestic sales organization as a whole did not have much enthusiasm for the car, the most important day for home sales duly arrived - the Mazda New Car Committee review - where a production prototype of the Eunos Roadster was to be shown.

Although some of the attendees expressed doubts about the car's marketing potential, President Iida of the Committee kept silent for some time. He then wiped his tear-filled eyes and said: "I have long been associated with the sales of Mazda cars, but I have never seen a vehicle as moving as the Eunos Roadster." His remark was enough to boost the spirits of domestic salesmen in time for the opening of Mazda Eunos showrooms all over Japan.

Production start

A lucky incident occurred at Mazda just prior to the start of production. Another new model due to join the production line just before the MX-5/Miata experienced some difficulty, which delayed its production start date. As a result, we got an earlier start than originally planned, by no less than

Before sales began, people were able to place advance orders at a hotel in Tokyo.

29

four months, and in order not to repeat the mistake with the other model that brought about such a sudden change of schedule, everyone concerned co-operated with the MX-5/Miata project much more than I'd expected.

In the past, a car for the export market usually entered production well after domestic production had begun. This was not the case for the MX-5/Miata and, despite the simple combination of three colors for one body, and a single engine choice, we carefully prepared for the production start-up.

Komatsu, Senior Managing Director in charge of manufacturing, was known for being a tough guy, guarding the production side's interest. After repeated discussions, which often ended up in him shouting, we got to know each other quite well, learning the important know-how of starting up production smoothly. Nakagaki and Ikemizu also learned the secret recipe from Komatsu, and implemented it by conducting the design review and design freeze, and fully utilizing the production staff.

On 31 March 1989, we were able to come to the production start without a single incident that would necessitate stopping the assembly line. Soon after the first production car rolled off the line and left for the parking lot, departing with a fine exhaust noise, I was standing alone, feeling deeply satisfied. When I called Komatsu to thank him for all his support and help. He said with a heavy Hiroshima accent: "Well done!"

Initial global market reaction

The first showing of the MX-5/Miata to the US market occurred in Nashville, Tennessee on 2 February 1989. In front of 2000 US Mazda dealer personnel, the car emerged from behind a theatrical screen of dry ice after the audience had been treated to a video showing the MX-5 Miata in action. When the MC introduced me with the car, I felt like I was floating in heaven, and all the problems and concerns I'd faced during the development stage seemed long forgotten.

I told people to come closer and see the car, and everyone came up to the stage, surrounding the six Miatas that were shining under the strong lights. I was shaking hands with everyone. They were truly thankful that we had made such a sports car available.

Chicago Show

Nine days after showing the car to US Mazda dealers, we held the first public showing of the MX-5/Miata at the Chicago Auto Show. At the same event, Nissan had its new 300ZX, and Honda had its NSX: the show became a three-way battle between Japanese sports cars. I was greeted by so many visitors, each making extremely nice remarks about the MX-5/Miata, and the business cards I'd prepared for the show quickly disappeared. After the event, I found four cards from Vice-Presidents of General Motors. It was way beyond my expectations to get a word of congratulation from GM executives.

When I returned to my hotel I found a fax message telling me to go back to Japan for an urgent meeting to prepare for the domestic press showing of the car. In Chicago Airport I met with a Japanese gentleman in a red sweater, who introduced himself as the President of Honda North America, Mr Munekuni. Behind him was Mr Kume, the President of Honda, who greeted me by saying: "Congratulations, you've made an excellent car."

Why the US before Japan?

As news of the MX-5/Miata in Chicago got to the Japanese media, they came to Mazda's PR Department, asking why Japan had not seen the car first? This had the effect of bringing forward the Japanese press launch. It was, however, a makeshift launch because there were not enough cars in Japan, and Mazda had to assemble a few for this special showing.

When I returned to Tokyo I was met by Maekawa and sped to

the Yokohama Technical Centre. The cars they had prepared were pre-production models that, although tested thoroughly, did not look like test cars due to much cleaning and polishing.

In the conference room at the TC, I spoke in front of journalists who were eager to take a first look at the car. I said: "This car has real blood running under the hood rather than oil and water."

I continued by describing my theory for an ideal sports car, in which there is "unity between the horse and its rider." After my speech, one of Mazda's executives made a correction by saying: "There was one mistake in Hirai's speech, it is not the horse and its rider, but the car and its driver." Following this press debut, the first test drive for journalists took place in April, again, ahead of the planned schedule.

Information driven society
US motor journalists applauded the MX-5/Miata, stating that it was a revival of the LWS spirit of the 1960s and 1970s. US consumers, both young and young-at-heart, liked the car so much that we could not produce enough to meet demand for more than a year. For a while, in the US and Japan, this shortage resulted in a premium on top of the official price tag, something previously unheard of for Mazda cars.

In August 1989, as I was going home from my office, I saw a number of young men sitting at the front gate of Mazda's headquarters at seven in the evening. They told me that they were there to make a reservation for the MX-5/Miata the next morning. I was so surprised that because of the news and media information, these young men were willing to spend a small fortune and wait in line all night for a car they'd never driven. I almost felt guilty. A similar thing happened in Tokyo the night before the reservation day, and special priority tickets had to be issued to make buyers go home for the night. These were, without doubt, encouraging signs for all of us who had worked so hard to realize the car, but I had never before appreciated the power of the news media in our society.

London Motor Show
The London Motor Show of 1989 had a new Lotus Elan on display, along with the MX-5/Miata. This seemed to attract the attention of the news media and I had seven interviews in one day, including one with the BBC. Most of the questions centered on the concept of bringing in an LWS from Japan to Europe, and the difference between the new Lotus Elan, which had an FF layout as opposed to an FR layout on the MX-5/Miata. My response was that it was my great pleasure to have the opportunity of introducing a Mazda LWS to the homeland of the lightweight sports car, and I believed that the FR layout was the best arrangement for such a car. I got the feeling that the journalist who asked the question was not very happy with the Elan's FF design.

It is my experience that to design a sports car, which must become a subject of love and passion for so many different individuals, is a very difficult proposition. The fact that we were able to make the MX-5/Miata materialize was entirely due to the focus and hard work shown by our team members. For this dedication, I would like to take this opportunity to thank them once again.

While our modern society is moving into a more hi-tech and science-oriented system, the Mazda MX-5/Miata seems to have been accepted as a car that brings spiritual satisfaction into people's lives. If it can continue to do so in the 21st century and beyond, it will give me a sense of joy and satisfaction far beyond my wildest dreams.

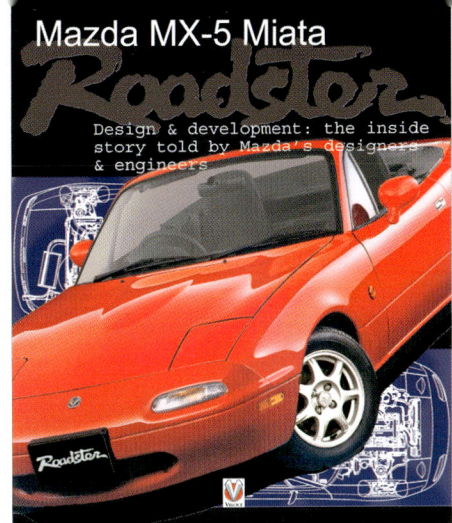

Mazda MX-5 Miata

Roadster

Design & development: the inside story told by Mazda's designers & engineers

2

The basic layout design
by **Masaaki Watanabe**

Prior to joining the MX-5/Miata project, Watanabe was in charge of the basic layout design section. The fact that the MX-5/Miata looks great and represents the ideal "unity of horse and rider" is due in no small measure to his hard work. He is one of the few engineers who truly understood the automobile culture I was talking about, and was remarkable in that he was capable of translating it into drawings.

T. Hirai

During the mid-1980s, the Honda CR-X and the Toyota MR-2 were becoming very popular as affordable and fun-to-drive sports cars. Under the circumstances, the only way Mazda could compete with these cars was to create a traditional LWS at the right price, and featuring an FR (front engine, rear wheel-drive) arrangement. At that time, the shift towards an FF (front engine, front wheel-drive) layout had reached the stage where Mazda had two FF platforms, one for the 323 and the other for the 626. Of course, there were arguments that it would be more economical to have another FF two-seater, or put the FF powerplant in the rear to create a mid-engined, two-seater similar to the MR-2, although it was not really that straightforward. The biggest reason for choosing the FR arrangement came from MANA (Mazda North America), the US R&D arm, where expectation of an affordable FR two-seater sports roadster was very high.

Why an open two-seater with an FR arrangement? The answer is very simply that it is the basic, very traditional arrangement of an LWS car with all the right fun-to-drive ingredients. Born in Europe and loved by drivers all over the world, LWS models came close to extinction because of safety regulations and anti-pollution laws, but an FR

open two-seater was synonymous with LWS culture.

When I first visited MANA in the early 1980s, I was asked to test drive an old Triumph Spitfire. MANA was located on Red Hill Avenue in Irvine, California, and the road in front of John Wayne Airport that connected to the Pacific Coast Highway was one of my favorite routes. As I drove the old Spitfire, I received many thumbs-up signs from other drivers. This experience demonstrated the strong attachment that American drivers have to a lightweight open two-seater. It never happened when I was driving a Mustang convertible, an American automobile. This was proof that the fun of driving (later we described the sensation as the "unity of horse and rider") could only come from a lightweight body, and a small, European-style engine was still an attractive proposition for many American drivers.

Hard planner

Basic Layout Design was an area I'd been assigned to ever since joining Mazda. The name of the department has changed, but basic layout design provided the bulk of the design stream, establishing targets of basic specification, layout and performance, and creating a package consistent with the product concept and available hardware. Other departments associated with this objective were:

product planning, design, testing and research, production engineering, etc.; and aesthetic designers who often became our greatest enemies, whilst also our closest allies. Basic layout design could result in a product with no hope of success, even if the other departments worked hard; on the other hand, it could also produce a fine backbone for a car that would be further enhanced by another's work.

To create a car from scratch is a chance that does not come often to an engineer. In this instance, all the given conditions were very exciting for me, because to create a car of this sort was my dream. As I think back, I remember that the following background situations helped to create such a successful product:

A very limited number of people were involved in the initial stage of development. At that time, Japan was entering an economic boom so all development manpower went into the design of new products, or design changes to existing ones. The LWS project which, in the minds of many, held no promise, could not be assigned many people. Ironically, this resulted in a clearer definition of the car, due to the small number of engineers involved. For the same reason, this became Mazda's first application of the integrated project process, from initial design to production start-up.

The most advanced design tools available were used. An advanced computer system, including GNC (Mazda's own CAD system), was fully utilized in the body analysis, vibration analysis of the PPF, and airbag simulations, etc., to find problems as well as solutions in a variety of situations throughout the development process.

The design concept was shared by all those who participated in the project following numerous reviews of competitive model designs.

Although manpower was limited, there was ample budget available to purchase, test, and compare competitive machines. Mazda's Miyoshi Proving Ground was frequently used for comparison testing, and the number of these sessions was unprecedented. The most notable was the driving school held for all team members. Through this training, all team members were able to fully appreciate the fun and difficulty of driving, as well as the effect of each member's work on the performance of the vehicle. Needless to say, the most vital part of an LWS is the feeling one gets when driving. In order to directly connect the driver's intentions and the car's reactions, the car must be as light as possible with a low center of gravity and low yaw moment of inertia, combined with an optimum wheelbase dimension.

Through these driving school lessons, designers and engineers came to appreciate the importance of these factors.

If any of the aforementioned elements were missing, we could not have created the MX-5/Miata. By the same token, if any of our project members were missing, we could not have achieved the same results, either. Even 15 years after development, the original team members often get together for a drink. This is not necessarily the case with other projects.

A tight space that creates proper tension

At the time of design approval and the prototype model review, one comment was repeatedly made. The cockpit was "too small" or "too tight." On these occasions, I always wanted to ask: "Are you a real car guy?" "Small" and "Tight" were key design points on which we placed a great deal of emphasis. We wanted to create a car that would put the driver in a completely different environment to daily life,

settling into the seat and gripping the steering wheel. Our target was to create a partner with whom to travel into a world detached from the daily grind. The opposite of this target was a vehicle with luxurious space and graceful ride, which seems to be more for the benefit of the passenger. Our car was to have none of this: it was a driver's car.

Basic layout

As with the RX-7, the powerplant had to be located as near to the driver as possible, in order to maintain the 50:50 fore and aft weight distribution we desired. Interior layout was also borrowed from the RX-7, but the real question was: how to create the 'tightness' that creates pleasant tension for the driver? We had no intention of duplicating the confines of a 1960s roadster, however, but wanted to create a minimum interior space that was compatible with the latest safety features, and other statutory requirements.

Hip-point height and interior length

The location of the hip-point, which determines the basics for driving, together with the pedal location, was based on RX-7 experience (Fig.1 and Chart 1 show the results). Interior length is in-between that of the original RX-7 and the second generation RX-7; the height of the hip-point from the floor is nearly equal with the two, whilst height from the ground is a little less. The interior height was intended to be equal to that of the RX-7 with the soft-top closed, and the height of the beltline, which greatly influences that open-air feeling once the top is down, was made 20mm (0.79in.) to 40mm (1.57in.) lower.

One automobile critic told me that the best height of a seat from ground level is one in which the driver can grind out his cigarette on the road from a seated position with the door open. This was obviously not possible in a modern automobile, in which an exhaust catalyst must be located under the body (raising the floor height). One thing we really wanted to achieve was an open-air feeling with good visibility when the top was down, whilst retaining a proper feeling of tightness in the cockpit. I believe this was reasonably well achieved via the combination of a large cross-section tunnel, low beltline, and front header, and the location and cross-section of the A-pillars.

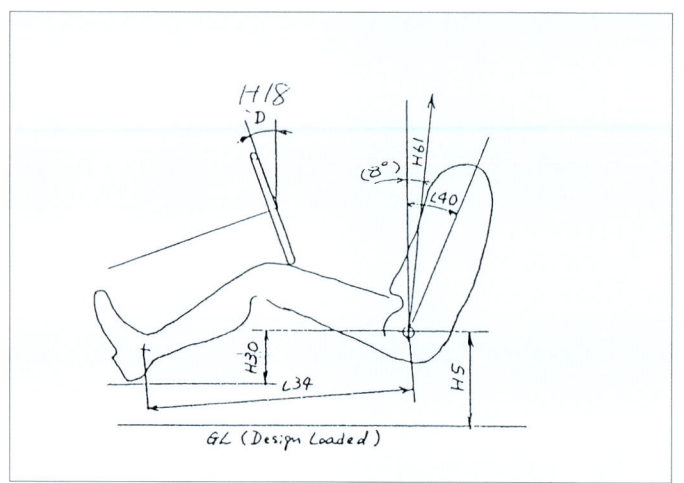

Fig.1

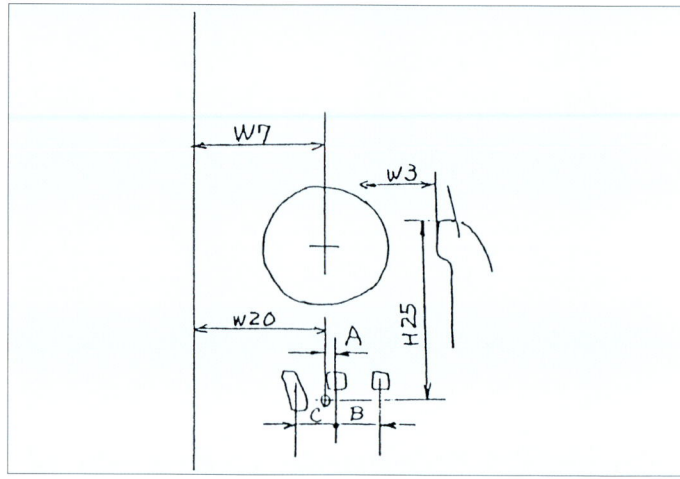

Fig.2

	W 3	W 7	W 20	H 5	H 25	H 30	H 61	L 34	L 40	A	B	C	D (DEG)
P 729 (LHD)	1280	350	350	360	434	170	943	1084	24	−25	120	110	19
P 132 (LHD)	1310	350	345	375	456	169	943	1055	28/30	−40	125	120	20.5
P 747 (LHD)	1346	350	345	378	475	172	944	1109	28	−35	120	120	20
MR 2 (RHD)	1350	340	340	360	476	196	948	1009	(24)	−39	120	105	24
Alfa Spider (LHD)	1206	300	314		424	150	942	984	(24)	30	106	95	19.5

Chart 1

Location of controls; interior width

Fig. 2 and Chart 1 show the relative location of the throttle, brake and clutch pedals, the steering wheel and door trim. The most important objective was to make the offset of the pedals from the driver's seat close to zero. By minimizing the effect of a large tunnel in the pedal area and the big side sills, the pedals and the steering wheel had almost the same relative locations as they did in the RX-7. The biggest difference between the MX-5/ Miata and the RX-7 was interior width: the MX-5/Miata is 30-60mm (1.2-2.4in.) narrower than the RX-7. It seems that interior width has much more to do with the tightness of the cockpit than any other dimension. Based on this theory, door thickness was increased to give the exterior body designers a touch more freedom.

Driving shoes versus winter boots

After a prototype was built, development staff took the car on various test drives. People came in varying attire, and when they left the site, Hirai always requested that they should come back next time with narrow driving shoes. A reaction to Hirai's remark came from Canada soon afterwards. A Canadian importer sent a fax to us stating that, in Canada, it is not possible to drive such a car in winter unless it has enough space to allow for winter boots. We were unsure, at first, how to reply to this announcement, but finally replied that the width of the driver's footwell was comparable with many other cars, and the request for narrow driving shoes was not a real issue, but more like mental preparation for driving a sports car.

Yaw moment of inertia

To swing a weight on a long bar, the force necessary to swing the weight depends on where the weight is attached. The further away from the pivot point it is located, the more force will be required and, for the same degree of force the angular velocity will be less, and the time it takes the weight to reach a target speed will be longer. The same principle applies to the handling of a sports car. Distribution of the weight of a car, including its passenger, will determine the force necessary to change its direction. This is called yaw moment of inertia. The smaller it is, the less force it takes to turn, or the faster it will turn. The value of the moment of inertia is calculated as the sum of mass multiplied by the square of its distance (or $\sum ml^2$). Therefore, in order to achieve the kind of handling we want in a car, it is imperative to locate all heavy components as close to the center of the car as possible, and too lighten any located near the front and rear.

Locate major components within the wheelbase

The Mazda RX-7 had a 'mid-ship' engine layout, which is the most effective way to minimize the yaw moment of inertia. Following on from this, the engine, suspension system, steering linkage, tunnel, and pedal layout were optimized with consideration for securing a crash zone under the latest and most stringent of crash safety regulations. In addition, the following considerations were taken into account in order to obtain the lowest yaw moment of inertia: location and weight of the battery and fuel tank, and reducing the weight of other fixed components.

Battery

Although the battery is normally located in the engine bay, we decided to place it in the trunk. Alfa Romeos and a few other marques have this battery location, but it was unprecedented at Mazda. Despite a longer and heavier cable, it helped to bring the parts count down (we no longer required components to protect the battery from engine heat), and helped enormously in achieving better front/rear weight distribution. One young engineer proposed to use a new battery that was proven in a motorcycle; it turned out to be very successful, despite some risks. This battery was also appreciated by assembly line workers as it was lighter to lift!

Fuel tank

In an FR arrangement, the fuel tank is normally sited under the trunk, with the notable exception of BMWs. For an LWS there were two problems to solve. In order to obtain the necessary crashworthiness required for the vehicle, the rear overhang would have to be incredibly long, and did not allow space for a trunk because a spare tyre and exhaust silencer would also have to be located there. Several alternatives were devised, including locating the spare tyre behind the seats.

As a last resort, we finally decided to stack the tank and spare tyre directly on top of the rear wheel center. This also worked well in our plan to achieve a low yaw moment of inertia. But difficulty arose in securing sufficient tank capacity, while the shape of the tank became very complex. Between the rear wheels there are two driveshafts, a differential case and an exhaust pipe; each claiming its own space. The fuel tank had to have a very complex shape, and because of our limited budget, the tank had to be made from stamped steel. The shape of the tank was thoroughly investigated by challenging the limit for stampings, and the way to install the tank on the vehicle. The amount of effort devoted to solving this problem is hard to appreciate, even if the tank is inspected from below.

After the tank design was more or less determined, a plastic foam model was made to confirm to its capacity. Although there was a computer program available to calculate the capacity, data preparation was too time consuming and we took a short cut by submerging the foam block into water. Finding a pool of water sufficient to submerge the mockup was another problem. Finally, a suitable tank was found in the Design Department, but another problem cropped up. The fuel tank mock-up had too much buoyancy, and it was impossible to submerge it even with three people! Finally we broke the tank mockup into pieces and found its capacity that way, which proved to be more than adequate.

Lightweight bumpers

Bumpers are located at both ends of a car, and a reduction of their weight is critical in bringing down the yaw moment of inertia. In those days, a bumper normally had a steel reinforcement bar inside that added to the weight

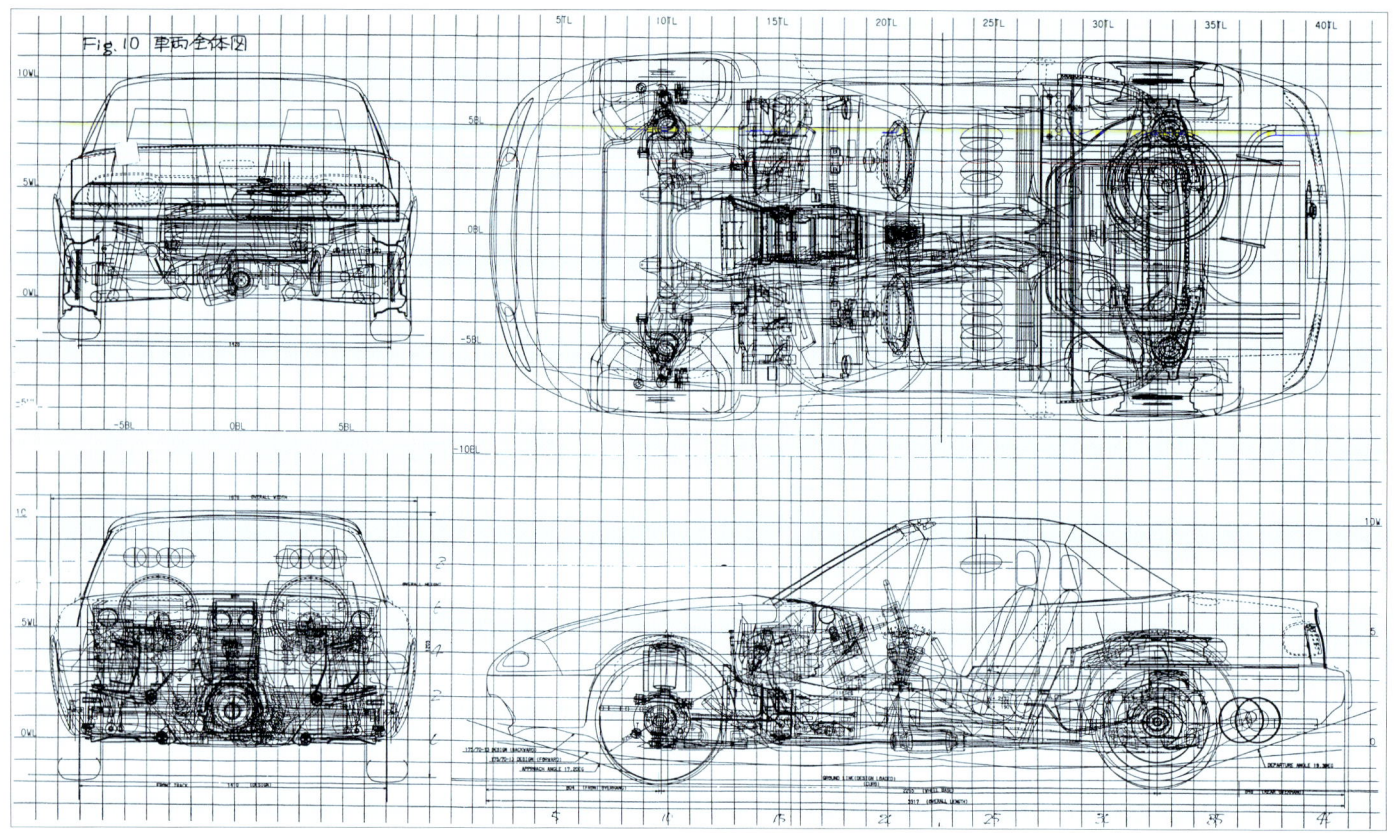

Fig. 10 車両全体図

quite considerably. A revolutionary idea proposed by the bumper designer was to fabricate the component using blow molded plastics. I knew a little bit about blow molding, but nothing beyond a plastic tank fabrication process. When I saw the final product, all of my concerns literally blew away. I have never been so moved by the fact that our engineers could devise anything if it was considered a necessity.

Amazing measurement result

Once the prototype was made and road tested, I felt that the car had excellent handling, just as we'd expected, but I was still not sure if the yaw moment of inertia was anywhere near the value we were looking for. One day a call came from the Testing and Research Division, inviting me to witness yaw moment of inertia measurement. What I saw was a prototype car hanging by wire from the ceiling. I was extremely happy to witness that the car had a very low moment of inertia, justifying all our hard work.

A final thought

In an American car magazine of the late 1970s or early 1980s, there was an article entitled: "What is a Sports Car." Among the many opinions expressed, I was struck by key phrases such as, "wind in the hair," and "no desire to smoke while driving." These words have stuck with me ever since, and I can still remember them vividly. When an American journalist had the chance to test drive a prototype, he left the car saying: "This car needs driving gloves to enjoy. Thanks for making such a fine car and congratulations." The journalist's name was familiar, and upon reading his name card, I remembered that he was the very person who wrote: "No desire to smoke while driving."

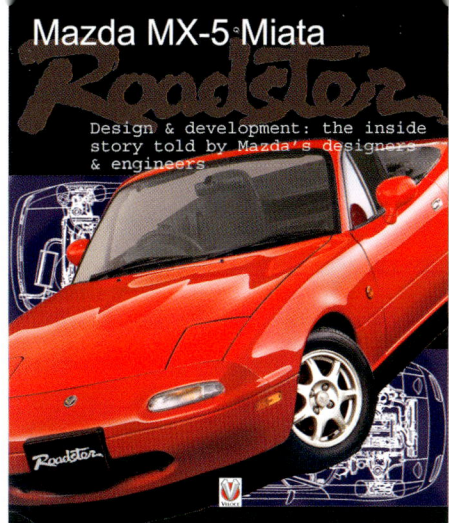

3

Vehicle engineering
by **Naoyuki Ikemizu**

Ikemizu was the group leader during the design, testing and production phase of the project. It is a tribute to his leadership that production start-up went without incident. He often hosted post-sunset communication meetings with the team members, something that has proven to be very effective ever since it started 16 years ago, and there is little sign of it stopping even now.

T. Hirai

What does vehicle engineering mean?

In general, an engineering designer is a person who is believed to be designing a product by himself. It is not the case with an automobile, where more than 100 engineers are involved in its engineering design work. There are various design sections including, but not limited to, engine, suspension, body, interior and exterior, electronics, and there are specialists in each of these fields. In order to realize a product, these engineers have to co-operate for the sake of consistency and in order to reach common targets in cost, weight, space and performance. At Mazda, that co-operation and adjustment function was called "vehicle engineering."

One day, when I was an engineer on bumper systems, my manager Abe called me up. He told me to join a new team as a vehicle engineering leader. I relished the opportunity, without even asking what the project was all about. I wanted to take part in the engineering of a whole car someday, but did not expect to do it so soon. Abe told me that the project was short of people and had no place to work, so find a suitable place first and do the work with minimum manpower.

Normally new car development at Mazda starts with Basic Layout Design, where the basic layout drawing and general design requirements are drafted. Design model proposals are generally proceeding concurrently, or slightly ahead. The Vehicle Engineering phase starts after such layout drawings and design proposals are made and the general design requirements are released. A Vehicle Engineering leader is nominated to co-ordinate the project with various engineering design departments. After the co-ordination work is over, the leader secures approval from the various engineering design managers, and the whole project is taken over by an assigned department, which is responsible for engineering drawing release and mass production.

Contrary to the above practice, I proposed a project team system consisting of a small number of dedicated engineers. The project responsibility would rest with the team (Product Program Manager, Vehicle Engineering Leader and

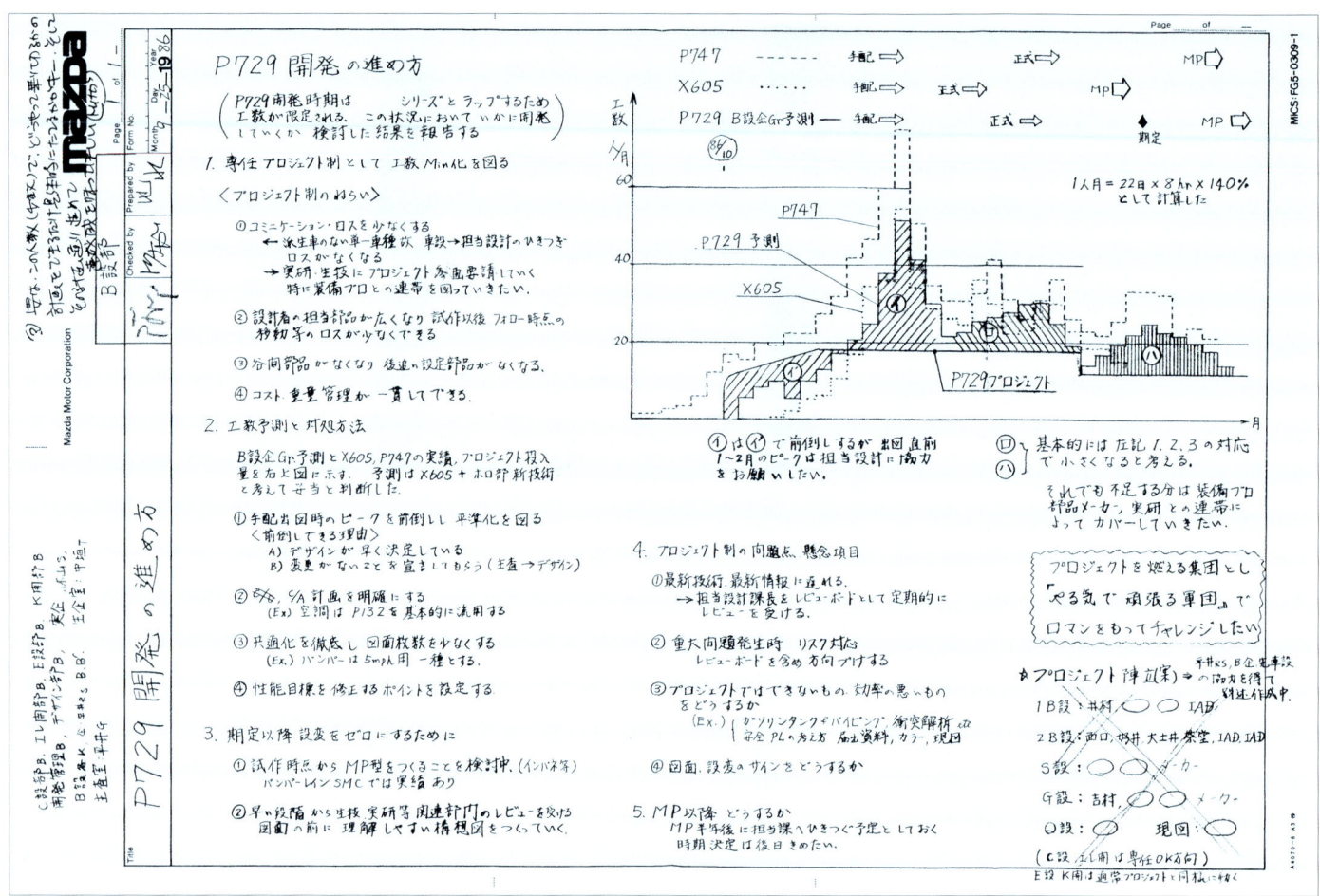

dedicated members), starting with five or six engineers, with possible additions as and when they were needed. For the work that could be time shared, such as the airbag, instrument and switch design, we would designate engineers ahead of time. With this approach, the number of man-hours would be reduced to 50% of the conventional process. I made a proposal and secured the approval of the management. The entire project approach was new to Mazda.

Engineers assigned

The entire activity took place in a primitive room on the fifth floor of the Design Building nicknamed the "Riverside Hotel." The project room had a carefree atmosphere and, mentally, was very relaxing,

however. There were no engineering or quality standards in place. In an ordinary design room, its walls are filled with documents containing all the engineering and quality standards that are generally called "design tools." Since the project room was a converted car park, it had no luxuries, but a convenient feature was the car lift, capable of bringing in any car we wanted at any time to place it right next to the drawing board. No-one had experience of designing a convertible, so there was no expertise in this field. But by fully utilizing the special feature of the project room, our car lift, we were able to bring in such cars as the Alfa Romeo Spider, Porsche 911, Lotus Elan and Lotus Super Seven right in front of our desk to

learn what a roadster was all about.

As mentioned earlier, Vehicle Engineering is not a formal organization. It is a function only effective during a certain time period, when all of the related design departments get together to make necessary design adjustments. For a period of three to six months, planners, designers, cost controllers, basic layout designers, component designers, testing engineers and production engineers get together at one location in order to determine the vehicle performance, quality and its structure.

Generally speaking, the early part of development is carried out by the Product Planning Division (which includes Product Planning

The design room - 'The Riverside Hotel' - was a converted car park. There were more drawing boards and tables than CAD terminal units - the opposite of today.

A cosmopolitan team was assembled, with Japanese members and five European countries represented.

and Basic Layout Design), and at a given point the project is taken over by the Vehicle Engineering team, where all of the related engineering design departments are gathered together to decide on the final layout design. A review will be conducted on the final layout design and, after its authorization, each functional design department brings back the requirements and prepares its final engineering drawings.

In the case of the MX-5/Miata, the small project started on its own without having the support of the Planning or the Basic Layout Design Departments, and all members of the team were asked to work through the detailed engineering design. By keeping all the project staff together, there was no loss due to personnel change, section change or location change, and the entire design work proceeded seamlessly and efficiently.

The project team members were quite varied. There were 20 members including, one Product Program Manager, Hirai, and four assistants, one cost planner, one basic layout engineer (a newcomer,

just out of school), ten component designers (five of whom were from overseas; two from the UK, one from Czechoslovakia, one from Poland and one from France), and one production engineer. The five overseas engineers were dispatched from a British consulting company. With these overseas members, there were some arguments on how to proceed with the development. They were fiercely opposed to making any design change after the basic layout design was fixed, and sometimes it took a week to convince them to come to an agreement.

At Mazda, a small change in the basic layout design is normally accepted if it improves function, productivity or cost, but the European engineers insisted that no changes should be allowed. They said that once a basic layout is established, component designers are to design each component within a given allowance, and he should never go back and ask to change the basic layout. In truth, they spend more time before they complete the basic layout which precludes later changes. Mazda's approach

includes much more flexibility, but at the same time it would be regarded as sloppy by European standards. Although there were differences in philosophy, I remember one day we all observed the nearby mountains on the other side of Hiroshima City, covered with snow as the sun was setting. We were all struck by the beauty of the scene, and soon after, the joint work seemed to go far more smoothly.

Total integration
Each component designer always wishes to put his best efforts into his designated component in order to make it the lightest, best performing and most economical of all. But in making a product package, it is important to combine those parts that are the best in the world with the most advanced technologies and those other parts that need to be simple and economical, giving the final product the right balance of cost, weight and performance. In order to achieve this balance, it is necessary to clearly identify what kind of automobile is to be made, with which engine and what kind

人馬一体

of suspension system is needed, all the way down to materials. After establishing these basic requirements, each component will have its final design requirements. There were about 1000 parts needing a new design, and each engineer had to have a good understanding as to the design targets for every component.

The most difficult job at this stage was to designate those engineers who were not expected to do much work. In other words, for those parts that needed to be the best in the world we allocated ample budget and design resources, but the other parts that did not require such a demanding target were compromised for cost and weight. For example, the MX-5/Miata did not have an aggressive target for quietness. Therefore, there was not much work for the soundproofing engineers, even though these engineers normally have their own goal images. If they worked towards meeting their targets, this would result in unnecessary quietness, combined with higher cost and weight. As a result, it was necessary to tell them that for this project, they need only do a limited amount of work.

State of the art technology often translates into higher weight and cost. In order to save weight or cost, or preferably both, my job was to select those parts that did not require such high technology, and convey this message to the engineers. Although engineers were told this, it is in their nature to want to do their best job. In order not to discourage them, it was often necessary for me to tell the engineers that their component was very effective in cost and weight reduction, helping to give the final product a very good balance of cost, weight and performance, and thereby making it affordable for younger customers.

Weight calculation & the mystery of weight totalling
The MX-5/Miata is assembled using about 3000 components, including roughly 1500 nuts, bolts and other fasteners. Of the remaining 1500 components, about 1000 were to be newly designed, meaning that new design drawings were needed. In order to estimate the weight of the completed car, the weight of these newly designed parts has to be estimated and added to the other 2000 parts.

Assuming the weight of the roadster to be 1000kg (2200lb), although it was actually 950kg (2090lb), about 1500 fasteners weighed 15kg (33lb), or an average of about 10g (0.4oz) each. Those parts borrowed from other designs weighed about 60kg (132lb) in total, or averaged out at about 200g (7oz) each. One thousand new components were estimated to weigh 925kg (2035lb), averaging about 925g (33oz) each. In totaling the weight of the MX-5/Miata, we requested to get the numbers in three digits, but many gave us only two digit totals. And if the third digits alone were rounded up, the accumulated total could indicate up to plus 5kg (11lb). Those designers having concern for their newly designed parts normally give, consciously or unconsciously, heavier numbers. If all of the designers estimated 25g (0.9oz) heavier for each component, weighing an average of 925g (33oz), this extra margin would come up to 25kg (55lb)!

Since these are calculated figures, there are often mistakes, and such mistakes often end up on the heavy side. Capable engineers are often very busy, and these engineers often gave us very rough estimates. This is only the beginning of weight estimation for a new car, however. After a prototype is made, and both the complete car and individual components are weighed, it is normally the case that the actual car and component weights do not match with the calculated weight. Weight calculation is theoretical, based on the drawings, and there are later numerous design changes, which have to be accounted for in order to know the exact weight.

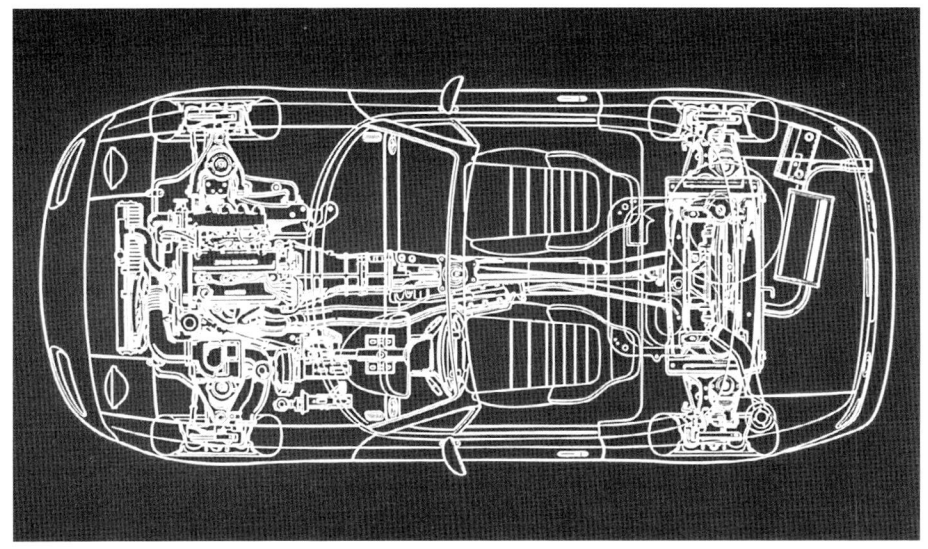

Basic layout drawing.

Weight control

Total weight control of a car starts with an accumulation of data from each design section. Starting from a meeting with each designer, weight for each of the parts, and weight for each functional group of parts is calculated. Risk of excessive weight and opportunities to save weight have to be calculated by judging the technical difficulties, and even including the character of each designer. The initial weight estimation was 50kg (110lb) heavier than our original target. As a LWS, our original target had to be achieved, and without question, we wanted it to be less than 1000kg (2200lb) because of the inertia weight ranking for emission tests in Japan and to achieve the "fun-to-drive" quality we desired.

While we studied ways to reduce the weight of some components at the sacrifice of additional cost, we also conducted more thorough interviews with each designer to sift out minor mistakes and over-estimations. In the end, we had to give weight reduction targets to some engineers, but we could not be confident. As a last resort, we asked our Product Program Manager to accept aluminum for the bonnet and PPF, as well as polycarbonate for the instrument panel. To further reduce weight, we asked that the weld flange of all body panels be reduced by 1mm (0.04in.), this in addition to weight reduction holes. The total length of body panel welding flanges is about 30m (98ft.) and a 1mm (0.04in.) reduction would save around 360g (13oz). The normal welding flange was about 17mm (0.67in.) deep, but where welding was easy, it had a smaller margin already. We asked Setsuo Nakagaki of the production engineering section to check every body panel to determine where reductions were possible, and we finally reduced weight by 250g (9oz) using this method.

The biggest headache we had during such tedious work was how not to have Shunji Tanaka, chief designer, and Minoru Nakamura, interior designer, do the work as they wanted to do it. They both wanted to put in door trim that had a nice contour with one-piece injected plastic. Against their wish, we proposed a flat door trim similar to those used in the Titan truck, and with a weight target similar to some micro-minicars. We told them to design only an inner door handle, and the rest must be left Spartan to comply with the "Simple is Best" ideal. In view of total cost allocation and to give the right combination of dynamic performances, such as the running and stopping capability necessary for a sports car, we could not have any luxury. They were simply very unhappy with such poor cost allocation. We kept chanting "Simple is Best" as our only weapon against them. We threatened them by saying that if the car was overweight by just 1kg (2.2lb), it would cost us vehicle certification, and that they understood.

I still feel guilty for giving them such a threat to this day. But weight is tougher than cost, and it is an absolute reality. I believe that they did a wonderful job under such heavy restrictions. There were no strong criticisms from the market regarding the simple and black only interior – customers seemed to accept our "Simple is Best" philosophy without question.

Yoshimura, who designed the instrument panel and center console, had a deep involvement with this project from the beginning. He finally achieved his cost and weight targets, although he fought with Hirai at times. He chose a rather expensive but

strong material for the instrument panel, to pass the crash safety test as the main reason, but really to achieve his weight target. In reality, Yoshimura cheated Hirai, who was not a specialist in interior materials, by omitting to use paint on the panel ... However, nobody knew at that time that this would pay off in allowing the roadster to its clear crash safety test so easily.

The ashtray was a ten-year old design, and we borrowed many interior parts from the Mazda parts bins. Some parts, such as the center console box lid, were a little bit difficult to use for the right-hand drive model customers because it was a common part with left-hand drive cars. One unexpected benefit of such common usage was the fact that the parking brake lever was located near the left seat, again focused for left-hand drive models, so that a right-hand drive car driver could touch his date's knee! Accidentally, of course ...

Territorial dispute

The period of vehicle engineering is also the time for territorial disputes amongst the different design departments. Each department fights for space in order to give its components the best position. Hirai, Product Program Manager, served as a referee.

If a good space is allocated to a component or system, detailed design will be much easier. Since the available space in a car is very limited, and restricted due to design considerations, nothing comes easy. And this, sometimes, resulted in new technology and invention. The proverb, "Necessity is the Mother of Invention," is quite often true in such cases. Design work is all about drawing pictures on a new white sheet of paper, but when there is little or no restriction, it is very difficult to start the work, and strangely the engineers are the people who feel pressured if complete freedom is allowed.

In order to give good protection against rain, we gave a great deal of freedom to the designers and requested their best proposal for the weather strip design. They proposed a weather strip about 50% thicker than normal. I then ordered the engineering side not to allow any water leaks, and the soft-top had to be made very light so as to enable single-handed operation from the driver's seat. At the same time, we asked our production people to come up with a good manufacturing method, while we requested our sales people to tell their customers that there might be a leak or two in this car. In production models, we did not experience any water leakage problems, but we had to be very careful as the soft-top would tilt if the car was parked on an incline and that might cause leakage.

It is generally true that engineers ask for more space than necessary when developing new technology. In a LWS, we had to eliminate any excess. In the development of the MX-5/Miata we did not stick with the ideal of new technology. Instead we sought a new way of thinking. At a time when automobile safety requirements seemed overwhelming, we chose a roadster. Rather than pursuing quietness, we sought a healthy and powerful exhaust note. We wanted good handling rather than a smooth ride, positive steering response rather than light steering, and a Spartan interior rather than a luxurious one. And as for the driver, we designed the driver's seat for an average size person, rather than making it adaptable to all sizes.

This way of thinking had to be

understood internally and had to be shared among all project members. The period we worked on the vehicle engineering phase was a period of propaganda. We became the missionaries, spreading the philosophy to testing engineers, production engineers, inspection personnel, and finally the PR and sales people. They had to be brainwashed with this idea so that the customers would share the same ideal with us. Our Product Program Manager was the guru of LWS culture, and he continued to be so.

The members of the testing and research group became our strongest supporters. They worked hard to allow as many internal people as possible to try the roadster, and have them understand this new way of thinking. They somehow got the exclusive use of Mazda's proving ground for days on end to have production engineers and inspection personnel test the prototype, and they even took them out at night for drives on winding roads in the mountains. All these activities were unheard of at Mazda. A high-speed test course was often available, and could be used exclusively, but the general road course was not. Therefore, they found a stretch of winding road suitable to test the handling of the roadster deep in the mountains of Hiroshima Prefecture. I remember taking one

such drive at night where we forgot about our work and simply enjoyed controlling the car.

Wheelbase

At a time when most of the basic layout design was firming up, the designers, led by Tanaka, proposed shortening the wheelbase. They said that the present wheelbase length would make it look like a Dachshund. Their claim seemed justifiable upon inspecting a clay model. But at that time the wheelbase was already very short, actually shorter than that of a standard micro-minicar. Upon inspecting the clay model, however, all the project engineers agreed, as if hypnotized by Tanaka, that they would work hard to shorten the wheelbase. A short wheelbase would make the car even more responsive, and that was a step in the right direction. We finally reduced it by 13mm (0.5in).

It is generally unthinkable to change the basic specification during the vehicle engineering stage, and it would have been impossible had the basic layout design been drawn by hand. Our Product Program Manager had instructed Watanabe to apply CAD from the basic layout design stage, and it was the CAD application that made this fundamental change possible. For this project, somehow the PPM had a higher authority for the basic layout design than the head of that

department. In a hand-drawn layout drawing, shortening the wheelbase would take at least one-and-a-half months to shift all the components in the drawing. With the use of CAD, the change took place immediately without fuss. The wheelbase was eventually fixed at 2265mm (89.2in).

The battery & spare tyre

The biggest headache in the layout design was the location of the battery and spare tyre. Normally a battery is located in the engine compartment. The MX-5/Miata had bulky and straight front frames for rigidity and crash worthiness. In addition, the retractable headlamp system took up a larger space than usual in

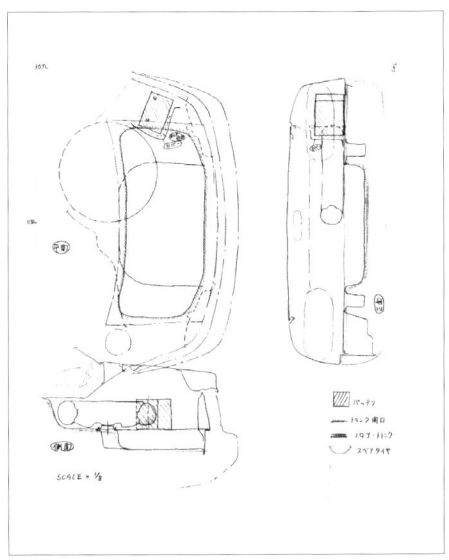

the compartment. All this meant the battery had to be located in the trunk (boot); however, in order to reduce the yaw moment of inertia, a heavy component like a battery should not be located in the overhanging part of the body. We thought we might find a space behind a seat, though it was later discovered that there was a conflict. A bar, necessary to lift the chassis on the production line, interfered with the lid for the battery due to the short wheelbase. Installing the battery after the final assembly would not allow the car to be moved off the line under its own power. We could not change the chassis lift hanger because this would not allow different cars to share a single production line, leading to a productivity problem.

The only space left was in the trunk, which had to be shared with a spare wheel. Locating the battery there would not allow enough space for two golf bags in the trunk, as originally planned, although, in any case, it was difficult to secure this much room from the beginning. We concluded that one golf bag was okay, although it was still quite a tight fit in the trunk.

At the beginning there was a lot of argument, in the interest of lighter weight, over whether a spare wheel was really needed. In the US, some states require a spare, and there were other countries that also required a spare wheel by law. So a spare wheel was a necessity, but we decided to use a temporary spare that was thinner and lighter than a standard wheel. For those countries that required a standard wheel as a spare, we simply decided not to sell the roadster there. As I remember, these were countries in the Middle East and South America.

Going back to the spare wheel, a question was raised as to how to put the standard wheel with its punctured tyre into the car after exchanging it with the temporary spare? There was not enough space. There was even an argument that the standard wheel would have be carried on the passenger seat, and to offer a vinyl bag as standard equipment for this purpose. If we put the spare tyre in the trunk, it would interfere with the space required for the soft-top link system.

Hirai was strongly opposed to raising the stack height of the soft-top, and we could not ask the designers to extend the body overhang again. Fortunately, though, the designers wanted to increase the height of the central body section in order to compensate for the appearance change brought about by rounding off the four corners of the car. This gave just enough space behind the seats above the differential unit to locate the tyre. A small increase in the yaw moment of inertia was compensated for by rounding off the corners of the car. But be warned, only a space saver type spare wheel will fit into the wheelwell!

Panel gaps

During the 1980s, stamping (panel forming by press) technology improved tremendously, along with the precision of the stamped parts. Whereas the gaps between the main body and the doors and bonnet, etc, had been between 7-8mm (around 0.30in.) in the past, 5mm (0.20in.) became the new standard, and some gaps were narrowed down even further; but it was understood that the smaller the gap, the higher the production technology required. At Mazda, the standard gap around a closed door was getting down to 4mm (0.16in).

However, for a convertible, where body rigidity is lower, it was a different story. A thorough simulation with CAE indicated 5mm (0.20in.) as the best gap, but the production people insisted on a smaller gap. Measuring the gap on a prototype under extremely rough road driving conditions showed about 3mm (0.12in.) movement and proved that a 5mm (0.20in.) gap was the required minimum. It was finally agreed to settle on 5mm (0.20in.) after Tanaka's statement: "The beauty of the line and surface, and the attractive curvature in the MX-5/

Miata's design will not be marred by a 5mm gap between the body and the door panels."

As exemplified by the above, some of the design requirements for the MX-5/Miata were different to those of the existing standards at Mazda. In fact, the Product Program Manager had to issue a specially-signed statement to the final vehicle inspection team to indemnify them regarding panel gap size variation on the roadster.

Vehicle design review

Several design reviews were conducted during the vehicle engineering phase but, due to the unprecedented nature of the design, they were not enough. In general, such design reviews were conducted to confirm how Mazda's internal standards and requirements were being followed. For the MX-5/Miata, this traditional approach was not applicable, as almost every aspect of the design was different to that found in existing models. In the design review, we took a reverse approach and pointed out those areas that were not in line with internal requirements, or potential problems in need of more design refinement.

We would say things like: "Yes, there is water leakage and we are increasing the cross-section of the weather strips to prevent it. This will be checked in the next test.

"The exhaust noise level is just within the allowable limit. Exhaust note is another important character of a LWS. We are working to get a lively and crisp exhaust note suitable for a sports car.

"Interior width is set deliberately tight so that the driver will be sitting properly with his elbow resting on the door trim. We will not increase the width.

"Front visibility is limited and may hinder the view of traffic signals in some cases. This is due to the exterior design and the desired level of wind intrusion into the cockpit when running with the top down."

Through this approach, we tried to win the confidence of the internal reviewers, allowing them to gain a clearer understanding of the LWS concept we'd established for this project.

Aerodynamic engineers endured many hours of testing in wintertime in the wind tunnel to choose the best windshield angle (they had to manually control a variable angle windshield) so that the draft was well controlled when the top was down. When the soft-top cover design had to be fixed, I joined the wind tunnel test because nobody was assigned as a responsible person. Interior designers maintained that it was the responsibility of the soft-top design group, and the soft-top design group argued just the opposite.

The wind tunnel tests not only tested the roadster design but also the endurance of the engineers working on it. The soft-top was tested even at minus 30 degrees Centigrade, although the owner's manual recommended not opening or closing the soft-top in freezing temperatures. Test cars were normally soaked for 4 hours under such extremely low temperatures before testing, but 20 minutes was the limit for the testing engineers.

One subject that provoked a big argument was the water leak inspection procedure. Quality assurance engineers argued that in order to ensure water tightness of the soft-top, a shower test of 30 minutes was necessary. For a closed car, they run only a five-minute shower test, with occasional 30-minute tests on a random sample basis so they can guarantee the model's water tightness. For the roadster, however, they insisted on a 30-minute shower test on all production cars. This would require a dedicated test line about 100m (328ft.) long just for a shower test. Finally, they agreed that such a lengthy test was not necessary, and accepted our argument that a larger weather strip cross-section would take care of production deviations in the body. We had also promised to provide special instructions to the sales and service group on the handling of the roadster. As is evident from the foregoing, one of the most important jobs for the

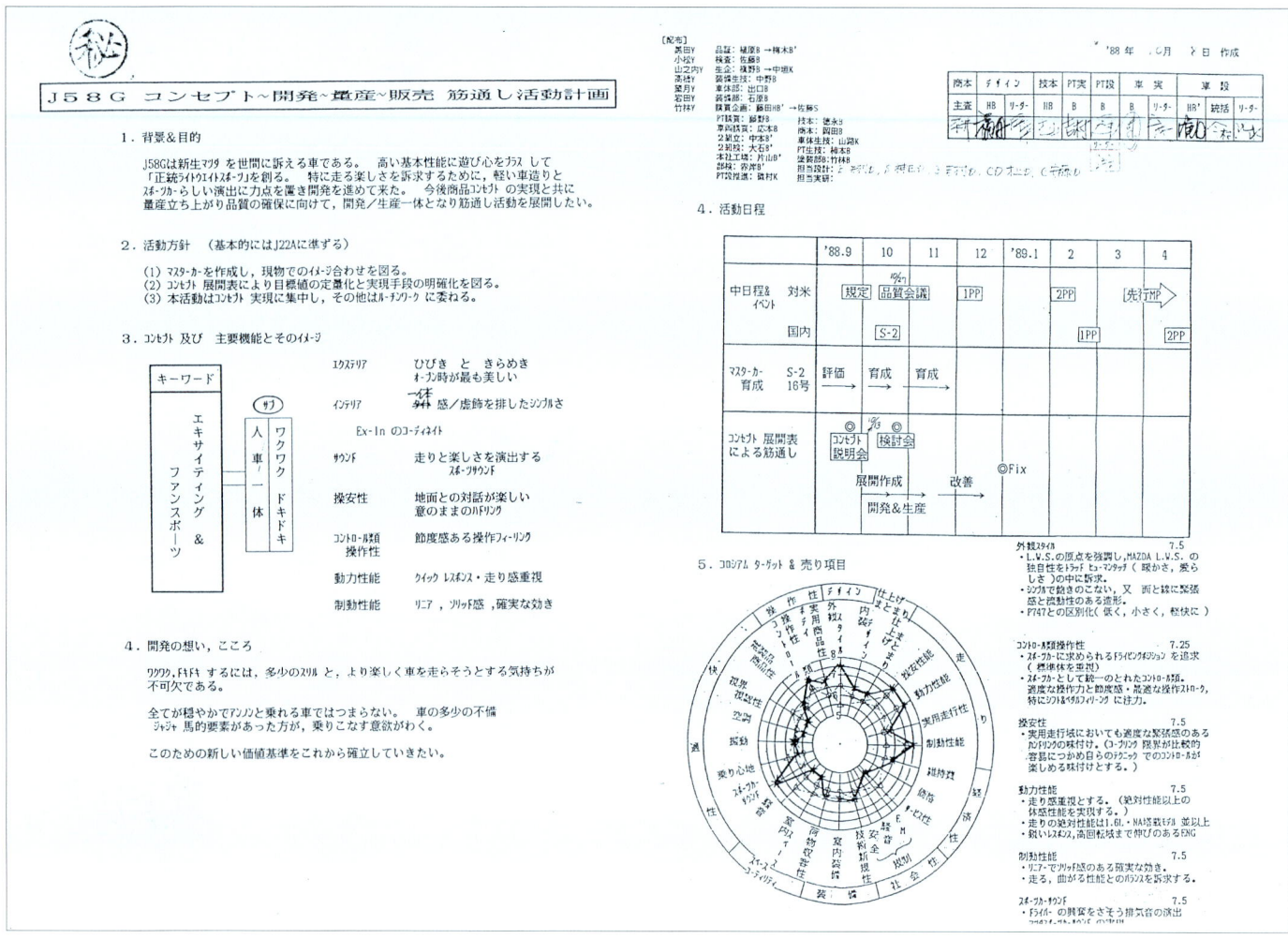

Product Program Manager was to negotiate with groups responsible for quality assurance, sales and service.

Design freeze & the direct production method

Everything about the roadster was lightweight, including its development, with scant funds and little manpower. But the design freeze and direct production method worked well, and saved the project. In a normal product development process, prototype parts are made with prototype dies, and after thorough testing production dies are made in preparation for mass production. The direct production method eliminated the prototype production process for specific parts, and mass production dies were made concurrently with the prototype. This meant no design changes were allowed for such parts, or the production dies would have to be redone. Therefore, we declared a design freeze early in the development stage.

When a competitor introduces a new car, the sales group will often request a design change to a model being developed. To prevent that, the PPM and Chief Designer gathered everyone involved and, after showing the latest version of the car, declared a design freeze. This does not completely eliminate prototype parts production, of course. Plastic parts, for instance, shrink after injection, and so we had to check them via a prototyping process. We made two plastic interior component prototype dies because, in the name of weight reduction, we had specified about half thickness for these parts. But for those parts that are similar in design or those using existing technology, we applied the direct production approach as much as possible.

The direct production approach eliminated a great deal of effort in development, too. We did not have to re-evaluate the final production parts from the production die. (It often happens that, even if a prototype part

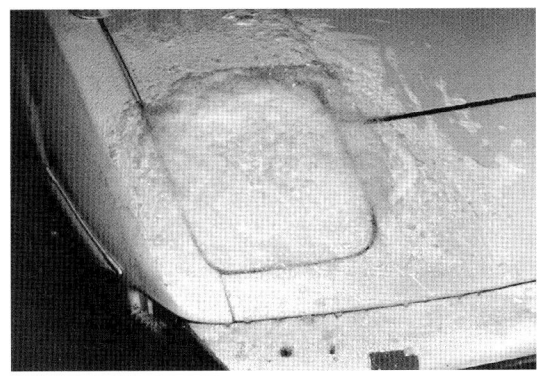

Retractable headlamp cold weather testing on the RX-7. This picture was taken during a test to see how the system would work after being exposed to sub-zero temperatures, and snow and ice. The room was kept at minus 30 degrees C.

passed all inspections, some do not pass the final evaluation due to the fact that they have been made with different dies.) Different dies meant different products and different performance, even though the dies were almost identical. This time, we had good control over the production problem, and technical issues raised during pilot production were resolved very quickly, helping us immensely when it came to the start of mass production. It all passed largely without incident.

Cost mystery

There is no one right answer when it comes to costing. To start with, all designers calculate each component cost and the data is compiled, but these calculations rarely come close to the cost target. Such data can be manipulated to make it look like it meets the target, however, and one also has to allow for the inevitable mistakes, as data from the purchasing section is not always accurate. Since everyone involved in making a part is responsible for the cost of it, no one person can really be responsible for the cost, and there seems to be no-one who can control the total cost. It is such a complicated issue.

I remember there was one particular part that was noticeably more costly than its target. Upon research, it was discovered that the component was supposed to

be transported from the supplier to the assembly line with a very expensive packing material for the fear of damaging the part. The decision to use this expensive packing was made by the receiving inspection group without consulting with the design or production teams.

In the planning stage, a large sales target volume would lower production costs, for it would lower the amortization cost of the production tooling. When the start of production nears, the sales side may become less ambitious, and target sales volumes may go down, which affects the cost. On the other hand, there is a continuous cost reduction program at any production or procurement facility. Cost is constantly changing, and it is very difficult to control during the development stage, yet cost management is always necessary. Furthermore, cost means different things to different people. Costs for internally produced components and costs for bought-in components are treated differently in calculation procedures. Furthermore, exchange rate variations affect the target cost for Mazda, because of the high export volumes involved. When the yen was getting higher and the rate was closing on to 100 yen to the dollar, I wondered how the cost accounting people could deal with such variances.

Unforgettable incidents

One year prior to the start of production, we tested several prototype cars in the US. By coincidence we met with a team of Australian Ford engineers who were also testing a small convertible. Since Mazda was supplying the engines we knew about the new car they had under development. Theirs was an FF vehicle, and ours looked much better. I sensed that our car would win over theirs, and at the same time I felt the strong responsibility to put the car into production as quickly as possible. During the same period, while we were testing in the mountains of California, we met a highway patrol. We explained to the police our purpose for being there, and they just smiled and left us alone. They came back over the next two days to see us testing the car – they, too, seemed to be enjoying it.

About six months prior to production, we took the car to the testing organization attached to an insurance company for a crash test. The car would be crashed into a concrete wall at a certain speed to estimate the damage repair costs. We saw the test car with its crushed front end and went back to the hotel. The next morning, the car was completely repaired and the person in charge said: "Congratulations. The insurance premium will be of an affordable amount. For a sports

Prototype testing in America.

car, its repair cost is less than average, and replacement parts are cheaper too." I shook hands with him saying "Thanks a lot." That was about all I could say in English!

Mass production started on 31 March 1989. I was walking along the assembly line with the first production car to see if there was anything I could do in case something happened. But everything went without any incident, and Nakagaki of Production Engineering, Kishino of the Inspection Department, and Moriyama of Testing and Research each told me that if there was any

problem they would take care of it, and that I should go back to my own work ...

For the MX-5/Miata, we purposely informed our associates of all the potential problems the car might have in meeting traditional standards, and had established a good common understanding on the allowable limits for an open two-seater. This was largely due to the fact that Moriyama took us all for test rides in open sports cars gathered from all over the world. Starting with a Lotus Super Seven, we then tried a Porsche 911, a racing kart, and even a dune buggy! Moriyama and

his group let us drive all of these vehicles, and that helped greatly in establishing what was acceptable for the roadster within Mazda.

Today, I commute to work in an early production model of the MX-5/Miata, taking about 40 minutes each way. On a fine day, I take a special route through a mountain pass with the top down. Driving leisurely on an open road helps dissipate all the daily stress and fatigue from work. I sincerely hope that our roadster will continue to provide driving pleasure to all sports car fans around the world.

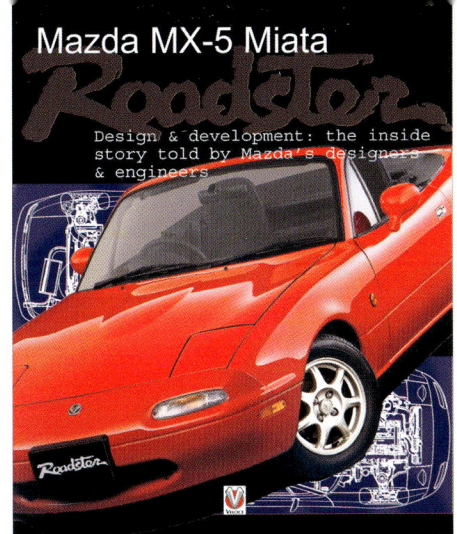

Roadster

Design & development: the inside
story told by Mazda's designers
& engineers

Roadster

4

The MANA proposal
& beyond
by **Tom Matano**

Tom Matano has a deep passion for sports cars, especially those of the 1960s (he owns a beautiful De Tomaso Vallelunga, and loves old Alfa Romeos). An inspirational stylist, he now lives in California, heading Industrial Design at San Francisco's Academy of Art College.

B. Long

On reflection, the MX-5/Miata program became a reality through a collection of coincidences. We had the right group of people in the right places at the right time, with the right economic climate. If the MX-5/Miata had come out a year or two earlier or later, it wouldn't have been as successful. If one of the key personnel had been missing, then the MX-5/Miata would not have happened at all.

The MX-5 project was a very special and emotional one in my life. I would like to spend the next few pages, if I may, to revisit some of the memories of that time ...

In the beginning
When I joined Mazda in 1983, the then President, Kenichi Yamamoto,

T. MATANO 8·85

Early design sketch.

also known as the foster father of the Rotary Engine, started to develop his vision of Mazda's identity. Addressing the entire R&D staff, Yamamoto explained his view of the automobile that Mazda should build by writing an essay entitled "Love Affair with the Automobile" and "Kansei Engineering."

In order to understand what Yamamoto was trying to illustrate, you need to understand his interpretation of the Japanese word *Kansei*. *Kansei* is based upon the realization that humans judge how they feel about the world around them by using more than just the sum of their five senses; they add aesthetics, and their personal values and emotions into the equation in order to complete their perception. All of these ingredients combined together create for us a world that is then infused with both physical and psychical sensations, not just one or the other.

Based on this philosophy, Mazda's designers and engineers started to create vehicles that became more than just the sum of their technology and parts. With Yamamoto's essay and the philosophy of Kansei Engineering as its guide, the design team started on the quest of finding brand identity by studying its own history – finding Mazda's roots. In doing so, we were able to find that our most memorable products

were each very innovative in terms of engineering, and highly attractive designs in their time. Combining this discovery of our heritage with the idea of a love affair with an automobile, we developed a design strategy that can best be described by the story entitled "Inspired Sensations" – the story behind our philosophy.

"Inspired sensations"

A car starts to draw more attention than others: it either passes on a freeway, or you see it for a split second on the TV screen. It makes you want to find out what it is.

You start to develop some expectations about how it might feel to drive, how you might look in it, or the lifestyle you might lead with it. After a while, you discover that it is a Mazda.

It is then that you may want to go to the dealership for a closer look. Upon closer inspection, you

are satisfied that your expectations and excitement were justified.

You open the door and the sight of the interior is so inviting that you can't help but sit in it.

At the first turn of the key, the engine starts with purposeful sounds, and it feels exactly like how you imagined it would.

The first turn of the wheel ... how it corners ... the way it stops ... the car goes beyond your initial expectations. By the end of the test drive, you would like to become a Mazda owner.

In the past, our product development efforts ended at that very moment, but it is here that our new philosophy begins. We continued to describe the type of life our customer would lead after the purchase:

You take the car home and, of course, take the family for a ride

Making the first design study model.

and show it to your neighbors and friends. After the initial excitement has subsided and just before you retire to bed, you stop for one last look, even say "Goodnight" to the car, or maybe you even sit in the car just once more.

On your daily route, you start to think of more challenging roads or new routes, in order to spend more time with the car. On your first out-of-town trip, you discover other aspects about the car's personality that you didn't realize from your daily routine. You discover the depth of the car more and more as days, months, and years go by.

Of course, even with the most prolonged driver-car relationship, there comes a time when you have to part with your beloved car – and you do part with it. But those fond memories – you will treasure them for a long, long time.

And further down the road, you seek out and find the same model, buy it again and restore it.

The first product developed under this philosophy was the MX-5/Miata, and the response to our design was overwhelming. For example, many MX-5/Miata owners are so attached to the car that they celebrate the date they purchased their cars (or "babies") as birthdays. Other stories told to me by owners described how some went so far as to spend the first night in the car. Instilling this type

of kinship and "pride of ownership" became a top priority in our design efforts and in developing our brand identity.

The MX-5 story (Part I)

At the beginning of the lightweight sports car (LWS) project, I wrote a memo that went along with the story of "Inspired Sensations." The memo covered more specific details about the "Dos and Don'ts" of creating a true sports car. At the time, I was driving a second generation RX-7 Turbo and I noticed many things that I didn't care for. Because I wanted everything to be perfect for our new and special project, I had to make sure that even the most minute details could not be overlooked. The following is an approximation of the memo I created for the LWS, based on my experience with the cars that I'd owned in the past:

The grip size of the steering wheel and the shift knob should be of the same thickness and feel. The gearshift linkage should be mechanical, and its feel should be direct. Its throw should be short so that it will shift as if you just used a wrist action. The cooling fan should be synchronized with the engine rpm directly, or an electrical fan of smaller diameter should be used, so that it doesn't sound like a regular passenger car. Movement of the tachometer needle should be

synchronized with not only the rpm, but also the torque increase. Turning of the steering wheel should be linear with the car's movement. I recommend switches from the RX-7, which have an extremely short-stroke and thus feel very solid and direct. In fact, every switch should feel direct with their mechanism. The exhaust noise should be carefully tuned, so I recommend an exhaust sound similar to the BMW M1's as a benchmark.

The feel of the two grips was something that could definitely not be overlooked because I did not want anyone to feel that awkward difference between their two hands after taking one hand off the wheel in order to grab the shift knob. For such a new and special sports car, even the sounds of the fan and exhaust were things that could not be ordinary, like any other passenger car. It was the attention to such details that would help drive the creation of a masterpiece.

I later received a call from the program manager for the LWS, Mr Hirai, asking me to send him a recording of the exhaust sounds from the various cars we recommended. I had to mention that American people not only hear these sounds with their ears, but through their body. I found out that he had gone ahead in recording several exhaust sounds

The MANA design studio.

and tested those with numerous people. Through his research, he was able to identify the ones with the most "sports car-like" sounds. He took those sounds and broke down the sound waves scientifically, analyzing every sound completely. The result of his research and development was a finely tuned exhaust muffler, one he created in a process much like the creation of a musical instrument. He not only recreated the "sports car sound," but also finely tuned the exact exhaust note to fit our MX-5/Miata.

In combination with the story "Inspired Sensations," my memo and other recommendations from our team helped engineers in Japan understand the true nature of the sports car.

The project was an off-line one, separated from the normal approval processes, and everything was directly reported to our executive officials, including President Yamamoto himself. This special process protected our freethinking designers, planners,

and engineers from being muddled by the on-line "production" mentality. It also enabled us to have a small team of very selective talents and helped provide for us a creative, but positive type of competitive environment to work in.

As for the design development, the easiest way for Mazda to build a relatively low-cost sports car was to build it based upon a front engine/front-wheel drive (FF) sedan platform, or to place a small FF drivetrain behind the driver (with a so-called "mid-ship" layout). An example of the first mentioned design is the Fiat Barchetta, while the Pontiac Fiero, Fiat X1/9, Toyota MR2, and MG's MGF are all examples of the latter. These model types were something I had predicted that the Japan team would attempt to build.

Our team at MANA (Mazda North America) in California, however, had other plans in mind – we believed that a true LWS should have a front engine/rear-wheel drive (FR) layout. So, for the

competition for selection, we sent a full-scale clay model to Japan. The two other models we were competing against came from the Tokyo studio. Sure enough, both designs were as I predicted – an FF model, and an MR variant. But by the time all the directors came to the presentation room to select a direction, the outcome was obvious.

Everyone was drawn to our model because it had the most "sports car-like" design. In fact, it was the only one that exuded the real emotion of a sports car. It looked nimble, warm, cute, and potent. So our design was the one chosen to move on to the next step for further development. A few months later, R&D management held an engineering meeting to discuss the powertrain issues. I was called into this meeting, which

Three months after work on the clay began, the first model was completed, and can be seen here in front of a full-size rendering and literally dozens of design sketches.

54

A drivable prototype based on the first design study.

also included other key individuals from Mazda headquarters.

The meeting started with Mr Yamanouchi (the Managing Director of R&D), who asked Mr Kato (the advanced program manager) to explain the concept, and then continued discussing the LWS development to date. One of the main reasons for this meeting was to bring the other part of the engineering community on-board for this project, because, until this point, any knowledge of the project was restricted to a handful of LWS team members.

Mr Kato's presentation came to point out the main issue regarding the drivetrain layout: For a successful LWS, the FR configuration was the most important requirement. In response to this, the head of engine development asked what engine Mr Kato was planning to use for the car, to which he replied that the twin-cam, 1.6 liter, four-cylinder engine we had for the 323 would be sufficient. The head of engine development said that this engine was originally designed to work for a transversely mounted layout, and in order for the engine to be placed longitudinally to fit our new design, it would need to be re-engineered so that the many parts could be replaced to fit the

layout design that the program called for. He further stated that it was not as easy as simply picking up a motor and turning it 90 degrees. Angrily, he then stated that he had never heard of this project before and that his group didn't have the manpower available to work on it.

At one point, Mr Yamanouchi put me on the spot and asked me why the North American team was so adamant about using the front engine/rear-wheel drive layout for the car, and I knew I had to do a damn good job of convincing everyone in the room of our convictions. My explanation went something like this:

First of all, our concept for the LWS was that it must be an 'everyday sports car.' I explained to them that it means that the car is like a pair of jogging shoes – you put them on and jog around the block. It is not a pair of spiked running shoes, designed to work at their best on a track.

The mid-ship layout is like the spiked shoes – such cars need a track to perform at their best and they require special skills to utilize their full potential. This layout is also artificially designed for maximum cornering capability, making it the best design layout for

racing and high-end, exotic sports cars.

The front-engine/front-wheel drive layout is like a horse-drawn chariot. It's also characteristically artificial in its maneuvering capabilities. You are pulled forward, almost forcefully instead of having a natural transition in the movement.

To sum it all up: both designs provide an artificial or man-made feel. The idea behind our everyday sports car is to provide drivers with as natural a feeling as possible, almost as if they are running with the wind on their faces.

At this point, I asked everyone in the room to close their eyes and to imagine that they are running the last corner of an oval track. I described to them the sensations of turning the corner by stating: "Just feel your legs kicking and driving forward. Feel your hands balancing your body and the power of your legs, as well as the impact on your hips. As you adjust your balance, feel the speed of the wind on your face. Read the curve – accelerate out of the corner to the home stretch and towards the goal line."

I further said: "Now imagine the last corner of a horse race: The horse's hind legs are kicking powerfully to propel it forward. It's forelegs are providing balance and you are feeling the lateral G's on your hips ... This is the natural way that all living things turn a corner. This feeling cannot be provided by

Although the overall concept never changed, the second model incorporated many detail changes. When the time came for the outdoor presentation, we were all concerned: there had been heavy rain in the area all night, but fortunately it stopped half-an-hour before the gathering was due to take place.

how we will achieve this objective." This concluded our layout arguments and we were able to move forward without ever revisiting the issue again.

However, after this critical path, the project faced another crisis – there were limited funds available to develop an "all-new" car. Due to this, management decided to go ahead with another project. So the LWS was to be put on hold to become an on-line program for another year or two, but Masataka Matsui, Director of the Technical Research Division (TRD), came to our rescue. He clearly believed in this project, especially because he had done some experiments on his own long before we had proposed a two-seater sports car. He requested that one of his staff who specialized in plastic bodies, Dr Hotta, and Mr Kato would develop a running prototype in the TRD as a plastic body experiment.

Kato, Hotta, Takiguchi (manager in charge of the drivetrain) and I were sent to England, Germany, and Italy to survey many companies who had the capability of building a running prototype. Kato and Hotta decided to go with a British consulting firm, so we shipped our clay model's casting to the firm. Headquarters sent the engine, transmission, and other parts from various Mazda products. It was going to be built on a backbone

a front-wheel drive layout, but only through a front engine/rear-wheel drive layout."

"Furthermore," I added, "based on my experience, only a full convertible would provide you with a true "wind-in-your-face" experience. A Targa-top or sunroof cannot give you the same free feeling as if you are running. In the early morning, you can feel the fresh morning dew on your face, or

you can smell the flowers in the spring on the warm breath of a breeze. The fully open convertible top will provide the driver with the closest feeling of nature in the four-wheeled vehicle."

When I finished my explanation, Mr Yamanouchi decisively proclaimed: "OK ... we will proceed with the FR layout. Please commence the study on

The third design study model.

chassis mated to an FRP body based on our design. The engine came from our B-series truck, which was the only engine available for the FR layout at the time. The transmission and differential came from the RX-7.

Santa Barbara delight
After completion of the drivable running prototype in England, Mr Matsui requested that it be shipped to Hiroshima via California. Much to our delight, he requested us to conduct a test drive on a city street to gauge the public reaction - but that is another story in itself. However, I can tell you that the result of this venture was the recommendation for Mazda to pursue the LWS program.

More debate
As our small team continued working on the second model with a much tighter package, two other issues plagued our team in North America. One issue was the mechanism for the convertible top, and the other was the design for the front turn indicator.

I wanted a convertible mechanism like that of the Fiat 850 Spider, which I had owned for three years, or like the Corvette, which gave a clean and uncluttered look when the top is folded down. Bob Hall, the product planner, insisted that we use a one-action top. He wanted to be able to pull the top and latch it to the windshield frame. My idea for the top required five actions to complete. You opened the lid, pulled the top out, closed the lid, hooked the top to the lid, pulled the top up, and latched it to the windshield frame. Bob won the argument and the team decided to go with a one-action top.

The front-turn indicator issue arose between Bob Hall and Mark Jordan in opposition to Shigenori Fukuda (manager of the North American Product Planning and Design Division) and myself. Bob and Mark wanted a very stylish turn indicator on the corners of the front bumper, much like the ones on a Corvette, with a set of pop-up headlights. The main argument was that while their idea was stylish, it was too commonplace, and a predictable

solution too. Fukuda-san and I wanted to add personality to our baby. We wanted this small light area to be a headlight as well. However, the technology to make this both a headlight and turn indicator was unavailable at the time. So the pop-up lights won the battle.

The running prototype being admired by car enthusiasts.

Early morning, and the prototype leaving the MANA car park. The tent in the background was used to hide the viewing yard from prying eyes.

Three years later ...

Three years after the project left us and went to Japan for the production design phase, its final design clay model was returned to the States for the pricing clinic organized by the North American Marketing Group. Our team saw the clay model and was really disappointed at its rear-end design. Shunji Tanaka (chief designer for the project, at the time) explained the results of the clinic held in Japan prior to the car coming to the States. He said that, in Japan, customers didn't like the rounded front end, but they loved the rear end. We voiced our opinion that the rear end didn't match the personality of the rest of the car, and it needed more fullness. Fortunately, the US clinic proved our concern and supported our opinions.

About a year after that, we received the first running prototype from Japan. We couldn't believe our eyes – the engineers in Hiroshima did everything we asked for and more. Our team wished for this car, but we never believed that we would get everything so perfect from Japan, a place that wouldn't be the best environment to produce

a true sports car. Much to our surprise and delight, it was absolutely perfect!

The MX-5 story (Part II)

The MX-5/Miata was introduced to the public in February 1989 at the Chicago Auto Show. It created a sensation and became an instant hit. Our dealers and sales departments were flooded with money-lined envelopes, and by the time the July sales date had arrived, some dealers had a waiting list with more than 100 names on it. The media hype that surrounded the MX-5/Miata had come close to that of the first Mustang introduction.

I remembered watching the news on TV one day, a few weeks after the initial release on 1 July. The newscaster was talking to this lady at a dealership and he said: "I understand that you've just taken delivery of this car. How come you were sitting in the passenger side with such a big smile?" She answered: "I fell in love with this car from the moment I saw it and I had to order it right away." Fortunately, she placed her order early enough to make it to the top ten on the waiting list. When the

dealer called her to come and pick her car up that morning, she didn't know that it was equipped with a manual transmission, and she didn't know how to drive it. At the end of her story, she finally gave her reason for being in the passenger side: "This young salesman will be teaching me how to drive a manual."

Stories about car clubs & customization

There was a third paper that I wrote to go along with the story "Inspired Sensations" and "Dos and Don'ts." This paper covered the proposed car club activities and accessories to support the development of an "MX-5/Miata Culture." In fact, I joined several car clubs at the beginning of the LWS project to study their activities. I strongly believed that in order to develop and nurture the culture, establishing a car club was an absolute necessity. In my opinion, it is the car club that fosters the culture of the car.

Without the culture, there is no legend.

So the MX-5/Miata Club of America was founded right after the car's introduction in 1989. Every year, I attended several club events, organized by a chapter in each region. These events were ran by volunteers from where the particular national event would be held. They were well organized; in fact, better organized than some professional conventions.

Accessories and provisions for customization were also an integral part of the equation. If you are a car lover, you can't leave the car showroom stock: you must add some personal touches, just like you do to your home. You could even have a seasonal makeover; after all, the MX-5/Miata is a convertible.

I used to customize every one of my cars as soon as it was delivered. I even started to think about how I'm going to customize it, sometimes long before buying it. From my personal experience, I also know that if you are connected with a car like you are with your loved ones, you want to keep it as close to you as possible – maybe even show it off. From these viewpoints, I explained why accessories and customization were vital to the plan, and I created a list of accessories that Mazda could prepare to coincide with the introduction of the MX-5/Miata.

The list started out with the typical accessory catalog items – aerodynamic spoilers, suspension kits, wheels, other body parts and so forth, for the exterior. Different seats, steering wheels, shift knobs, gauges and pedals were listed for the interior. The list beyond the car contained items such as memo pads, coffee mugs, pens, clocks, paperweights, and other desktop accessories. After that, apparel items were listed, such as sweaters, T-shirts, hats, sunglasses, keyfobs, socks, shoes, blankets, picnic baskets, and so on. I even considered including underwear to the apparel list, as well! Please remember, just because I placed it on the list, it didn't mean that Mazda had to market all the items, but there was a good chance that Mazda could link-up with companies like Benetton or Esprit to co-brand some of these accessories.

As for the car's basic design to be easily accessorized or customized, we made an extensive list of the potential items, but some of them could not be accommodated due to safety regulations, costs, manufacturing limitations, or a combination of all these factors. In the final design, those thoughts were built into the interior of the MX-5/Miata. A good example of this is the center stack fascia – a separate piece in the car. Normally, this would be molded in one piece as part of the whole instrument panel to make assembly easy. This way, it would allow either the aftermarket suppliers or the customers to alter the finish of this part.

Today, there are so many creative ways to customize the MX-5/Miata. In extreme cases, there are totally different front and rear end kits available, which retain the car's standard middle section. I've seen a Lotus Elite and Elan version, Ferrari Lusso and Daytona versions, bug-eyed Sprite version, and even a Dodge Viper lookalike kit. I don't necessarily subscribe to these lookalike kits, but they were done quite well and each captured the original's flavor. What amazes me the most is the fact that the mid-section of the MX-5 is so neutral that it works with all of those different front and rear ends.

The story continues ...
There is a fourth paper – one that describes the life cycle of the first generation MX-5/Miata after its introduction. In 1986, I wrote a market condition in relation to the car year by year: a paper that came out three years prior to the actual introduction of the MX-5/Miata in 1989 but that, too, is another story to tell in the future. Now all of this is history, dreams have been realized and the elements have combined to create a long-lived and well-loved automobile that will be around for many more years to come.

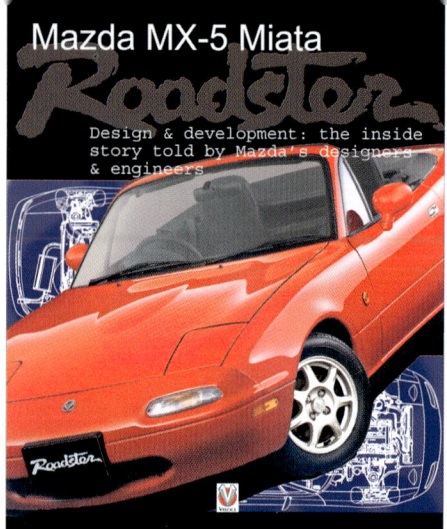

5

Design development by Kouichi Hayashi

Hayashi was fortunate to be assigned to do the advance design of the MX-5/Miata roadster when he was working in Mazda's Californian design studio. Among many demanding designers in the studio, he must have been one of the happiest project members. The advanced model he worked on in Los Angeles was sent to Hiroshima, when his boss, Tanaka, took over the production design work. The design came through the shape-up exercise to become Mazda's first LWS.

T. Hirai

California and an LWS

Laguna Seca Circuit (known as Mazda Raceway since 2001 because of Mazda's title sponsorship for the track) is located about two hour's drive south of San Francisco. It is a Mecca for sports car enthusiasts and, every year, in late August, hosts an historic car race. This event seems to signify the strong attachment American people have towards various types of sports cars. After the Second World War, European lightweight sports cars captured the attention of American drivers. The image of, and yearning for, the LWS seemed to grow even stronger during the 1960s.

An LWS is FUN, and that is its purpose and its value. Although there was a healthy demand for such cars, by the end of 1980,

there were no new LWSs available on the market due to tightened safety regulations and the decline of the British automobile industry that had previously supplied most of them. Those still running in the 1980s were the same as those sold in the 1960s and 1970s, although due to its fine weather, California was the place where most of these cars survived, cherished by their owners.

An LWS is produced with a clear concept and has a simple purpose. They are built to give the owner pleasure through the joy of driving at a level not possible in today's sporty specialty cars. Although it must conform to various regulations and safety requirements, it will not appeal to

Laguna Seca circuit (courtesy Kazuki Saito)

Triumph T.R.3 Sports

A typical example of a classic British LWS - the Triumph TR3.

everyone, and certain things must be ignored to appreciate the car. It is not expected that the car will undergo frequent minor design changes, so its design must have a timeless look with a distinctive character that is not affected by fashion.

Aim of the Mazda LWS

Mazda's share of US car market was only 1.9% at the time this project started, and with this level of sales, no clear brand image existed to speak of. Other than the RX-7, there were many Americans who didn't even know of Mazda. In order to capture the heart of consumers, we had to produce a car that would best express the concept of the design and heart of Mazda directly through the hardware. MANA (Mazda North America: Mazda's R&D arm in the States) proposed a small and simple lightweight open two-seater, having all the good, traditional LWS characteristics, but born in the 1990s. LWS qualities were broken down into the following elements:

Responsive handling.
Lively performance.
Timeless design.
Pleasant space for two adults.
A simple and user-friendly open top.
Affordable to anyone who loves to drive.

We did not want a simple re-creation of a British LWS of the 1950s and 1960s. We wanted to rearrange their elements in a modern package that would make the car acceptable in the 1990s environment. In the age of high technology, we wanted to bring back a human touch and the snug feeling one gets in a LWS, and wanted to expand this design theme to other Mazda cars.

Start of an off-line project

An "off-line project" at Mazda means a project to research future products, a scheme which started in late 1983. There were three potential projects, one of which was the LWS. A MANA PP&R (Product Planning & Research) Division member started the

project with great excitement. After completing the sketch proposals we submitted them to headquarters for evaluation. MANA even made a presentation outlining the desirable concept of an LWS for the American market. Approval for procedure to the next step was given.

LWS design study models
First design model
(May 1984-July 1984)

Masao Yagi, who was dispatched from headquarters, was assigned to make the first design model with the assistance of Tom Matano and Mark Jordan. By then a small design studio had been completed at MANA for design activities and fabrication of a full-scale clay model. Two expert clay modelers, Shigeru Kajiyama and the late Takeaki Mori, were sent from Japan to join the team. Bill McIntyre was recruited for this

A second-hand Triumph Spitfire was one of several cars purchased in America to provide the MANA team with inspiration.

Design proposal sketches drawn as part of the off-line project.

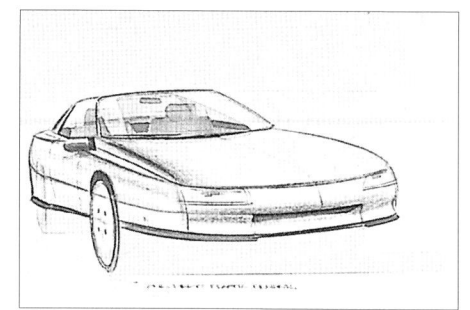
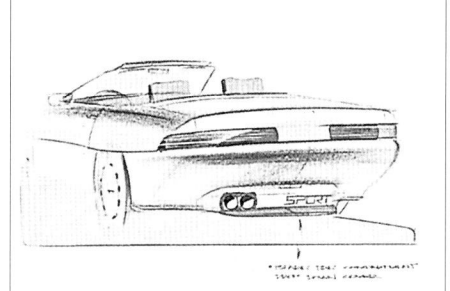

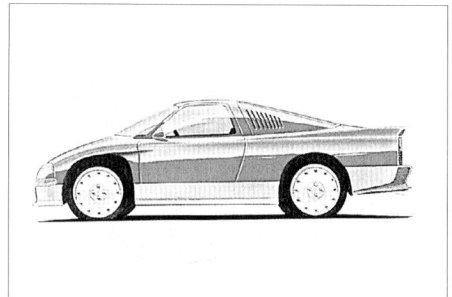
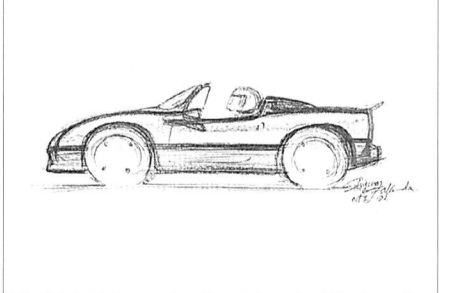

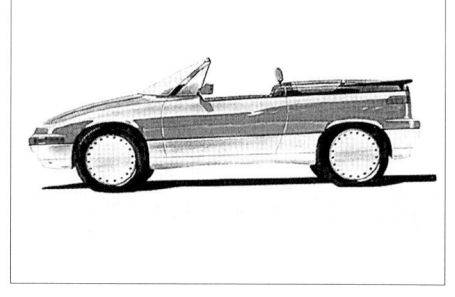

job, also. Bill was an expert in hardware work, and besides fabricating a space rocket component for NASA, had created a stretch limousine by himself. At the beginning, these people were new to each other and a little restrained for a while but, as they learnt their respective capabilities, they worked extremely well as a team, and the first clay model was completed in about two months. The red painted model seemed as if it was ready to run and fascinated everybody involved. It was sent to Hiroshima immediately.

At the same time, in the Tokyo studio, designers Youichi Sato and Hideki Suzuki were working on two other models, one RR and one FF. All three models were evaluated in Hiroshima as a product base for the future LWS. The MANA proposal was chosen, along with its FR drivetrain arrangement, which MANA had long been promoting. This original MANA model had a lasting influence on the design of the next advance model, as well as the final production car. This first model clearly expressed the concept of a desirable LWS for American consumers. The key words for the design were "neo-classic," based on a British LWS of the 1960s, and it certainly impressed the reviewers with its fresh look, whilst managing to provide a nostalgic feel for the customer who was familiar with the traditional type of sports car.

The MANA design studio, pictured here during the off-line stage, well before the MX-5/Miata project was officially given the go-ahead.

Kajiyama-san (nearest the camera) and Fukuda-san working on the clay. Fukuda, the head of design, can be seen working on the shape of the roof.

Second design model
(September 1985-November 1985)

More than one year after the first clay model was shipped to Hiroshima, the LWS project was still in the "Study" stage, and not included in Mazda's cycle plan. When I visited the headquarters in May 1985, the atmosphere was not very clear. The people at MANA wishing for an early project start were getting impatient. But luckily, at the same time, a prototype model for plastic body development was being assessed. The project, led by the Technical Center, was in progress at a consulting firm in the UK, along with a basic body study within Mazda's advanced body group.

Soon after, a budget for the second design model was approved for MANA to start design study under new package conditions. The new conditions, however, included a wheelbase 50cm (19.7in.) longer than the original, which would make it difficult to call the car a LWS. We had a rather dim view of this request, even though expectations regarding the styling were high.

In addition, head office asked that in order to transfer the design to production smoothly, the engineering hard points should be strictly followed, since the LWS project was already two years behind schedule. As the first model had left a very good impression of an LWS, there was a glimpse of their mixed yet strong expectations surrounding the second design model, as well as their desire to bring it into production as soon as possible.

For the second model, there were two modelers from Japan, veteran modeler Naoki Tanaka and young Toshi Furuta, the English modelers Martin McLease and Bryan Innocent, American Bill McIntyre, and the Mexican hard modeler, Luis Romo. This was indeed quite an international design team.

For the second model, we carried over the design concept of the first model. But because we used the old FR Familia (323) as a base, the height of the first model was a little taller than ideal, and could not fully achieve the desired atmosphere of a LWS. In particular, the beltline of the first model was higher than we would have liked. We wanted a low, compact and exciting little car that was emotionally inviting for a quick

MANA's FR LWS proposal.   *The Tokyo studio's FF proposal.*   *The Tokyo studio's MR proposal.*

drive. In addition, Shigenori Fukuda, the first Manager of MANA's PP&R Division, requested us to put more presence into the design, somewhat similar to the first RX-7, small and cute but distinctive. Although not specifically stated anywhere, it was our understanding that this design would set the direction for Mazda's car styling in the future.

I first started with the height of the beltline. As a former pipe smoker, I could not wipe out an image of a driver who strikes a match on the surface of the road to light his pipe while seated in an LWS. I first tried to set the beltline very low, similar to that of the Triumph TR3, MGA, Morgan or Lotus Super Seven, with a minimal door that was so low it wasn't necessary to open it to get in and out of the car. But that attempt

gave a result that was too similar to the traditional British LWS. I tried to modernize it, but was not satisfied and had to abandon the idea. The second model attempt was not 100 percent satisfactory to us as a team either, because of the lack of character and presence, although it did display a very low beltline, compactness, and a certain measure of overall excitement.

The third model
(April 1986-June 1986)

After three years as an Off-Line Project, corporate authorization to proceed to a production model was finally granted, and Toshihiko Hirai was selected as its PPM (Product Program Manager). Hirai came over to MANA in March 1986. Together with Hirai, the MANA members had a joint test drive of

competitive cars, and a heated discussion trying to solidify the image of a LWS followed. After this joint working session, we felt that Hirai had a full grasp of the US market needs, and relief that the project stagnancy of the last three years had been broken. In the meeting with Hirai, he made clear the basic conditions that critically affect car design. They were the height of the beltline, the clearance between the engine and the bonnet, hood height, bumper clearance, and so on. The wheelbase was another subject of discussion. Although it was shorter by 30mm (1.2in.) compared with the previous design, it was still too long. Hirai, Fukuda and I felt that sticking to it would not benefit our work. We knew we could change the wheelbase later somehow, and we stopped arguing about it. At

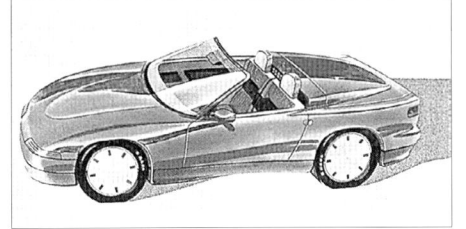

this stage, then, the model kept the requested wheelbase.

This time the work had a definite target and someone to take over the project and continue the work in Hiroshima. It required accuracy in millimetres, and there was a deadline to meet, which was something we, as an advance design team, were not used to. The work on the clay model started under this sort of pressure. Before making the third full-scale model, I and Wu-Huang Chin made a one-fifth scale model of the second design for review. We then concluded that in addition to the neo-classic atmosphere of the first model, the low and traditional proportion of the second model was to be combined in the new design. This time, the clay model work was carried out with the addition of Tony Ashpool, another British member (Bill McIntyre and Luis Romo were in charge of hard modeling, as before). Chin further supported the design work, including the fine detail and wheel designs.

Work on the third model progressed calmly. We kept a simple design, creating tension through controlled highlighting of surfaces and lines. Attachment design, such as the door handles and mirrors, was kept straightforward so as not to interrupt the rhythm of the entire body. But then, I felt that something was missing ...

Since it was formally decided to proceed as a production design, I tried to mature the design by verifying the engineering requirements. I was getting used to California living and my indulgence with sports cars was getting deeper, and I was feeling in tune with carrying out the LWS design. For the second model, I could not get that feeling so easily, but in the third model it was more natural. We put emphasis on compactness and lowness on the second model, but we could not achieve the kind of presence we wanted in the LWS, a Mazda sports car image that would follow the RX-7, and the Mazda design identity that would lead future Mazda design. These subjects

stood in front of me like a big impenetrable wall.

In making the second model, we tried hard to achieve a certain dynamic expression and an image of speed by creating a wedged character line (or highlight) on the body side. After a great deal of trial and error with the modelers, we figured out that in order to make a highlight on the side lines, it was necessary to add a flare to the front fender of about 50mm (2in.). But such additional work could lead to changes in the whole body design that would delay the schedule, so I was reluctant to do this. Our modelers, then, requested that they wanted an extra day to do final adjustments. We came back to the model room late in the

Comparing the first and second models, the former's waistline was perhaps a touch too high. The beltline was kept as low as possible to give the car an exciting and compact character.

Fukuda-san inspecting the clay. He requested more emphasis on the door cut lines, and the beltline, which he wanted lower.

Cockpit of the second model.

The members involved with the second model's development proudly standing next to their creation. From the left: Shigenori Fukuda, Martin McLease, Tim Pine, Bill McIntyre, Norman Garrett, and Kouichi Hayashi.

Rear three-quarter view of the second model.

A full-scale clay was made based on these emotive drawings by Wu-Huang Chin.

Fine-tuning of the third clay in progress.

evening, and found a body with a clean highlight running through the body side. This cross-section was retained in the final design.

After this incident, I was beginning to see a form that was new to me – it was something quite different to those I had known in the past. Ferraris and Porsches have a very rounded cross-sectional design, yet they somehow express lively, crisp lines. How they achieved these lines was my question, and I could not find an answer easily. Every weekend I attended automotive events and shows. Because it was California, I was able to easily find some sort of event where vintage sports cars or supercars were shown. I took many pictures, sometimes more than ten rolls a day. As I was taking the pictures, I noticed that a car would look different according to the light and shadow. The design work I was doing was to draw a sketch, and based on that image, I made a series of drawings that represented a three-dimensional shape. A clay model was made from these drawings, and we made fine adjustments by changing the model's surface and lines. We

accepted lines if they had a smooth curvature, and surfaces if there were no indentations, but I recognized these were still only two-dimensional design considerations.

Light and shadow on a clay model does not represent that on a real model. In order to simulate conditions similar to those experienced in the real world, a very thin film called "Dynock" is normally applied over the clay model. A clay covered with this

film shows many different forms and expressions with changing light conditions. The expression of the body design changes with time, and reflections of the surrounding scenery added many variations. I felt that cold steel panels could unite with nature by combining light, shadow and reflection, as if 'warmth' and 'humanity' were integrated in the curves of the body.

Since that time, I have intentionally tried to design body

Dynock film was placed on the car to bring its contours to life.

The modellers went to the viewing yard to control highlights on the body.

Clouds reflecting on the bonnet of the second clay. Light and shadow played on the car's surfaces to give it a different character as the clouds moved above it.

Front three-quarter view of the third car.

Rear three-quarter view of the same car.

The main members involved in the development of the third model. From the left: Wu-Huang Chin, Norman Garrett, Kouichi Hayashi. and Bob Hall.

cross-sections that bring attention to light and shadow. I especially favored the sunset during the Californian summer, as blue sky changes to pink as the sun drops onto the horizon. Often rendering sketches from overseas makers had this pink color. Such expressions would have remained a mystery to me had I not lived in California.

In the initial design, a bulge was added on the bonnet in order to create a powerful image, but the bulge was later removed and replaced with a delicate curve. This small accent would create a delicate difference in light and shadow, and reflection of the scenery. The form added a dynamic expression and created an emotional atmosphere that would excite people. A small but tasteful design with enough presence that would excite warm-blooded people was born.

Although we were certain as to how to express our motives in the US environment, we were still not sure how to control other environments. Since the 'light and shadow' design was made under the California sunshine, the design had unnecessary volume under the weaker light of Japan. In the production design, therefore, the body went through a trimming process. The simple lines, with their clear light and shadow message, were duly inherited by Mazda cars that followed.

Design development
A true backyard special
At the time of advanced design

Work in progress on the second clay. This picture was taken in the viewing yard, with the studio clearly visible in the background.

development, the space allocated to us was a small area within the rotary engine refurbishment factory. There was no adequate space to inspect the clay model under the sun, and we had to improvise by sealing off part of an outdoor parking lot with a tent. Many British LWS models are said to have been built in private back yards, and our roadster was no exception. The modeling space had no painting facility, so we had to build a makeshift booth from wood bought from a home furnishing center, then covered by vinyl sheet and with a ventilation fan in the corner for when we were spray painting. Because of our makeshift facility, the paint flaked off from the clay due to the unusually high humidity in autumn. We learnt then that even sunny California had seasonal changes.

As usual with any design model making, the week before a presentation is normally hell, with all workers spending sleepless nights. The three models made at MANA were no exception, and the problem of the paint flaking off must have been a great surprise to Bill, who was quite a perfectionist.

The international team, however, got their job done by working all day and night, and we made it by the presentation day. The fact that Bill, who is normally quite calm and expressionless, had turned pale, and his voice had gone up in pitch with tension, was later to become a conversation topic among the team members. I guess all of these incidents were quite appropriate for a true backyard special.

Prototype roadster testing
The Technical Center's plastic body development project duly

A clay model in the temporary, handmade spray booth. Panic set in when the primer peeled off the clay, causing everyone to rally round and repair the damage.

made a running model using the first LWS design from MANA. This prototype was produced by a British consulting firm (which was also contracted to dispatch engineers to Mazda later on). In September 1985, the British-made prototype was shipped to Hiroshima after testing in the US. We chose to test drive the car in Santa Barbara. Norman Garrett, who is familiar with the local roads of Santa Barbara, became the leader, and we loaded the car on a trailer and took off. As soon as we unloaded it we were surrounded by people and bombarded with questions. Some took pictures and asked for money or they would sell it to car magazines. We had to stop these people from doing that with

all our effort, by saying: "If you do so, this project may be scrapped. Isn't it better to sell the photos ten years from now?"

As I think back, though, what happened on this day determined the fate of the MX-5/Miata, as the incident was immediately reported to Hiroshima. All of the development team members must have quietly grinned with satisfaction.

Active utilization of a plotter

The third model of the LWS was in the process of reaching the pre-production design stage, and we could therefore not change its shape using our viewpoint alone. Hirai, the PPM, often warned everyone that we designers would change everything if left with a

model, but on this project we could not even change a line in the clay model without the authorization of vehicle engineering. As a result, without permission from Japan, we could not change the existing design. In those days, cross-sectional drawings of the model were sent to Japan for engineering feasibility study rather than measurement data. Today, this is all accomplished by electronic data communication.

The most useful tool at that time was a small, mechanized drawing machine called a plotter. Although it is easy to execute engineering drawings with a home PC nowadays, at that time we only had a plotter that would draw pictures in A3 size. It was a very

Santa Barbara, a famous resort, two hours north of MANA's base via the Pacific Coast Highway.

The running prototype, made in England, on the road with a 1973 Triumph Spitfire.

After the adventure in Santa Barbara, Matsui-san (head of TRC) joined the MANA members to toast the success of the prototype and the stir it caused with the public.

Halfway through the second model, it was proposed that the front foglights should be made more prominent.

A drawing made before the third clay was started. Fixed headlamps were a feature, but were not adopted until some years later.

Second generation MX-5/Miata, introduced for the 1998 season. Note the fixed headlights.

primitive machine and very sensitive to input. A single input error would stop the machine dead. We utilized this machine to the fullest extent in order to send the latest drawings via fax to Japan, and then receive another facsimile back for correction in detail the next morning. Using this simple process, we spent many days and nights toeing the line, because we didn't want to be criticized by the PPM. We were desperate to see the product, originally conceived and designed in America, go into mass production in Japan.

Headlamp design

While the first and second model had retractable headlamps, we wanted the third model to have fixed headlamps. The reason was to give a carefree character to the face. In those days, retractable headlamps were already generally considered to be outdated, but there were no small lamps available with sufficient power. We really wanted two small but powerful eyes. We tried to use foglamps, instead, to symbolize eyes in the second model, but the balance, with the eyes under the mouth, did not work. We still couldn't achieve a perfect combination on the third model, although the turn signal lamps were added in the process. (Our desire to give the roadster two fixed bright eyes finally materialized with the roadster's facelift of 1997.)

On the first day of my assignment at MANA, the first model was just being shipped to Japan. Later, after working for almost two years at MANA, I shipped out the third model to Japan. I wrote a fax message to Fukuda, General Manager of Design at head office back then, and who'd left MANA just before the third model was packed off. It said: "I've just shipped off the final proposal model. As I stand beside it, I'd like to drive out under the California sky, if only it could move. I am still excited as I write this message, and simply cannot wait to see the MX-5/Miata running on the California highways."

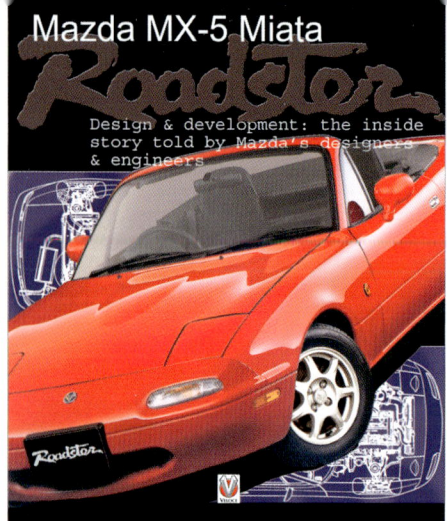

6

Product design
by **Shunji Tanaka**

While working on the Mazda 929 luxury sedan, Tanaka was assigned to the LWS project that was thought to have a very slim chance of reaching mass production. This assignment was considered a bit reckless, but the fact of the matter was that there was no-one else, back then, who could work in Hiroshima on such a challenging project. Without complaint, he handled the two projects concurrently, and showed his ability as designer in both – he was like a samurai in his approach to this difficult problem.

T. Hirai

Shigenori Fukuda came back from MANA (Mazda North America) and became General Manager of the Design Division. He brought back with him a clay model of a sport convertible. This was the third advance model designed by Kouichi Hayashi and the team at MANA. It was evident that Hayashi and the MANA design staff had put a lot of effort into the design, but it seemed, to be frank, very Americanized to me. At the time the model arrived in Japan, Mazda's design staff was extremely busy, and the advance model was left in the corner of a warehouse for a while, despite the strong

Over 50 different chisels are used in the art of Noh mask making. One starts with a solid block of Japanese cypress wood ...

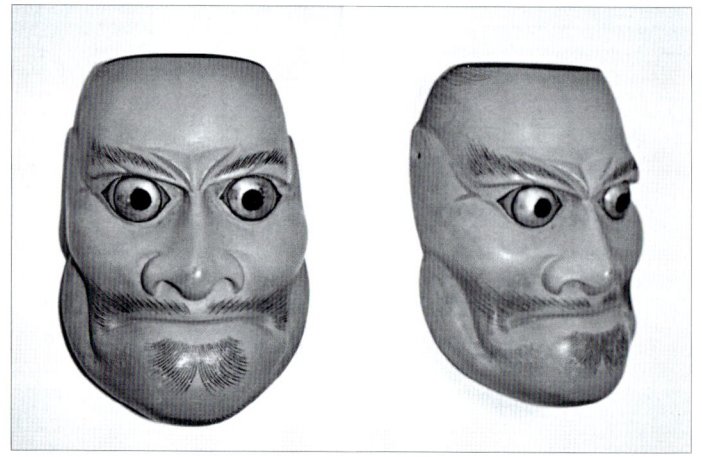

A male Noh mask depicting a goblin-type character. As a designer, this time-consuming hobby is an exciting field in which to develop new skills, and one that provided a great deal of inspiration.

Side view of a girl mask. One can almost imagine the shape of an open car, with the forehead as the bonnet and chin as the tail.

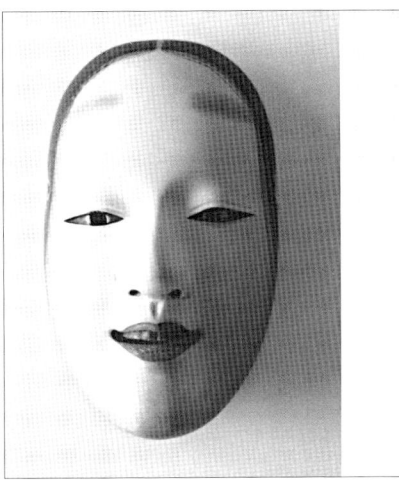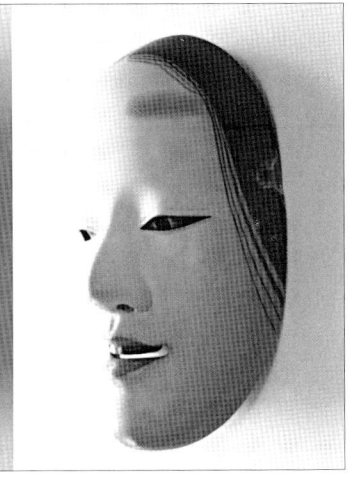

Whenever I had an interview in the US, it was not easy to explain the Noh mask concept. In reality, the MX-5/Miata was created in the image of a young girl, like the one illustrated here.

expectations of the people at MANA.

I was completely immersed in my work on the 929, trying to create an original design. Many models were made and scrapped, and I took refuge overseas for a while in an attempt to create a new design. As I look back, it was a very difficult time for me, and the thought of quitting repeatedly crossed my mind.

At the time, my wife had just started to learn *Noh* mask making from Master Ai Nomura. She asked me to sharpen her carving knife, and after testing the blade for sharpness, I was also attracted to the art of *Noh* mask making. As I indulged in the art, I realized that I'd been deeply lured into the delicate curvature of the mask that was only found in Japan. "This is it," I thought, and I suddenly felt that the curtains hiding the daylight were torn open in front of me. Before being a car designer, I realized that I was simply Japanese. I was determined to search for my original design motif in the Japanese tradition. The design for the 929 followed the image of Beshimi, and

a one-fifth scale model was made accordingly. This was subsequently presented to the Mazda management and approved. It was Christmas 1986 when I felt that I was finally free from a long and dark tunnel.

The LWS project miraculously revived in February 1986 with a new code name J58G and Hirai as its Program Manager. I was summoned by Uchida, Deputy General Manager of the Design Division, and he said: "The 729 came back thanks to Hirai's effort. I hope you will take the job." Why me, I thought, for I was already very busy with the 929, but, at the same time, I knew that whatever Hayashi had done in US would have to be finished by me, because Hayashi had been my subordinate when we'd worked together on the design of the Bongo, Luce, B2000 and MPV in the past. I finally accepted the job of Chief Designer for the LWS project.

Start of product design

My first job was to take over the mass production model design that was subcontracted to a British design consultancy. After Hirai

came back from the UK and after a series of long negotiations with the firm, the project somehow got started with a few engineers. One-hour concept meetings were held daily in the converted car park known as the "Riverside Hotel," but it was difficult for me to attend these meetings for the work on the 929 was getting close to its peak at the time. Even when I did attend the meeting, it was complete chaos with conflicting opinions among the project members. Despite this creative chaos, the basic layout design was established, and the conditions necessary to start the product design were settled in May 1986. The basic layout design that resulted from the heated discussions was excellent, and I felt that I had a good grasp of a final image in my mind at that time.

While I was conscientiously building my own aesthetics around traditional Japanese culture and creating an original design for the 929, the design theme of an open two-seater sports car was clearly forming within me. Also, through more heated discussions, a consensus was established to

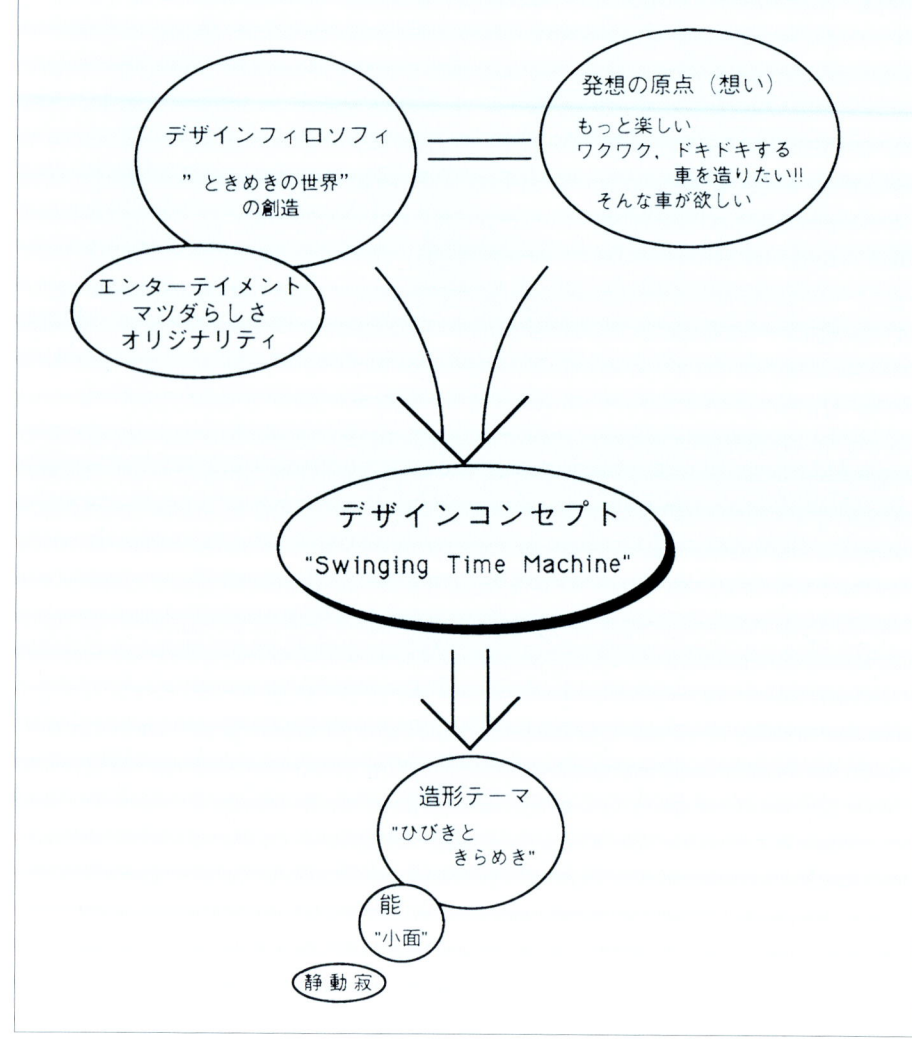

The MX-5/Miata's original design concept scenario.

create a car that would be beautiful to look at, fun to sit in and pleasing to drive. In order to realize this product concept, I needed to further clarify its design concept. Hisashi Takei, of the Design Planning Department, helped me immensely in establishing the design concept scenario for a traditional LWS in a new era, and one that would appeal to customers. This concept scenario was instrumental in creating a new global market for the two-seater open sports car then codenamed "J58G."

Our conclusion was that modern automobiles are over-equipped, with advanced mechanisms, functions and comfort, and that they might have reached a state beyond appealing to human senses. Could we have lost a sensible relationship with cars? We simply wanted a car that was more fun – something exciting that would make the heart flutter. Among these thoughts, we were determined to pursue the pure fun of driving that is inherent in a car, and to design a vehicle that would re-establish the most pleasurable

relationship between a car and its driver.

The key catchphrase for the design concept was "Swinging Time Machine." This would be a car that would take anyone who loved freedom and nature to another, more thrilling world any time. Takei and I had lengthy discussions about this machine that would take the young, and the young at heart, into this other world which made the pulse race faster.

Formation theme: Hibiki & Kirameki (echo & sparkle)

A car design must be soft yet flexible and resilient, while having echoing tension in a simple form. Such simple forms must reflect complex shadows with limitless change, and a transformation that would resonate within the viewer's heart. I wanted the car to be an organic design that would melt into nature, yet possess sparkling presence via the harmony of simple lines and the resulting curvature. During the design stage of the 929, I was convinced that this sort of emotional design could only come out of human sensitivity, borrowing from the traditional beauty of Japan.

As I carve out a mask from a piece of wood, I always appreciate the perfection of the simple yet delicate curved surfaces of the *Noh* mask that was handed down to us over several hundred years. The

人馬一体

thoughts and wishes of a mask maker are sealed into the simple curvature, and they appear as facial expressions with the delicate reflection of light and shadow. This abstract expression is uniquely Japanese and quite different to a Western expression that is set in stone.

I also wanted to express, in the form of a sports car, the stillness, dynamism and silence that are in the mind of the Japanese. When the car is still, it should have static beauty with the richness of a woman, as in a Matisse sculpture, and, when in action, it should have the dynamism of a beast in pursuit of prey. And it should have a silence, like a resting beast after a fast run through winding roads, feeling the wind through the woods and hearing the songs of the birds. I believe that a sports car is there to grasp the fact that you exist and you are alive. A sports car must reflect and absorb the natural scenery, and meld into it to become a part of silent nature. My image for the MX-5/Miata's creation came about during a fleeting moment whilst such silence existed.

Our preparation before starting design work was completed with the concept, the design image, and the basic layout design, but we did not have any modelers to make a clay model, or even a clay model table allocated to us. The only thing there was the red Dynock film-covered model sent from MANA. Its front window area was still rough and the interior was full of garbage. There was no way to recognize it as a LWS, rather it seemed to me to be like a heavyweight sports car in the image of an RX-7, the MX-5/Miata's big brother. I felt sorry for Hayashi that after many years of staying in the US, he must have eaten too much steak and forgotten the delicacy of Japanese cuisine.

I started first by shortening the wheelbase by 30mm (1.2in.) and took off excess clay from the entire body by as much as 25 to 30mm (1.0 to 1.2in.). I wanted to establish early on the overall proportions and cowling line, as well as the root of the A-pillar in the car, and then start the interior design. Doing both interior and exterior design single handedly was almost impossible, and I went to Uchida asking for one interior designer, using Hirai's support. Kenji Matsuo, a freshman, was assigned to the J58G project. Interior design of a car is a very complicated job, and it would normally take five years or so for a designer to become fully-fledged in the art. This job was too much to handle for a newcomer, but he was all I could get after my negotiations with Uchida. The interior design therefore started from ground zero with only a complete beginner to help.

Next, I went to Hirai asking for one engineer from his six or seven staff. He was furious and said: "Don't you know how few engineers I have?" We were, after all, trying to do the impossible and I could not expect anything to go as normal. After some discussion, I was able to convince Hirai to have the interior design proceed concurrently with the engineering, in a new attempt to spread the workload. Toshiteru Yoshimura was the engineer who helped me with the interior design.

It was at this time that international value of the yen went very high, and we had to design the car to be competitive at a rate of 100 yen to the dollar. Hirai requested us to re-estimate the costs using this absurd exchange rate, but it was Yoshimura who took care of the design and cost, and he was the one who made it happen.

Image of a tearoom

I wanted to design the interior of the roadster using the image of a tearoom with its simple and organic atmosphere. I visited a Japanese tearoom many times to grasp the ideas needed for such an interior. In Hiroshima, there is a tea school named Ueda Sookoryuu, teaching a style which was mainly practiced among the Samurai class from about 400 years ago. The old tearoom named "Enshou" miraculously survived

Interior of the Japanese tearoom that I visited on many occasions. Several tea ceremony styles are followed, so not all tearooms are the same.

First sketch of the interior, drawn in half-scale to enable Yoshimura-san to work from it.

the atomic bomb, and still stood among the mountains of Kogo. I had the luck to be acquainted with the master, Munetsugu Ueda, and frequently visited the tearoom.

In the room, you realize the spirit of the warrior who chose each column and designed the tearoom 400 years ago. The tension contained in each design element was well harmonized to create a comfortable atmosphere that filled the entire room. To be there was to travel back in a time machine. This is the image I wanted in the interior of J58G. A tearoom is made simple so that the host can express himself via flower arrangements, hanging scrolls and tea ware. I wanted to transplant this atmosphere to the car, so that the driver would be the host in a simple form surrounded by comfortable tension.

To make it simple and light also meant low cost. Yoshimura collected a mountain of components from the current production lines that seemed usable in the car. Yoshimura checked the usefulness of each component he collected, and once it passed his scrutiny, he would make a layout drawing for the component. Matsuo, standing by him, would then draw

a tape for clay model instruction, as well as for design review pictures. There was only ever one sketch of the interior of J58G, drawn by Matsuo and based on a layout made by Yoshimura. This black and white sketch has the air of an old Chinese ink painting, and perfectly matched my image of a tearoom.

New ideas
"No more ideas are needed. Go on to make a life-size clay mock-up." That was my instruction. The main part of the instrument panel needed to be rigid because of cost requirements, but I wanted it soft where people touched it. In order to achieve this contradicting request, Yoshimura came up with a solution which allowed a horizontal padded cushion across the width of the dashboard with a centralized control panel. Air conditioning and stereo components were redesigned from the parts bin components we'd collected, and a minimal independent instrument panel hood was added. After thorough evaluation of existing combination instruments for a compact car, large letters were chosen to express the sporty nature of the car whilst

still carrying over the basic components; also chromed rings were added to the instrument dials. Speedo and tachometer needles were made narrower to suggest precision.

With respect to the steering wheel, we had to design a four-spoke wheel with an airbag to cope with US safety regulations, but it could hardly be called sporty. I was in favor of a three-spoke wheel, but had to abandon the idea for US models. This was the time airbag application was just beginning, and it was very difficult to design around the new regulations.

As a continuation of the horizontal pad on the instrument panel, the upper door trims used urethane padding, whereas the lower door trims were plywood bonded with plastic, the cheapest system of all, even at this time: I was a bit concerned that the cost cutting might have gone too far. Ironically, the same designer was also designing Mazda's first luxurious car, priced at well over 3,000,000 yen, at the same time and adjacent to our project office.

From interior to exterior
The rear end of the interior was a storage space for the soft-top and its structure. With the low beltline, soft-top links would protrude over the body. It was, however, the

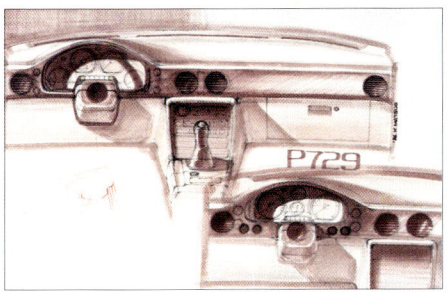

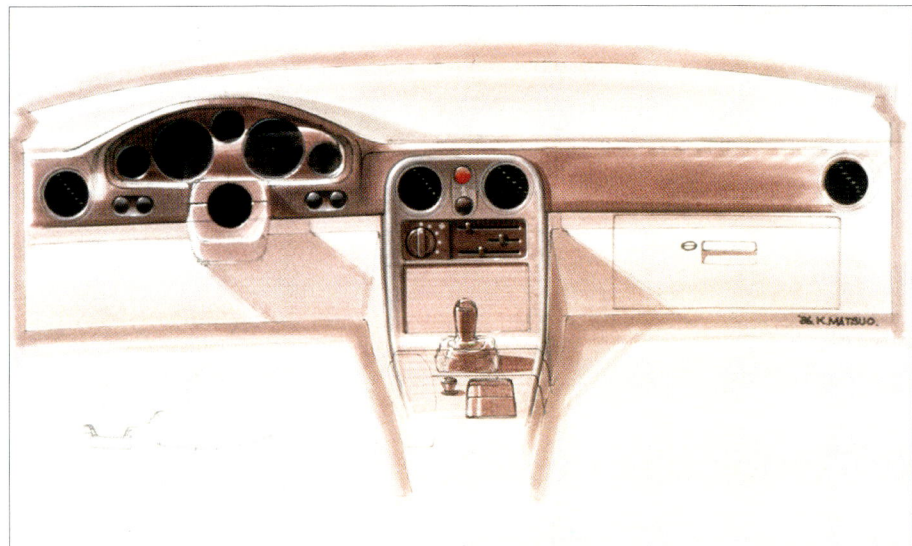

Following a feasibility review, the design was refined slightly. A model was produced after just these two drawings were made, as available parts defined certain areas of the design, and it fitted in perfectly with my image. There was no need to go any further.

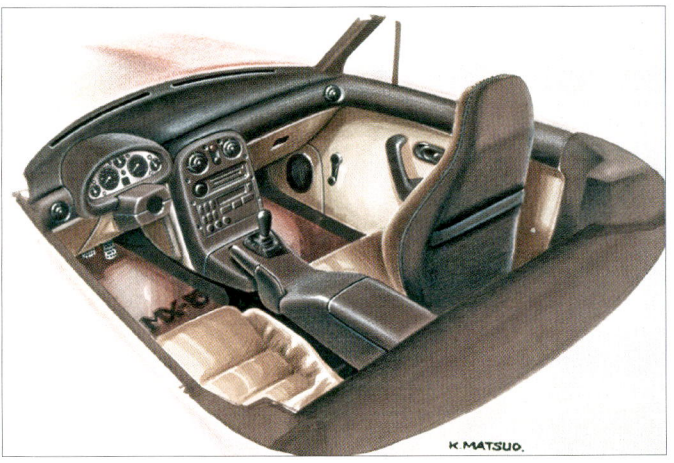

Final rendering of the interior, drawn after the mock-up was completed.

First design mock-up.

most critical part of the body design, and I made repeated requests to Hirai to make the soft-top structure as small as possible whilst giving ample space to store it over the fuel tank. In order to achieve an ideal rear fender line, the fuel tank capacity had to be sacrificed, giving the PPM a hard decision to make. After through study, fuel capacity reduction was held to a minimum by choosing a slightly waving rear fender line in Coke bottle fashion.

After deciding on the most important lines in an open bodied car, those that determined the beltline, the next point to establish was the A-pillar and front cowling line, which connect to the beltline. The design had to take into consideration the airflow over the body, and necessitated a series of wind tunnel tests. Normally, a wind tunnel test is carried out to reduce the drag coefficient of the body design, but this time its purpose was to create a pleasant relationship with the wind. In order to achieve this, the angle and height of the windshield, as well as A-pillar cross-section, were

adjusted to achieve the best position. Since the wind tunnel test was conducted with a rough clay model, I assumed an approximate seating position and duly sought the most suitable wind combination. While the angle of the windshield is very important in controlling the airflow over the body, I also discovered that a small triangular window behind the A-pillar was quite effective in wind control. Through these activities, the front windshield and A-pillar design was getting close to its final shape.

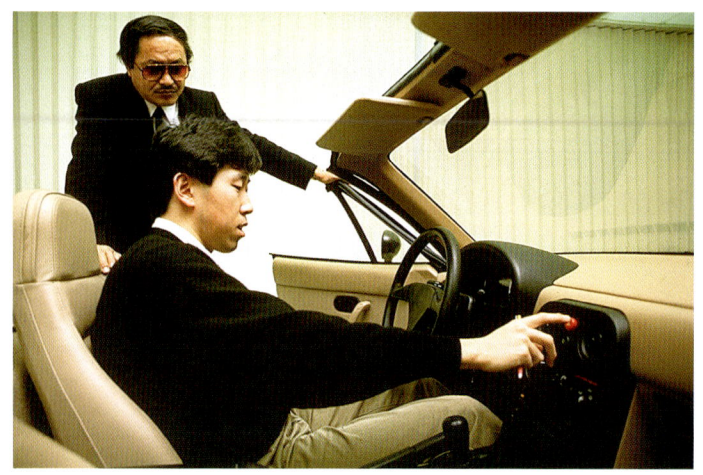

Reviewing the interior design with Kenji Matsuo.

The interior of the production model.

Beginning body design

Although we were just beginning the body design, there were no modelers and not even a surface plate was available. While the interior design was somehow proceeding with Yoshimura and Matsuo, there was only a rough clay model that was used for the wind tunnel test. At that time, my work on the 929 got past its peak and I was a bit more relaxed. Satoru Akana, EX (exterior) Chief Designer, who worked with me on the 929 design, Eiichi Hamana, IN (interior) Chief Designer, and Shigeru Kajiyama, Chief Modeler, came to help me while I was working alone on the J58G. The J58G clay model was eventually placed on the surface plate after removing the 929 model, and Kajiyama and I worked on the clay during the holidays. Because of the many trials and tribulations in the earlier 929 design work, our team worked well, and the J58G clay model was beginning to take shape just as it was in my mind. I showed Kajiyama a new *Noh* mask I had just made with my wife's coloring, and asked him to re-create this image in the clay model.

While we were busy working with clay, there was another change in the market. The exchange rate for the yen went higher, and marketing people in the US and Europe started to say that there was no market anywhere in the world for such a car concept. Hirai duly told me to slow down the work. At the same time there came a rumor that MANA designers were angry that I'd destroyed their design. This sort of thing was a big blow to the project, although it was true that I'd made vast changes to the original MANA proposal. MANA designers, Tom Matano and Mark Jordan, and a product planner, Bob Hall, complained to their former boss, Fukuda, although it seemed that Fukuda was too busy with other projects that were nearing production and he'd forgotten all about the J58G. My worry reached its peak, however, when Fukuda commented that the original MANA design looked better upon seeing our clay model.

Despite these criticisms, Uchida, Deputy General Manager of the Design Division, supported me by saying: "Your design concept, originating from Japanese sensitivity, is wholly appropriate." Hirai also supported me from a different angle by saying: "I cannot accept a design that does not fully satisfy my design requirements, and Tanaka's design, which is following the engineering requirements, seems more fitting for an LWS."

A prototype used in wind tunnel testing. The movement of the wool tufts was monitored to establish airflow in and around the cockpit.

Discussing product design in Hiroshima.

One-fifth scale model. It would later be used to evaluate the final design.

Again, Kajiyama and I went back to work during a holiday to finalize the design surfaces. A line from the front fender would flow to the rear fender, turn around the tail lamps, and continue to the opposite rear fender. A roundish design was completed. Its surface nearly duplicated the sensitive tension one finds in a *Noh* mask.

Concept image

Many of the previous car designs were dealt with within the domain of industrial design. An image sketch would be translated into two-dimensional lines for communicating with the clay modelers, and the surface would be understood to be a membrane between the said lines. The modeling of the LWS car overturned conventional methods, and fully utilized a new modeling method that we were beginning to establish through the design work for the 929.

By visualization of my concept images, I wanted to share a common image with my modeling staff. I handed them a real *Noh* mask to have them share the delicate shades and curvature of its simple surface. The mask is lifeless, yet it talks to a person if the viewer is willing to empathize

with it. So, a handful of clay was molded to the center of the form with the same kind emotions as if we were making a sculpture. This method is only effective for a clay modeler with strong artistic senses. A final form is born through repeated highlight checks, applying film on the clay model, and through careful observation by the designer and clay modeler working closely together. Kajiyama, a modeler of God-given talent, had worked with me for a long time on the design of the 929, and this long association with him yielded a great result.

I kept hearing objections from MANA, nevertheless, and within the company there was a rumour circulating that "Tanaka is wasting time and money," this at a time when there was shortage of manpower.

The clay model, completed by Kajiyama with tender loving care, was then covered with a thin colored film to simulate a real car. We put the filmed clay model on a turntable located on the roof of the design building. The model, under the fading natural light, showed endless highlights and delicate changes in reflections as if it were alive. We looked at it with awe for a long while. It was a time of sublime appreciation for a piece of

clay that had taken another form, and it was a happy moment for a car designer.

Theme of a circle

We presented the model to Fukuda immediately, and he looked at it without saying a word. I said: "I would like to call it the final model after the addition of an interior design." He said to go ahead, and added: "It will take many man-hours to create a mock-up. It cannot proceed like a hobby, so please consult with Uchida." With these words of support from Fukuda, our job became much easier, although it still had no formal approval as yet. And those engineers and designers who were helping us with an uneasy feeling in the back of their mind, now felt much better, and the work progressed at a much faster pace as a result.

Mating of interior design and exterior design got started, and hardware design of interior parts was also put in progress. In parallel with these activities, I started the design of controls and switches. The controls and switches have to be easy to handle first and foremost, but I concentrated on their design to be such that their functions are directly transmitted

81

The first clay model made in the image of a Noh mask.

The glassfibre model based on the first clay. The rear overhang was a touch too short at this stage, giving the car a rather abrupt tail.

to the driver. The design theme of the interior parts was a circle. A circle is a simple shape that is flexible yet resilient. A circular motif for the interior design would match the exterior design, adding simplicity and tension whilst producing a sense of playfulness.

Door handle
The circular motif was extended to the exterior design also. I spent much time on how the door handle should be shaped. A sports car is an escape from daily life, and is accompanied by a comfortable kind of tension. Opening the door of a sports car, therefore, should be the first ritual in entering into a different world, a world apart from daily routine. Likewise, the entrance to a tearoom is a small low door, and you have to crawl in. It may not be very rational, but when one crawls into a tearoom, one sheds his worldly self and returns to the basic person. And on seeing the tearoom, one would feel the depth and width of another world in a small room. I imagined many situations, wanting a design that would commit a driver to open the door and enter a less rational world.

With the design theme of circle, the door handle had to be

The side mirror was shaped in the wind tunnel to control airflow into the cockpit.

light and minimal, and I wanted it to be attractive as a piece of metal can be. Several models were made and tested. The designs proposed by the designers were not well accepted by engineers. "Not easy to use. Not an industrial design," came the remarks. One big question mark was raised over whether to operate the door handle with one finger or two fingers. Three fingers made it too big. We finally settled with a small slender

handle that is operable with one finger. From the start of door handle design, it was a unique design approach, and the result was an equally unique door handle. It exemplifies the kind of philosophy I wanted to carry through the entire design of the automobile.

Side mirror

The shape of the side mirror came directly from the wind tunnel test. We tested various angles for the

windshield and different shapes for the side window in order to control the airflow over the body, but it was difficult to control the airflow over the driver's shoulder. A long drive in a tank top would chill the outside shoulder of both passenger and driver, while enlarging the front windshield would affect the overall design proportions of the car. Initially, we tried to put a side mirror on the fender rather than the door, but finally, by attaching the mirror on the door and creating proper turbulence, we were able to control the airflow over the shoulder of the occupants. The mirror shape was formed in such a way as to control the airflow so that any conceivable angular position would result in a pleasant breeze for the driver and passenger.

At the first public showing of the car, several journalists questioned the shape and position of the door mirror, saying that it was not easy to use and its shape was not suitable for a sports car. I retorted: "Would you rather have your girlfriend chill her shoulders?" Then there were no more questions. One journalist finally said: "This is a completely new concept for a sports car, and it should not be regarded like an LWS of the past."

The door handle. Originally, an even slimmer design was proposed, but for practical reasons, the final dimensions were slightly larger. It's a great shame that the next generation used a conventional pull handle.

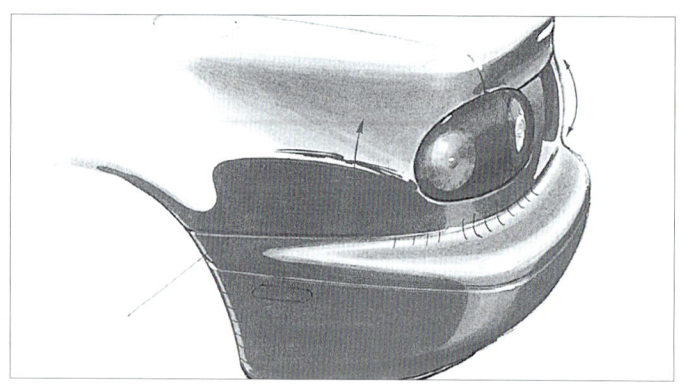

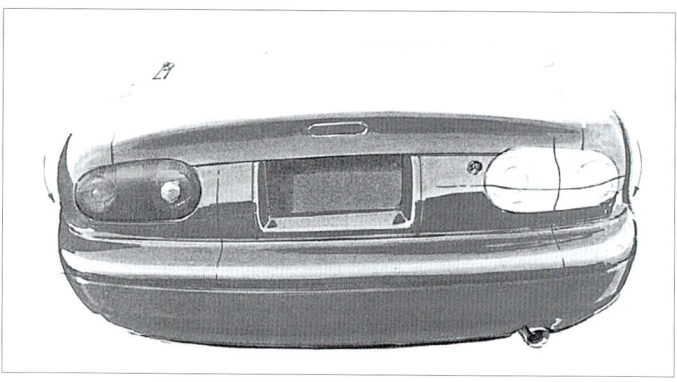

Tail lamps

Tail lamp design was based on the circular motif, too. Two circular lamps were combined in an oval outline within a minimum space, satisfying all functional requirements. The design conformed to all regulations worldwide at that time, which was quite a challenging puzzle to solve. The rear end of a sports car must be attractive and the shape of the tail lights plays an important role, so I wanted to spend all the money available in this area. The lamp cover was made with simultaneous injection of three different colored plastics, which was new at that time. The lamp maker was quite skeptical and hesitated at first, but finally agreed to proceed with the support of Saeki, the Manager of Exterior Component Design.

Everything in the tail lamps was modeled. Although we could make the prototype rather easily, it was more difficult for production. Saeki and I spent many late night hours figuring out ways to make it feasible for production. Saeki made our ideas into rough sketches, and negotiated with the lamp manufacturer the following day. One problem was left with a reflector. Because of its small size, there was not enough brightness. We tested a prototype in a lighting lab all night. By filing and attaching fine bits and pieces to the lamp reflector, when we finally achieved what we were looking for, it was dawn!

An object that is made with an all-out effort often strikes people's hearts. When we were fighting over the tail lamp, I never thought that it would be accepted as a piece of art. When I was asked by the curator of MOMA (New York Museum of Modern Art) what was the most memorable part of the car, I answered: "The entire car is, of course, but if you ask for a specific part, then it is the tail lamp." The curator said: "I agree. Because of this tail lamp, we do not want the whole car, just the tail lamp. The whole essence of the car is concentrated in the tail lamp."

I majored in sculpture at art school, sketching nude models all day before making life-size clay figures. Later, I turned to metallic sculpture, and at that time I wanted some day to have my work shown at MOMA. Somehow, I became an industrial designer, and after so many years of detour, the tail lamp that I'd designed became a permanent resident in the New York collection. I can live with that!

Pop-up headlamp

I originally proposed to adopt retractable headlamps for the car to continue the image of the RX-7, but there was opposition from MANA and the Testing & Research Department because of the additional weight caused by the pop-up mechanism. However, I insisted on round, pop-up lamps in order to continue Mazda's identity, and eventually got the go-ahead. There was another reason, stemming from a US regulation requiring the lamp bottom to be over 500mm (20in) above the ground, and without the pop-up mechanism, this could not be achieved. A simple and light one-axis pop-up rotation mechanism was chosen over the more costly two-axis design used in the RX-7.

The 3-D CAD system showed real usefulness in the pop-up lamp design. When we were designing the RX-7, any change in pop-up axis took two weeks for drawing changes, and it took three months to find the best position for the axis. With the 3-D CAD on hand, we could figure out the location of the pop-up headlamp in a few hours. After the first model was made, it was judged to be too high

for the overall proportions, and another 3-D CAD analysis was made to lower its highest point by 20mm (0.79in.). This change was acceptable and was nicely balanced with the rest of the design. All this took just four days in total.

Bumper & wheels

From the beginning, I had it in my mind to fabricate the bumpers via the urethane rim injection molding method that was only used for luxury cars at that time. The know-how gained through fabricating bumpers for the RX-7 was utilized to achieve light weight and conform to US safety regulations. I determined that the design could not be achieved without the injection molding method but, to my surprise, no-one seemed to raise objection to this expensive choice, despite the severe cost requirements.

At about the same time, Mizunaga of the Exterior

Reviewing a clay model. At first, the pop-up headlights sat too high when erected, so were lowered by 20mm (0.79in.) in the final design.

Component Design Department brought me the news that a new formation method for the bumper beam was now available which would cut down weight. This method created what was called a "blow molded bumper beam." This new technology was said to reduce weight by 8kg (18lb) per car without any significant change in the bumper design. We adopted this new method and made slight changes in the design to facilitate ease of manufacture, and added turn signal lamps and side lamps to the front bumper within a minimum space. In order to avoid damage to these lamps, a small recess was made in each side of

the bumper that added some expression too. The opening under the front bumper gave the car a smiling look, but was carefully balanced with cooling airflow requirements and tow hook location.

I was also convinced that a spoke pattern wheel would look most sporty for the car. Because of a lack of time, I wanted to clear the wheel strength requirement by adding more spokes. Mazda's internal requirement for curb (kerb) override strength is the toughest in the industry, and there is a special test course for this verification. The test condition is so severe that few other

manufacturers could pass Mazda's requirement. I have had terrible experience in the past with many design changes to my earlier wheels. Bearing in mind the importance of low unsprung weight, I designed, within a short time, an eight-spoke wheel. The design, however, was changed to a seven-spoke wheel by the PPM, without my agreement, in order to reduce its weight. I was furious, but decided to accept it due to weight considerations and a guarantee that the manufacturer would make them strong enough to pass the test.

As I think back, I was very busy with the design of the 929

Discussing seat fabrics.

going on in parallel, and did not have much time to consult with others. Many of my decisions were made alone, and I often felt depressed with the loneliness. This was my first such experience in the development of a new car.

Seat design

A lightweight seat was another necessity. Yoshimura brought me the lightest seat he could find within Mazda. In order to secure a survival space in case of a roll, the headrest was integrated into the seat back. I would have liked a separate headrest, but could not do it for safety reasons. A lightweight seat was ultimately achieved via the use of thinner

padding in urethane foam. We did not go through a detailed comfort check for the seat, and accepted the first prototype after thoroughly informing the manufacturer of the design concept of the car.

I immediately had the prototype seat installed in an interior mockup and adjusted the padding, saying: "My torso is of international size, it's only my legs that are sub-standard." When I said to the seat manufacturer that their first prototype was acceptable with only minor changes, they were very surprised. As for the seat fabric, I chose a tatami mat pattern from the many candidates in order to identify Japanese nationality. Since the interior was

all black, no-one noticed it. When people commented on the sporty but funny fabric, I felt a cold sweat.

Trunk space

With respect to the trunk space, the PPM requested we secure space for two golf bags. However, the most important part of a design in a sports car is its hipline, and a cute hipline was vital for this car. While the request was in my mind at the beginning, it was completely out of my mind by the time I was finishing the design: I was going all out to design an attractive hipline. The PPM was not satisfied with the limited space available. I said that there is no way to store

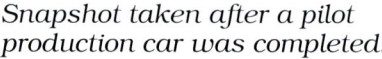
two golf bags with today's long driver shafts anyway, and I would do my best to make room for one bag. Furthermore, I said that the sports car was not really for going to a golf club, as the image was all wrong. After many arguments of this sort, we agreed to stay with the existing design rather than increase the rear overhang to accommodate an extra golf bag.

There were many arguments and associated drama over each part of the car, but we finally came to a point were we could build a final presentation model.

Marketing of concept and design

When I had a chance to visit the US for other business, I brought some pictures of the final model and made a presentation. The Mazda US staff, including the Vice-President of Sales, were of the opinion that no matter how we might look at it, there simply was no market for an LWS and they told me to go home ... The US was going to be the main market for the LWS, and we worked hard to make the car competitive at 100

yen to the dollar, doing all we could to meet the target cost. I felt desperate.

Fujimoto, the President of Mazda Germany, also told me on another occasion that he did market research into the LWS at the request of Hirai, and found no market potential in Europe. And in Japan, marketing people told me after my presentation that they would estimate a monthly sales figure of perhaps 150 cars through domestic dealers. This figure was too small for mass production.

These remarks from sales people sounded like a death sentence for the project. The only hope came from the gentleman responsible for new car sales in Austria. He said: "Tanaka, this car has the potential to be a great hit. Do not give up hope." He and I had earlier shared some success in introducing a new model to Austria, and I trusted him. When I visited New York in connection with the 929, I visited one of the Mazda dealers for his opinion. After seeing a few pictures of the car and a long pause, he said: "When will the car be ready? Is

Mazda really serious? I am so happy to be a Mazda dealer if I can sell these." His eyes were full of tears.

Although I had located some strong supporters for the car, there was also strong opposition, and MANA kept complaining that because of my changes to the design, their brainchild was distorted and had lost its chance forever. The real enemy of the LWS was the poor forecast of US sales and, in reality, MANA should have complained to the sales side rather than me. I was furious, and my relationship with MANA was terrible.

A little earlier, we'd experienced a sharp difference of opinion from US sales on an MPV project. Because of this, the project came close to being abandoned. But when we took a model and had a blind user clinic, where the proposed model was compared with other competitive vehicles using randomly selected consumers as judges, the result was very positive and the MPV survived. Due to this experience, I had a discussion with Hirai and we jointly made a request to Michinori Yamanouchi, a Senior Managing Director, to secure a chance to get a direct response from US consumers. After shipping a clay model, Hirai and I left for the US to join the clinic. We were both desperate and ready to abandon the project if a positive

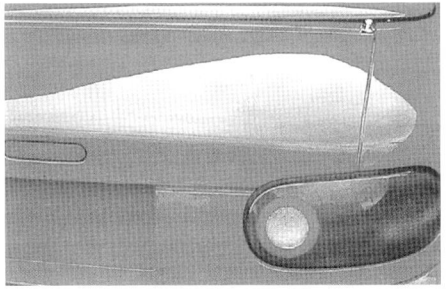

The model that was sent to America for a styling clinic was very well received. The wheels used for that event led many to think the new car was an Alfa Romeo.

reaction was not forthcoming. Hirai said: "I only wish we could make a prototype and test it at Miyoshi Proving Ground." I had the same thought. The mood on the flight to LA was a dark and gloomy one.

When we passed the airport customs, there was Bob Hall, Mark Jordan and Kouichi Hayashi, all with big smiles. They greeted us with a loud "Congratulations!"

I could not understand what was happening. After getting into a car, I asked Hayashi for an explanation: "What's going on here? You have been tearing us down all along, and now you're here to greet us. Why?" He told me that when the model was unwrapped and the MANA staff saw the model, they all loved it!

Clinic

On the day of the clinic, randomly selected consumers arrived at the auditorium we'd rented. These people would fill out questionnaires and inspect the model all day. After inspection they were randomly gathered into focus groups, and with the guidance of professional leaders, they would comment on the questions for which we most wanted answers. We observed the event in a backroom with a monitor TV. It

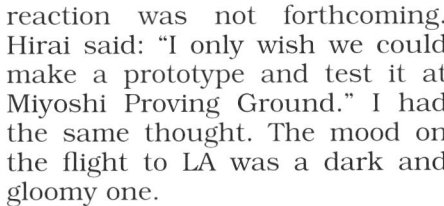

seemed to me that those who liked the model outnumbered those who did not. I said to Hirai: "It seems positive!" He replied: "Let's wait until we get the final result," but he was obviously relieved by the look on his face. Two days later, the result of the meeting was made available. Although I cannot recall in detail, the result was roughly as follows:

60% of the people liked the model and 40% disliked it. The main reasons for disliking it were that they had owned a LWS in the past and had trouble; there were safety concerns if the car rolled; the high price of a convertible, and/or they currently owned a Porsche.

80% of those who liked it would consider buying it.

The average price they would be willing to pay was $17,000. We were prepared to sell at $12,000 and still make profit.

30 people thought it was a new Porsche, 20 an Alfa Romeo, ten a BMW, ten a Honda, seven a Mazda, four a Toyota, and the rest could not tell. Among those who could not tell, most said they wanted to get the car whatever the make was.

Hirai and I were in tears and dancing with joy – we were so happy that we had not quit early in

the proceedings. The environment for the project had been so bad, although there were times we thought we might have to quit, and there were times that I got so mad that I was ready to walk away from the project. But these rough patches were all over, I thought. We went back to Japan ahead of schedule and reported to Yoshihiro Wada, the Executive Vice-President. Wada said that if the market wants it, accelerate the schedule.

A week later the model came back to Hiroshima. Although the final model should have been presented to the Executive Committee for approval, we put

I enjoyed my first drive of the MX-5/Miata at the Miyoshi Proving Ground. I can clearly remember it, with the top down and a breeze wafting through the cockpit. I felt a great sense of freedom ...

the agenda in motion with the model that was sent to the US. The public had clearly voted for it and, basically, that was enough.

Mass-production stage

After securing Executive Committee approval in record time, the model that grew up in the shadows sprang onto to the main stage. The Riverside Hotel was filled with engineers, and everything went on concurrently in order for the car to reach the production stage quickly. We were so busy making up design line drawings. One production problem was the necessity for the deep pressing of the rear fender panel. There were no precedents, and there was a danger that a steel sheet might tear under such stress. I told them that the rear end of the roadster was the most vital part of the design and couldn't be compromised. Press technicians insisted that steel is steel, and impossible is impossible. By moving the trunk lid parting line outward by 12mm (0.5in.), the original hipline was maintained and the engineers were satisfied, although the fuel tank lid was changed into an oval shape from the original circular design.

In order to save weight, the engine hood (bonnet) was to be made from aluminum, but forming the delicate power bulge in the center was another problem. Production engineers' comments were quite abrasive towards my strong convictions regarding the design. I told them: "Western sculpture expresses only one thing. Rodin's Thinker is thinking all the way to his toe. That's Western culture. We make this car with our Eastern aesthetic philosophy and, as Zeami said in his Fuushi-Kaden, hidden is the flower. Please take my word for what's required and produce the hood as I designed it." Somehow I persuaded them to take the challenge. As for the one-piece urethane bumper, there were previous experiences with the RX-7 bumper, and more discussions were held on crash safety and weight reduction rather than the problems of production. Eventually, we got there ...

Soft-top

One of the few things left to review, using the 3-D CAD system, was the link mechanism for the soft-top. The shape of the parcel shelf was also done with a 3-D view on the screen. With regard to the design of the soft-top, I remember the comment made by an older British engineer dispatched from the UK. He said: "Tanaka, I tell you, a soft-top is an umbrella. Everybody is trying to make a cabin with the soft-top. You must understand, Tanaka, it's just an umbrella."

Upon discussion with the PPM, we chose a simple design for the soft-top. I did not like the sharply pointed center when it was raised, but accepted it for it would look good folded down. The material for the soft-top was chosen from fabric made in Germany where the temperature in winter is much colder; it is also used on the VW Cabriolet.

Final check

Various parts were ready for mass-production. Press dies for body panels were completed, and went through a final press trial witnessed by our design staff. The pressed rear fender did not have the tension I wanted. Therefore the die (it weighs five tons) was disassembled and whet stoned and then another test pressing made: this process was repeated over and over. A manager in charge of press working came and stopped the process claiming that it would exceed the tolerance of the die. I insisted that we continue, because I was not satisfied. Then, an old press worker came along with various sheets of paper in his hand. He put a carefully selected sheet of paper between the die and the steel. "Go on, press," he said. Then, after the 10,000-ton press was released, the panel had a perfect profile! However, pressed into the sheet of paper was a little mosquito that had wandered between the die and the paper: the flattened mosquito on the paper is something I'll always remember!

Body color

Originally, blue, yellow, and red were the colors we chose, but I was convinced that a purplish-red, not an orangey-red, best matched the design. I requested that a new kind of red paint be developed, but when there was no positive response I visited the paint maker and had them develop the color of my choice. This was called "Tanaka Red" for a while and later renamed as "Classic Red." Blue was a proposal from a color designer at MANA. When I first got the presentation from her, I felt it too bright, but took to the idea for she had bright blue eyes! Yellow was the most difficult color. After many unsuccessful trials we gave up on this color. White or silver were the two alternatives we had in mind. The US insisted on white, whereas Japan insisted on silver. Since both these colors were already in use, there were no production problems.

Pilot car

After all the parts were assembled, we had the first pilot production model. The first internal viewing was hosted by the Quality Assurance Department. A red pilot production car was covered with white marks all over the body. Each of these marks indicated a quality problem. As I checked them, all but three were acceptable to my eyes, but the Quality Manager insisted that he would not give his approval "as long as his eyes were black" (which means as long as he was alive!). I told him: "I don't care if your eyes are black or white, I'm responsible for the design. If I say OK, it's OK. All I want you to carefully check is the flowing highlight line from front to rear. This must be observed strictly." I requested that QA check the car not only part-by-part, but from a much broader point of view, as if it was the customer looking at the vehicle.

Of course, I really wanted to take a test drive in the car. One sunny winter day in 1988, we all got together at Miyoshi Proving Ground. Many project members and managers from the Development Divisions were there. It was the first time I'd seen the pilot car run. As the red pilot car accelerated in front of me out of a corner, its tail lights got blurred with the tears in my eyes. After the PPM, I got into the car and after checking the function of each component with my shaking fingers, I started the engine. I lapped the test course first with the top up and then with it pulled down. As the latches were released, the world suddenly opened up. With the physical release of the top, my mind was also released: this was the moment we had waited for with the soft-top ...

The "Global Circuit" at Miyoshi Proving Ground consists of the many kinds of road to be found in the world. I lapped the course gradually increasing the speed. This was an experience that gave extreme pleasure. Slightly sliding its tail, the car went into a corner and then downhill following a downshift. The pleasure of maneuvering was fully reflected to the driver.

"Moriyama, you are a genius!" I cried out with joy, praising Hiroyoshi Moriyama, our testing and research co-ordinator. The wind over my shoulders was better controlled than in the wind tunnel test, and a dream from my childhood had finally come true.

The Mazda MX-5/Miata in right-hand drive guise.

7

Chassis design
by **Takao Kijima**

From the very beginning of the project, Kijima was watching the entire car develop in addition to his chassis design assignment. One day, he came to talk to me about a PPF (Power Plant Frame), and proposed that one should be installed. After trying a test PPF fitted to an RX-7, I confirmed its effectiveness and that it was the best way to provide the driver with a feeling of direct response from the car. We proceeded to develop the system, but found that there was not enough manpower to do the necessary work. Consequently, Kijima worked on the PPF (even though it was not really within the scope of the Chassis Design Department) and released its production drawings from his department. It was quite an unusual situation. Fittingly, Kijima is currently PPM in charge of the RX-7 and MX-5.

T. Hirai

Any engineer who works in the automobile industry would like to make a sports car. In a big corporation like Mazda, it is very difficult for an engineer to develop his own expertise whilst dreaming about his ideal car, and even more difficult to have a chance to participate in the building of such a dream car. But if the chance is granted, of course, anyone would muster all their strength to face the challenge.

When Mazda committed to develop a LWS, I was determined to be a part of the team and take the challenge by all means. My boss, Ito, then manager of the Chassis Design Department, told me that although he agreed to me taking the job, there was not enough manpower and I'd have to work on holidays or do overtime to make up for it. The conditions I was given were tough, but I was pleased that I would be able to contribute to the project. I didn't care about the overtime work, and felt much happier each and every day that I was able to take part in a job that I had previously only dreamed about.

As I look back, we went to the Riverside Hotel whenever we had time, in between our main work, and after five. The place was filled with engineers with the same passion and vigor. The discussions we held there were so exciting that we often went home past midnight. Despite such heavy work demands, however, I do not recall anyone getting ill during the development time. It must have been the fact that creating a sports car was so exciting. We all exerted our best efforts, and that resulted in the great success we have on our hands today.

Driving stability development
The definition of a chassis became less clear after the birth of the monocoque body. The department

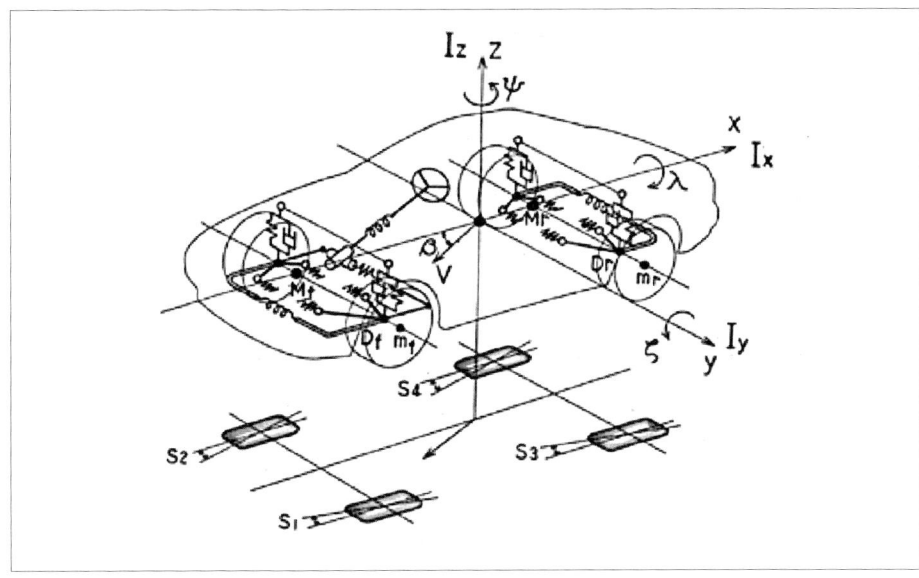

A DEMCO model, allowing handling stability analysis.

I belonged to was called the Chassis Design Department, although the name must date back to the days when Mazda was manufacturing three-wheeled trucks. The scope of chassis design included frame, suspension system, brake system and various control mechanisms, with the exception of the powerplant. Therefore, it meant that our department was responsible for making those parts that create the best basic performance of a vehicle, providing the best handling and stability for the car.

Mazda already had a long history of sports car making with the Cosmo Sports in the late-1960s and the RX-7 from the mid-1970s, and we had our own sports car philosophy firmly established. The first and the foremost priority for a Mazda sports car was to make it fun to drive. Mazda firmly believed that a vehicle that only went fast on a straight road was not a sports car, and that the fun of driving was to go through a winding road at speed according to the wishes of a driver. This was the key, and the conditions for achieving this quality were:

Front engine, rear wheel-drive.
Low weight (less than 1000kg/ 2200lb).
50:50 weight distribution.
A low yaw moment of inertia.
A low center of gravity.

In order to satisfy these five conditions and realize a car that is fun to drive is actually beyond the domain of chassis design. It is not an overstatement to say that the design layout determines the basic potential of a vehicle's dynamics. In the development of the MX-5/ Miata, I clearly remember that Hirai, the PPM, paid great attention to establishing and maintaining a basic layout of good quality from the very beginning.

Suspension

The specification of a suspension system is the second most important element in determining the vehicle dynamics of a sports car. At a time when the outline of the project was becoming clear, I had in mind a suspension scheme which would have a double wishbone system for all wheels. There is no compromise allowed in the suspension system of a sports

car, although particular adherence to a specific philosophy may be allowed. The suspension system of a sports car must have the greatest freedom of adjustment for suspension settings, and that meant adopting a double wishbone system. This choice also helped convince our team members that we were creating a car that reflected our ultimate choices in each respect of the design. This decision later created a few arguments, which troubled Hirai, but this aspect will be discussed later.

The suspension system specifications necessary to realize the targeted vehicle dynamics were quite varied, but interrelated. In order to achieve the target performance, one must understand these interrelations and establish ultimate characteristics through repeated bouts of trial and error. Our work was to design and create the suspension parts that would realize our ultimate goals for the LWS.

In the development of the MX-5/Miata, we deployed a new approach to transforming the design philosophy into hardware more efficiently. This approach worked very successfully in achieving the desired handling and stability, and came about as a result of ideas developed to fully utilize the limited manpower available for the project. The accompanying chart was used to

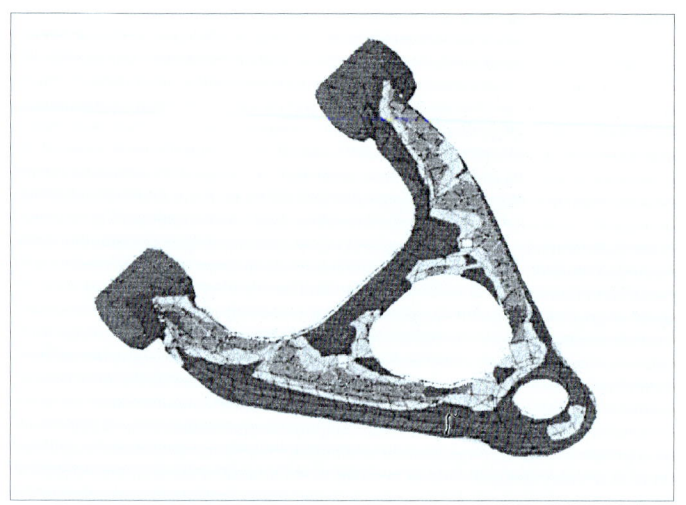 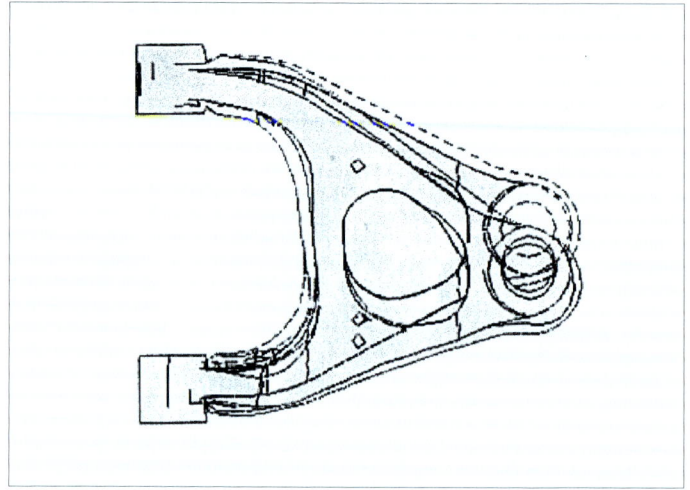

FEM analysis allowed us to see exactly what would happen to the MX-5/Miata's suspension upper arm during braking. The lighter shaded areas are those that were under the greatest levels of stress. The right-hand picture shows distortion. Without the need to produce an actual part, the FEM system allowed many variations to be evaluated before a final design was selected.

guide our approach, and is still a valuable tool for those who engage in suspension system development: we found that suspension tuning could be executed most efficiently with this chart, too.

Mazda had an exceptional chassis analyst by the name of Nishioka. He had developed a design program named DEMCO in the early 1970s (much earlier than the ADAMS programs for handling and stability analysis), which proved to be an excellent design tool. Mazda had a leading position in the industry with respect to handling and stability analysis since the days of our three-wheelers in the 1950s, and this design tool was powerful and indispensable in creating a fun to drive sports car. We fully utilized this technology along with experimental results in determining the chassis specification. The details of this process will be described later.

A tunable suspension system

By adjusting suspension tuning, the handling and stability of a car may be altered to extract more enjoyment from driving. For a sports car, the chances of driving on a racing circuit are high, and proper settings are then vital to be competitive on the track. To design a suspension system for ease of tuning depends on the chassis designer's philosophy. Most of the cars today are designed with fixed tuning and a maintenance free quality in mind, eliminating adjustable mechanisms. Although it may be optimum for its chassis, there is no facility for tuning and adjustment, depriving the customers of further enjoyment. Rationalism certainly has economic merits and Mazda cannot neglect it, but for this roadster, we were determined to provide a fully tunable suspension system for our customers. Fixing bolts for suspension arms were of the traditional cam shape to provide freedom for camber and caster angle adjustment. Likewise, we avoided press fit or caulking of the joints for dampers, springs and stabilizers to give ease of disassembly, simply using nuts and bolts. The suspension of the MX-5/Miata was an exclusive

design to give tuneability and enhanced sports performance.

Weight reduction

The Finite Element Analysis Method (FEM) was used for the design analysis of all parts in order to save weight and give enough strength where needed. This was a critical design without any margin for error. Since the reliability and durability of a car is directly related to the ongoing reputation of the car manufacturer, it is normal to apply ample margins in the design of each component to give it sufficient strength in order to avoid any claims from consumers. On the other hand, for this LWS, we could not afford to give any excessive margin of strength for its components. Our target was to design each part to have the ideal strength for its function, to give it just enough strength and durability, but no more. In the development, there are many confirmatory FEM tests conducted at each stage, and each of the test codes contained a certain amount of built in standard margin. Therefore, we had to optimize

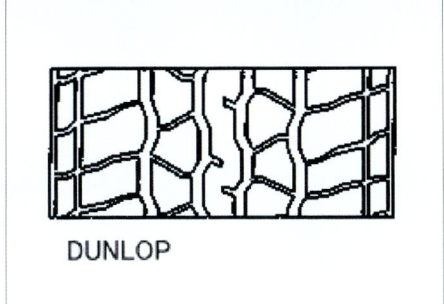 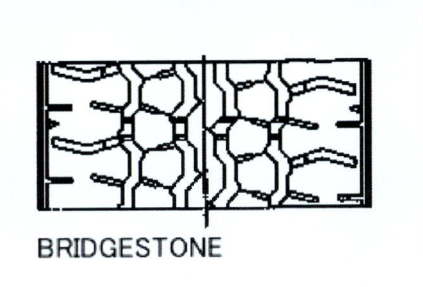 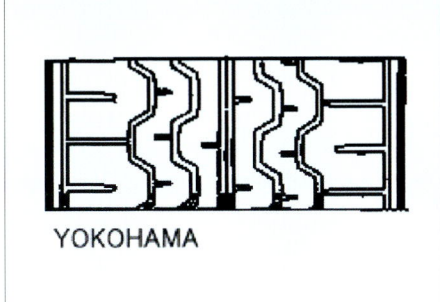

Tire patterns from the different manufacturers.

those margins in the test code for the LWS. Hirai had to go through repeated arguments with engineers in the Testing & Research Division in order to make them optimize their test codes for the MX-5/Miata. Every time these arguements occured, Hirai insisted on his LWS philosophy and convinced his opponents: this hard work was an important hidden element in the success of the roadster.

We set ourselves the target of designing a double-wishbone suspension system within the weight of a strut-type system. In order to achieve this target, we allocated a weight target for each component. The toughest challenge was to work out and allocate a certain weight for the upper arm that does not exist in strut-type suspension. By repeated FEM analysis of the suspension components, we reduced unnecessary weight in each part and finally achieved our goal. It is quite common that many components of a prototype need uprating after actual testing, but in the case of the MX-5/Miata, such beefing up was held to a minimum despite the critical minimalist design. After so many years since the first introduction of the roadster, we are extremely proud that the car has attained a reputation for unprecedented reliability and durability, in addition to its fun to drive qualities.

Cost saving

Among the many materials from which to fabricate a suspension system component, pressed steel is a very common approach. The press die necessary to press a steel sheet is normally very expensive, and efficient design is needed to keep the cost to a minimum. The suspension system, like human legs, is symmetrically designed, but if the arms are symmetrically designed, dies for both the left and the right arms will be required, coming with an associated cost increase. Our goal was to design a common suspension arm for both right and left sides to save cost. Likewise, the chassis design engineers worked hard to use a common press die for the following parts and components:

Suspension arms
Front upper arms (L&R) were from a common die.
Rear upper arms (L&R) were from a common die.
Rear lower arms (L&R) were from a common die.

Suspension crossmembers
Brackets for rear suspension crossmembers were from a common die.
Front and rear crossmember upper panels and lower panels were from two common dies.
Left and right bracket for rear suspension crossmembers, and upper and lower parts of front and rear crossmembers were from a common die.

Damper unit mount rubber
Damper unit mount rubber bracket for the front and rear suspension were from a common die.

The front crossmember was designed to provide a mounting function for the engine, steering, and suspension arms. When we designed the front suspension crossmember, which was made with one large press die for precision, we integrated a mounting function for the vital components at the front of the car. As a result, we were able to produce the front suspension within a cost and weight target which is comparable to a strut-type suspension system. With this design, the man-hours required for production were also reduced considerably.

Tyre tread pattern
With the co-operation of tyre manufacturers, we were able to have them design special tread patterns for the MX-5/Miata. Automobile tyres are normally made for general application, and this must have been the first time for Mazda that tyre tread design was made to suit the product image of a sports car.

Tyre manufacturers compete with each other for better performance day by day, but they

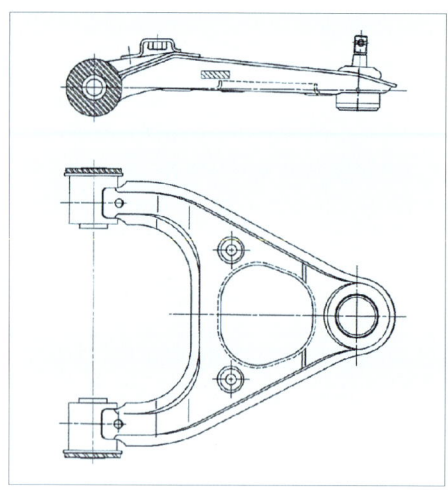

Front suspension upper arm.

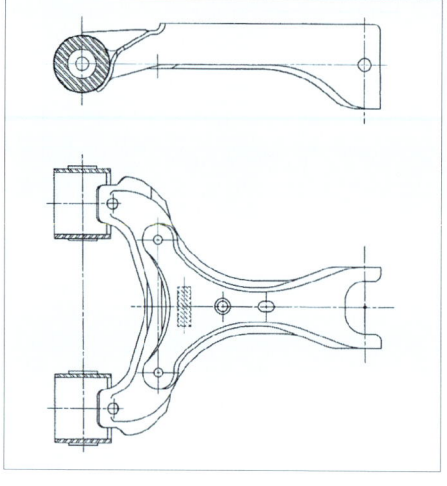

Rear suspension upper arm.

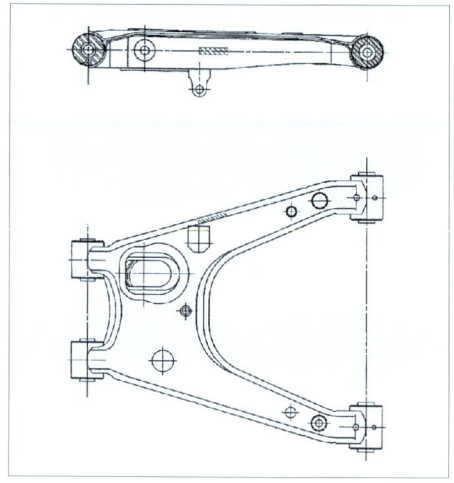

Rear suspension lower arm.

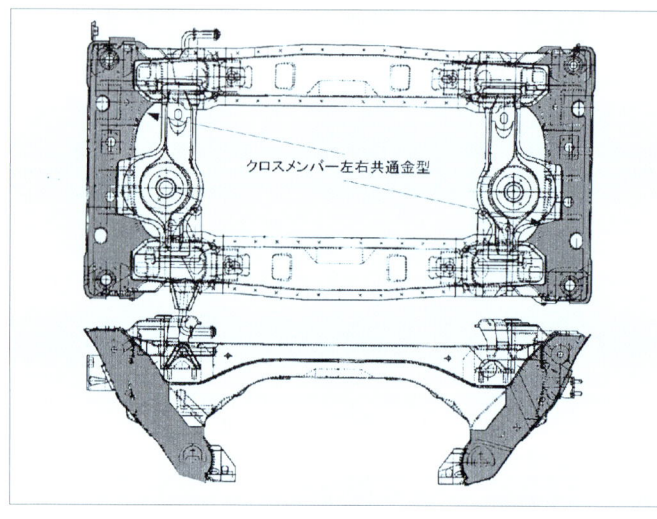

クロスメンバー左右共通金型

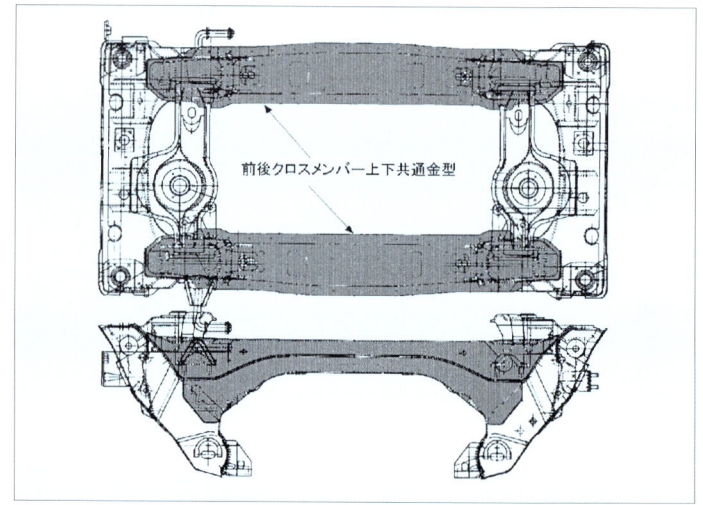

前後クロスメンバー上下共通金型

Rear suspension crossmember.

Damper unit mounting rubber.

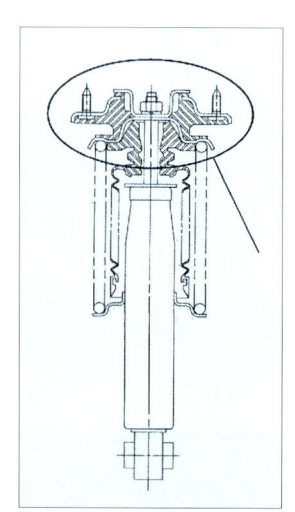

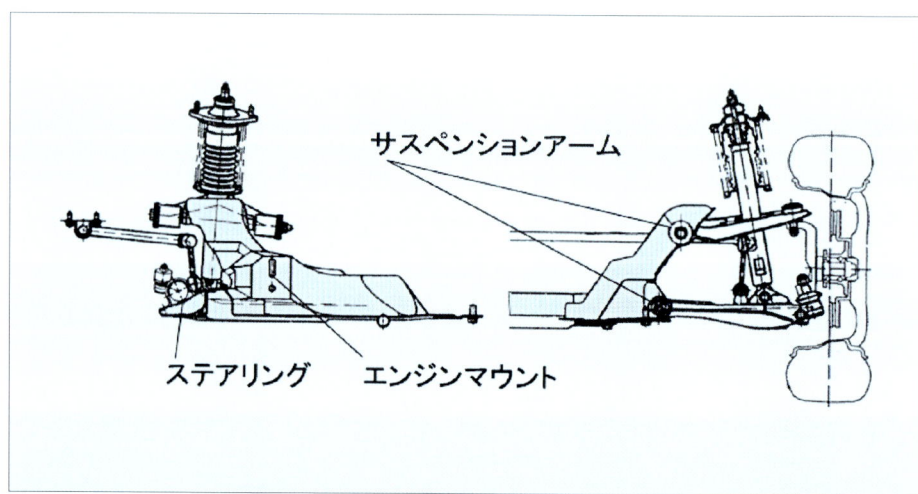

サスペンションアーム

ステアリング　エンジンマウント

were not ready at the beginning of the LWS project to design a special tread pattern for the roadster (tread pattern is most vital in controlling tyre performance, including grip, traction, braking, water dispersal, noise and durability). However, after our thorough explanation of the product concept, performance targets and showing our strong passion towards this project, they agreed to develop their own individual tread patterns for the LWS. The tread patterns shown in the picture were the ones finally selected from each of the manufacturers.

Handling and stability: background of technological development

The MX-5/Miata was Mazda's first sports car to feature a double-wishbone suspension system on all four wheels. In order to achieve the original design concept of the car, we had been making drastic decisions with particular emphasis on the following items:

Low yaw moment of inertia, and ideal front/rear weight distribution.
Ideal geometry for a double-wishbone suspension system.
Toe control mechanism.
Damping force selection.

As a result of this design focus, I believe the roadster attained an unprecedented level of driving satisfaction.

Concept

We wanted to revive a traditional LWS with a traditional layout, but incorporate the latest technology from the modern era. To achieve this goal, we eliminated everything that was not necessary to achieving the fun to drive quality we wanted, and unity of the car and its driver. Among these, our concept for handling and driving stability was:

Linear handling that will create a proper amount of tension for the driver within a normal driving speed range.

A suspension design which gives a clear indication of cornering limit to the driver, and one that provides the driver with fun even during normal driving.

In order to achieve these aims, low weight, optimum front and rear weight distribution, a low yaw moment of inertia, and body rigidity were the most important targets in the design of the MX-5/Miata from the very beginning.

Characteristics

Among the many characteristics of the roadster, the following items were very closely connected to its handling and driving stability.

Chassis layout following a traditional FR arrangement: the engine located in the front midship position.

A suspension system employing double-wishbones with unequal length upper and lower arms for both front and rear. This system allowed freedom in the geometry, to shift the roll center and to change the camber angle as

99

Steering mechanism.

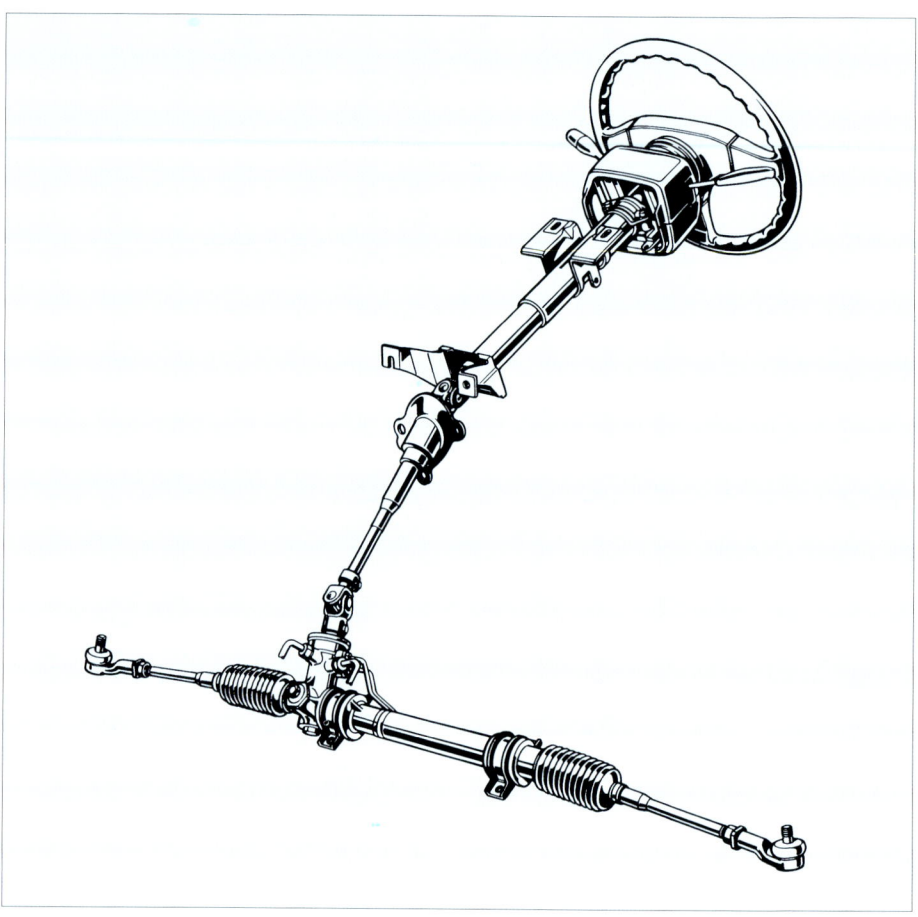

desired. By changing the rubber bush hardness of the rear lower arms, front and rear, a simple lateral force toe-in function was easily achieved. Because of the lack of side force common on the rod in strut-type suspension, the friction loading on the damper was reduced, and its damping force was raised in the low piston speed range and reduced in the high piston speed range to achieve a good balance of stability and ride comfort.

Suspension arms were attached to a subframe through a rubber bushing, and the subframe was rigidly attached to the body. Very high overall suspension rigidity was achieved as a consequence. An advanced structural analysis method was deployed for the body, suspension arms and other structural components to give a lightweight and rigid body design. The resulting body had unprecedented rigidity for an open monocoque body, and the suspension system had a high level of controllability and linearity with plenty of freedom in the suspension settings.

The transmission and differential gear casing were connected by an aluminium powerplant frame (PPF) to form a highly rigid, single drivetrain. This drivetrain system reduced the wind-up effect, vibration caused by resonance of rear suspension and differential gear case, rear

suspension pitching, and power transmission time lag, that were all common in traditional FR cars. The PPF eliminated the phase lag in the handling and stability, and improved linearity.

The tyres were newly developed for the MX-5/Miata with particular emphasis on tread design. Weight was reduced by 1kg (2lb) per tyre with optimum balance between lightness and performance – seven-spoke, lightweight aluminium wheels to match were developed for the roadster. A highly rigid rack-and-pinion steering mechanism was employed, with an 18:1 gear ratio for the manual rack and 15:1 with power assistance.

Methodology and effects

I would like to describe in the following sections the design methodology and effects on four of the most important areas we were pursuing: Low yaw moment of inertia and optimization of front/rear weight distribution; variable suspension geometry settings for the double-wishbone suspension system (camber angle adjustment); toe control mechanisms; damper force tuning.

Low yaw moment of inertia and optimization of front/rear weight distribution

In order to improve steering response, turn-in ability and controllability at the limit, yaw moment of inertia reduction and optimum front and rear weight distribution were pursued. There were eight items to cover in order to achieve these goals:

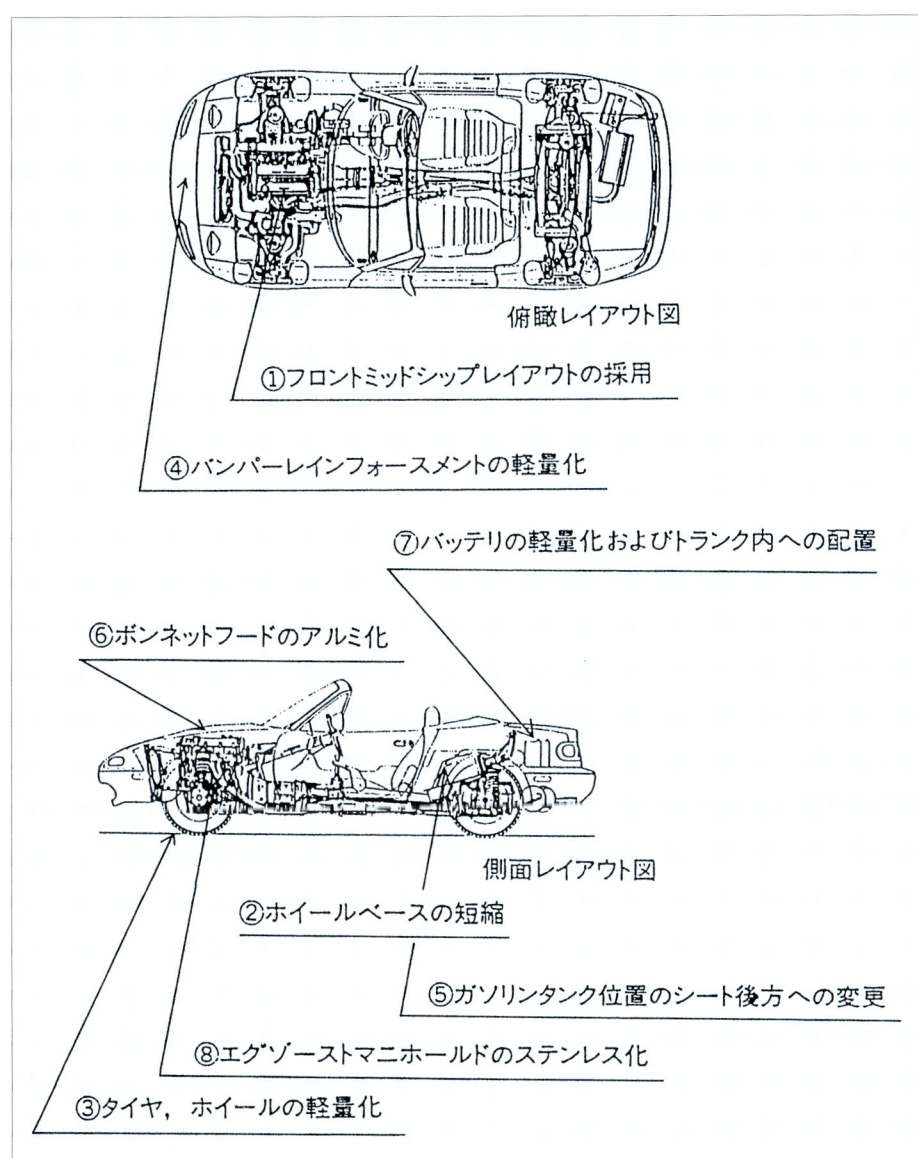

俯瞰レイアウト図

①フロントミッドシップレイアウトの採用

④バンパーレインフォースメントの軽量化

⑦バッテリの軽量化およびトランク内への配置

⑥ボンネットフードのアルミ化

側面レイアウト図

②ホイールベースの短縮

⑤ガソリンタンク位置のシート後方への変更

⑧エグゾーストマニホールドのステンレス化

③タイヤ，ホイールの軽量化

A front mid-ship layout.
A short wheelbase.
Light wheels and tyres.
Light bumper reinforcement.
Fuel tank location behind the seats.
An aluminum bonnet.
A light battery located in the trunk.
A stainless steel exhaust manifold.

The reduction of yaw moment of inertia to 1340kgm for the roadster meant it was 12.8% lower than a conventional design's 1536kgm. Fig.2 shows a comparison with other sports cars and is plotted via the difference of front and rear weight distribution and yaw moment of inertia, divided by total vehicle weight. The figure demonstrates that the MX-5/Miata has a very low yaw moment of inertia and good weight distribution.

The following test results indicate how effective the basic dimensions are in relation to actual performance, by changing yaw inertia moment without changing vehicle weight.

A frequency response test was conducted to verify response and tracking to steering wheel movement. With steering angle as an input and yaw rate as an output, their gain and phase lag were measured and plotted in Fig.3 and Fig.4. From Fig.3 it can be seen that a large yaw moment of inertia will cause low peak gain and a large phase lag. Fig.4 shows that the MX-5/Miata demonstrated higher peak frequency and a smaller phase lag compared to other sports cars. This data shows that the roadster was able to achieve superb response and tracking, and unprecedented handling characteristics.

In order to evaluate the directional stability against disturbances, a hands-free stability test, in which a certain amount of steering deflection is given at 60mph (100kph), is performed and convergence time measured. Crosswind stability tests were also conducted, in which the roadster was subjected to a strong crosswind of 25m/s at 87mph (140kph). See figures 5, 6, 7 and 8.

Despite a short wheelbase of 2265mm (89.2in), the MX-5/Miata showed exceptional stability against disturbances and an excellent recovery time for convergence. This means that its suspension settings were effective,

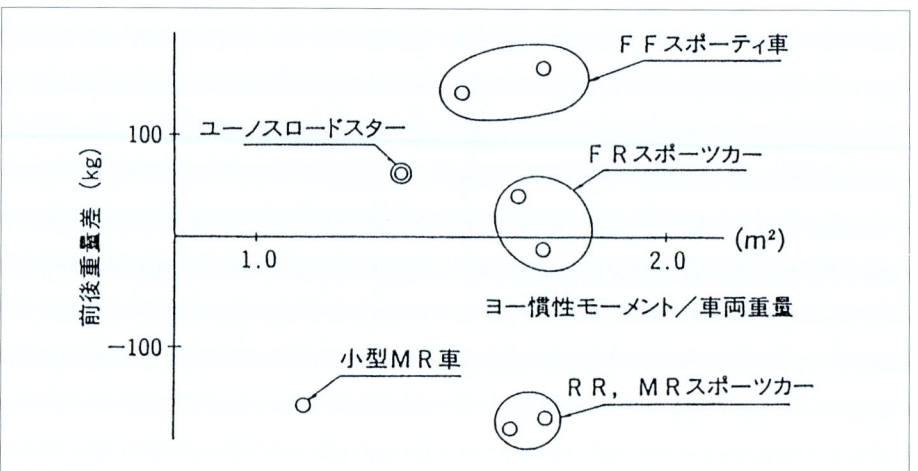

Fig.2: The effect on yaw moment caused by various drivetrain layouts.

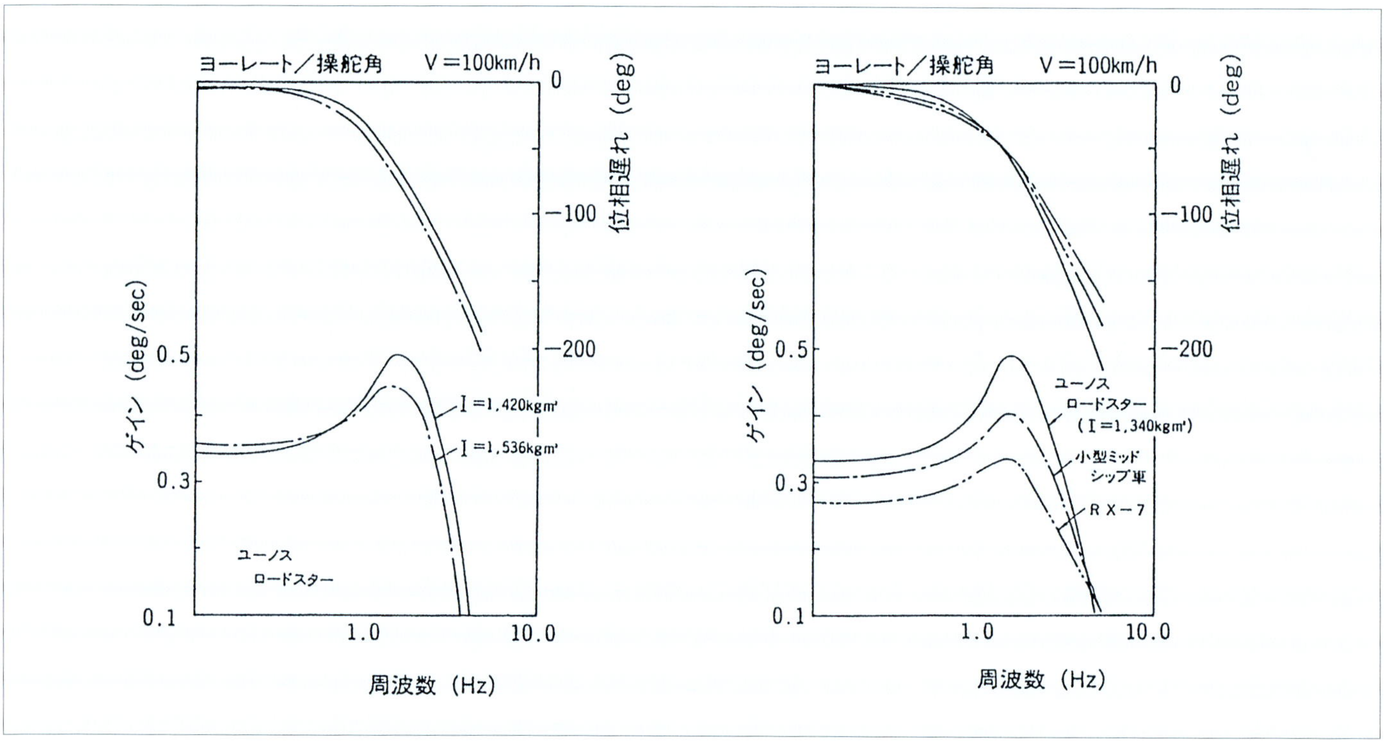

Figs.3 & 4: Steering response test, showing steering input versus yaw moment reaction. The graph clearly illustrates the MX-5's excellent response.

helped by the low yaw moment of inertia.

Suspension geometry settings (camber angle adjustment)

The double-wishbone suspension used in the roadster has a wide range of geometry adjustment to achieve excellent roadholding under all conditions. Fig.9 shows the arrangement for the front and rear suspension. Both systems used a short upper arm and a longer lower arm, each connecting to a hub carrier.

As the suspension moves, the difference in location of upper and lower arms results in the camber angle change. Optimization of this camber angle change was achieved through simulation during the design stage, and through actual running tests with a special test vehicle.

One of the evaluation methods is to measure the temperature distribution of the tyre over varying

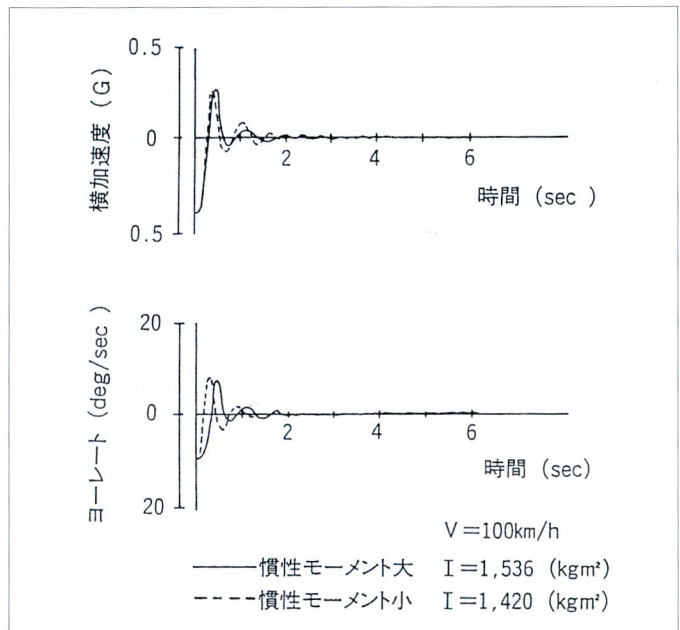

Fig.5: Stability test results without holding the steering wheel.

Fig.6: Stability test results in crosswinds.

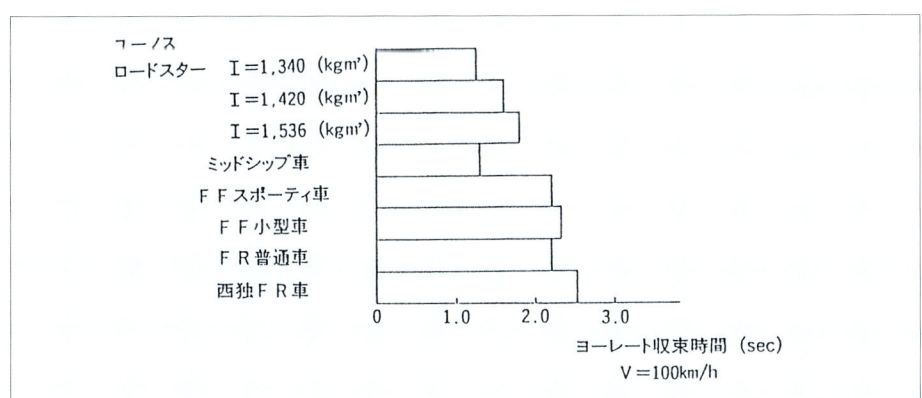

Fig.7: Another chart showing stability test results without holding the steering wheel, but this time including MR, FF, and FR layouts.

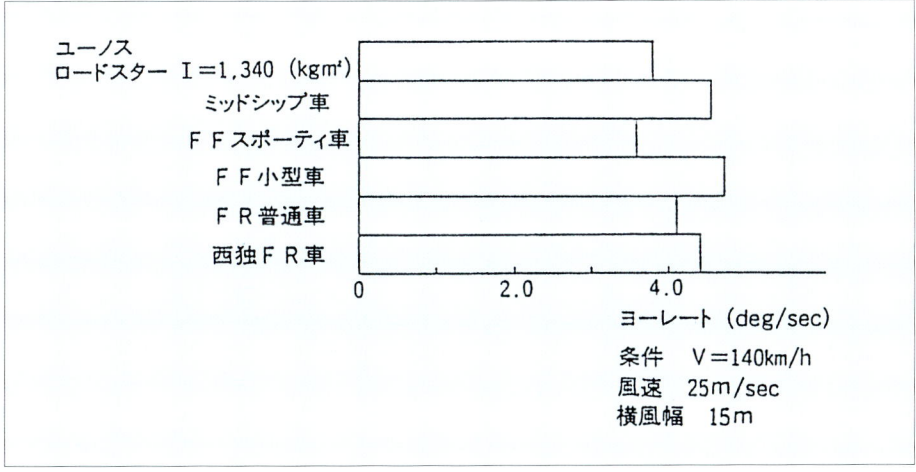

Fig.8: Crosswind stability test results using various drivetrain layouts for comparison.

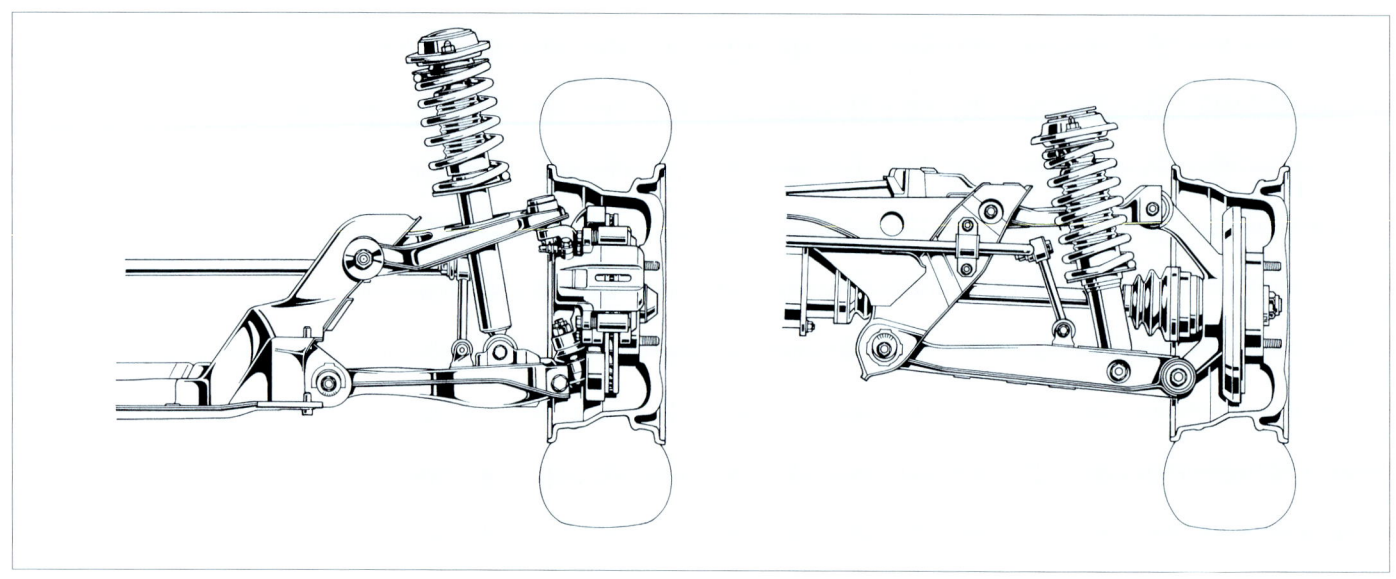

Fig.9: Front and rear suspension.

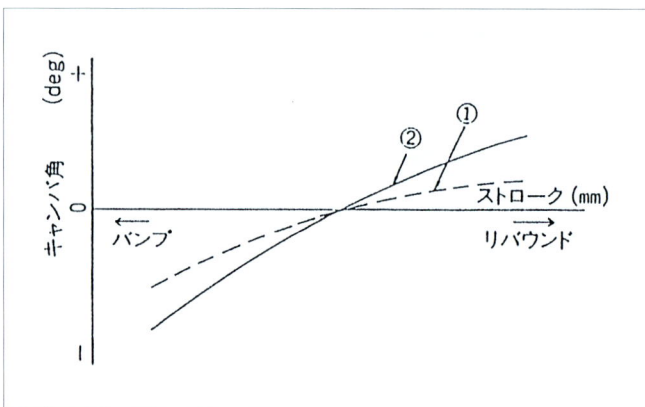

Fig.10: Camber angle change in relation to the body (front).

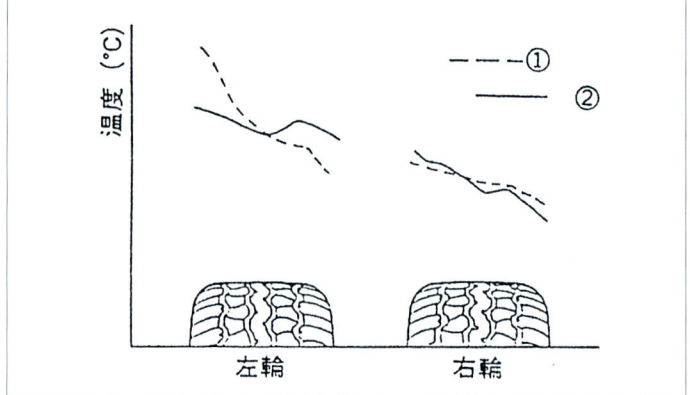

Fig.11: Tire surface temperature (front).

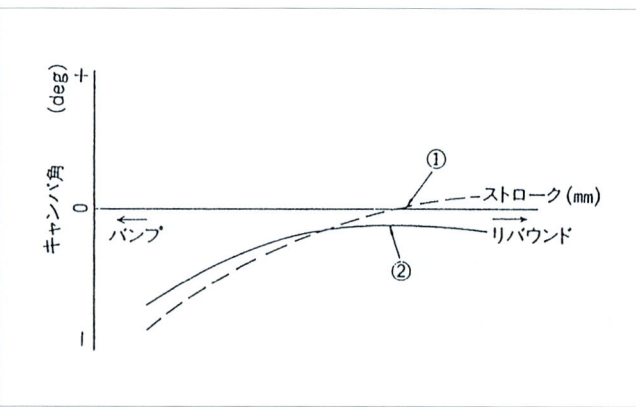

Fig.12: Camber angle change in relation to the body (rear).

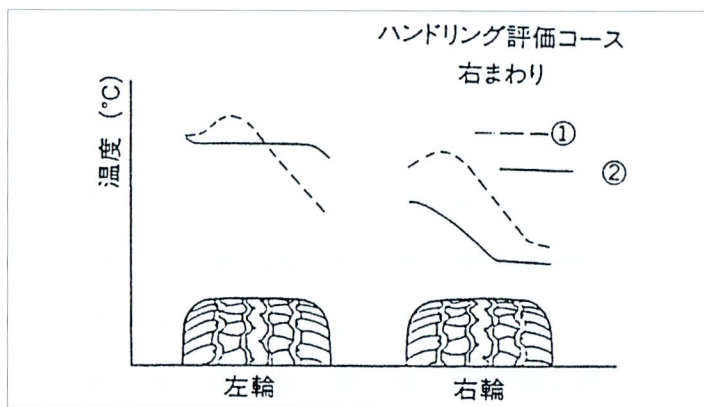

Fig.13: Tire surface temperature (rear).

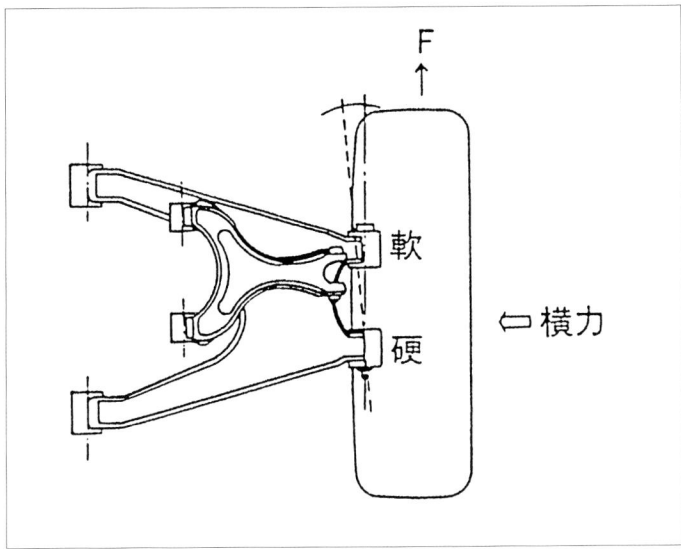

Fig.14: Toe-control mechanism.

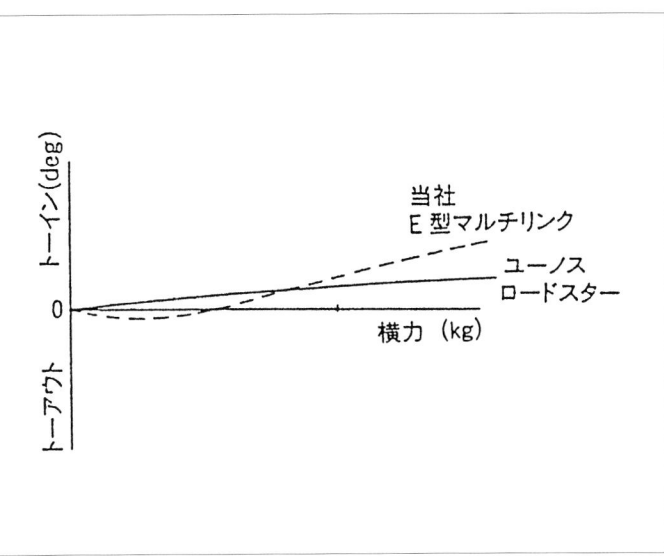

Fig.15: Rear suspension toe change whilst cornering.

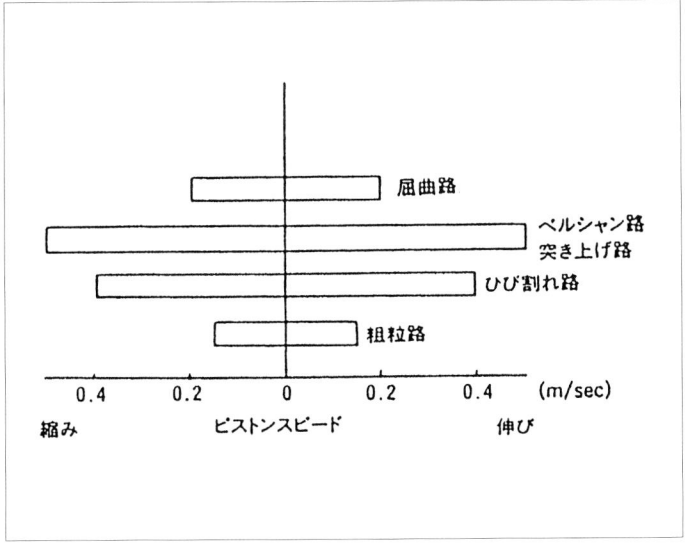

Fig.16: Damper speed in relation to road surfaces.

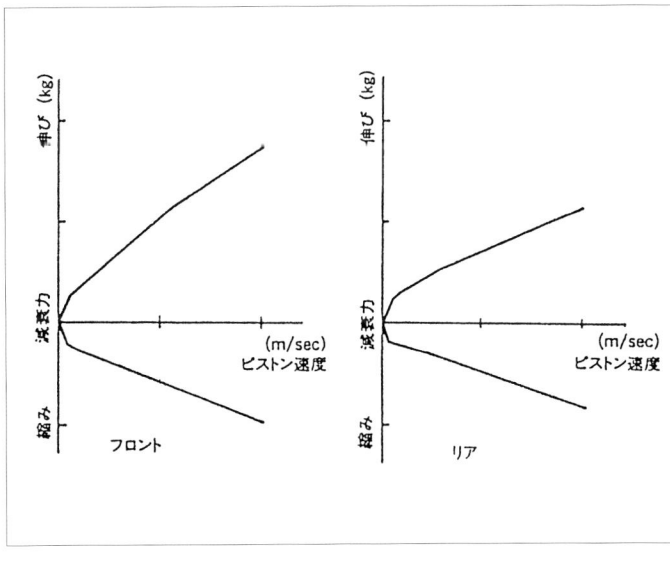

Fig.17: Damping characteristics.

camber angles. Fig.10 and 11 (front tyre) and Fig.12 and 13 (rear tyre) show the results of such an evaluation. From the graph, it is evident that there is an optimum point. Fig.10 and 11 illustrate that '1' shows smaller camber angle change in a corner and results in higher shoulder tread temperature. This means that the tyre to ground contact is uneven and inefficient. '2' shows smaller temperature variation over the tread and road contact is good. With respect to rear tyres shown in Fig.12 and 13, '1' has a peak temperature in the tread center, and this may have resulted from too much camber change. In contrast, '2' shows better road contact with less camber angle change. In the MX-5/Miata's development, we utilized both computer simulation and actual test evaluation, as illustrated above, to arrive at the optimum suspension geometry for the roadster.

Toe control system
In the development of the MX-5/Miata, in order to achieve the typical taut feel of a true sports car, we paid great attention to the rigidity of the body, subframe, suspension arms and hub carriers. These design considerations

resulted in quick and responsive handling for the roadster.

The rigidity of the suspension system components also helped to achieve a desirable level of compliance steer (toe angle changes according to a side force applied to the suspension). The MX-5/Miata's simple toe control mechanism is an extension of the suspension design philosophy of several Mazda cars, including the 323, the 626 with its TTL rear suspension system, the RX-7 with its toe control multi-link rear suspension system, and the 929 with its E-type multi-link rear suspension. As shown in Fig.14, a different hardness of rubber bushing for the front and rear of the lower wishbone arm/hub carrier on the rear suspension effectively gives a steering effect to the suspension system when a side force is applied. This effect is caused by the fact that softer front rubber bushing near the hub carrier crushes easier than the harder rubber rear bushing, thus making the hub carrier deflect slightly to give the desired toe-in effect. (See Fig.15.)

The MX-5/Miata was designed with a low yaw moment of inertia

and other specific qualities to give it quicker turn-in ability, while this toe-in effect induced compliance understeer to achieve the best possible balance. As a result, the car had excellent stability in cornering and high-speed lane changes.

Damper tuning

In order to achieve a balance between driving stability and ride comfort at a high level, damper tuning was carried out with a focus on the difference in piston speed ranges. Fig.16 shows the distribution of damper piston speed as tested at Mazda's proving ground during driving stability tests and ride comfort evaluation. As shown in the illustration, a low piston speed range is the key for driving stability and a high piston speed range is critical for ride comfort.

For the MX-5/Miata, therefore, strong damping force was applied for low piston speeds, setting the quality standards there, and set low for faster piston speed to eliminate harshness against reactions to road surface. Such damper force settings resulted in a good compromise between stability

and comfort. Fig.17 shows damping force characteristics for the front and rear dampers.

The foregoing descriptions detail the four major items we gave special consideration to in the design of the roadster's 'chassis.' As a result, the following four specific characteristics were achieved:

Direct and linear steering response.
Quick response to sudden input.
Absolute straight line stability at high speed.
Controllability near the limit via the steering wheel or throttle.

We are confident that we were able to give the MX-5/Miata unique and unprecedented handling characteristics, and successfully realized the key engineering catchphrase used during the development of the roadster – "unity between horse and rider."

Powerplant frame (PPF) development

This section describes the design considerations including structure, performance and technical ideas that led to the adoption of a PPF for the first time in a Japanese automobile. The PPF rigidly connects the transmission (gearbox) case to the differential gear casing, via a rigid framework.

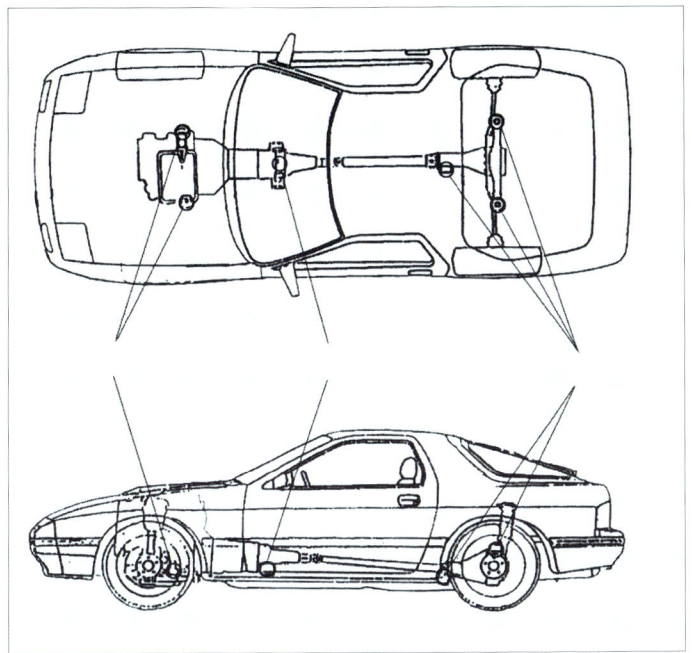

Fig.19: Traditional FR layout, as illustrated by the Mazda RX-7.

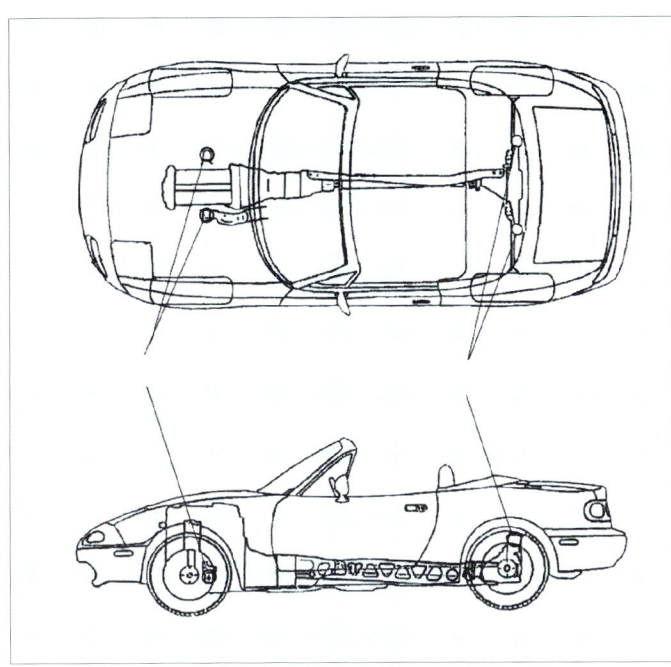

Fig.20: The MX-5/Miata's FR layout, using a PPF.

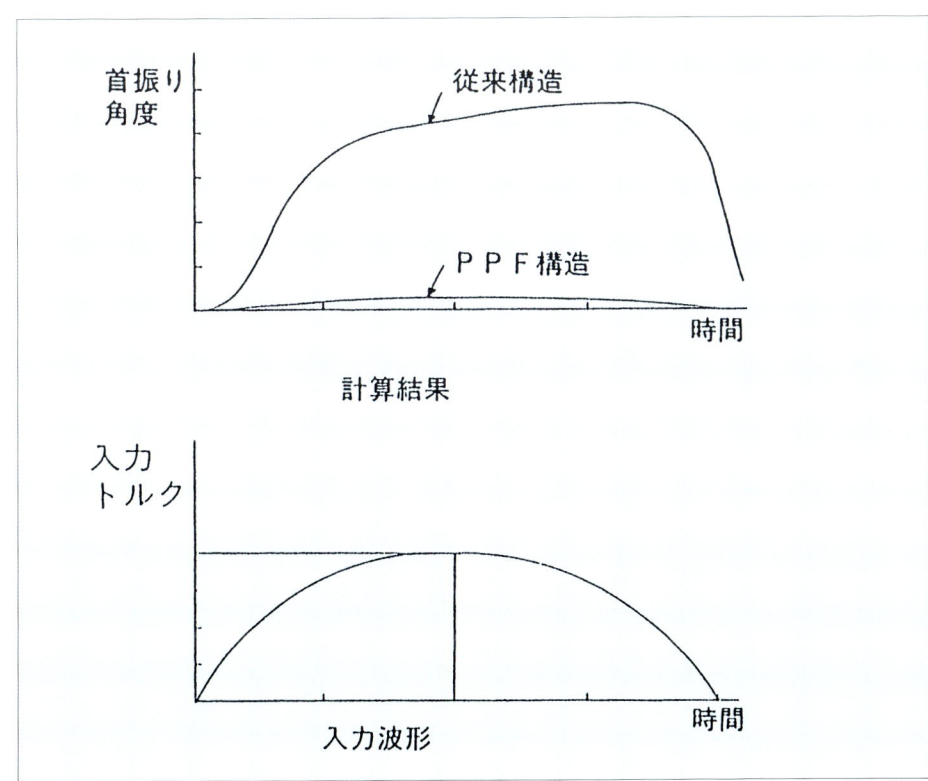

Fig.21: Differential casing deflection under acceleration, with and without the PPF installed.

By unifying the powerplant system of the car, the PPF plays an important role in providing the sense of unity we were targeting.

In sports car development, the most important point is to decide on its basic performance in running, turning, and stopping. These basic, fundamental elements are derived from its basic specifications and layout. I have already mentioned that we thoroughly examined the basic specifications and layout of the roadster from the very beginning. Our efforts are shown in the product, with its low weight (940kg/2068lb) for an open bodied roadster, low yaw moment of inertia, and ideal 50:50 front/rear weight distribution.

Adoption of the PPF was to further enhance the basic performance of the car. The PPF stops the relative movement (wind up) of individual components as torque is transmitted through the powertrain from transmission to differential, and gives direct

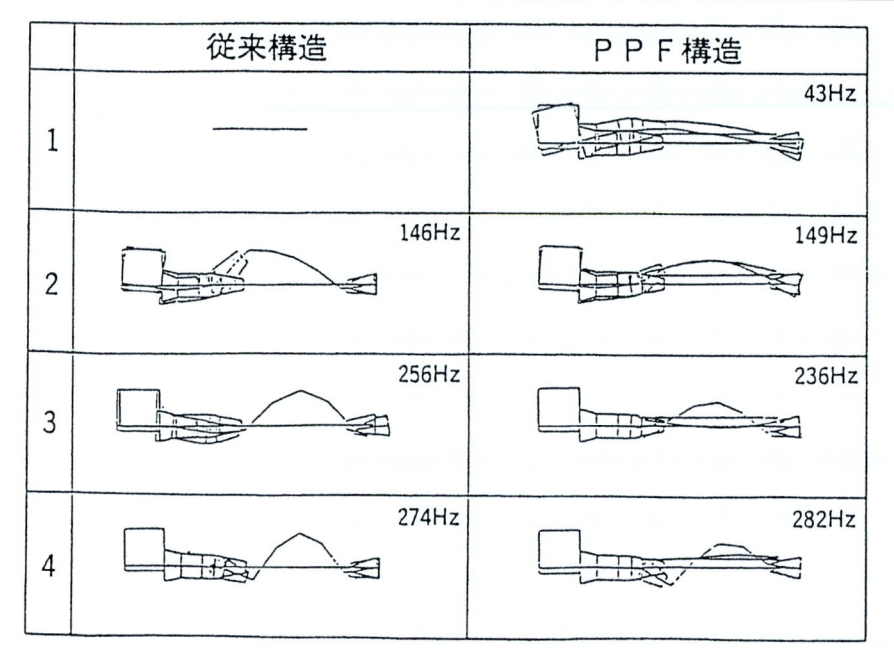

従来構造	PPF構造
1	43Hz
2 146Hz	149Hz
3 256Hz	236Hz
4 274Hz	282Hz

Fig.22: Drivetrain oscillation.

throttle response for the driver. This was an indispensable part of the package in realizing "unity" and a responsive feeling for the roadster. Fig.18 shows the powerplant of the MX-5/Miata mounted on the front and rear suspension crossmembers and joined by the PPF. The PPF is located to the right side of the propshaft, and bolted to the transmission and differential gear casings.

Aim of the PPF

Fig.19 shows a contemporary RX-7 without a PPF, and Fig.20 shows the MX-5/Miata with its PPF. The difference between the conventional arrangement of the RX-7 and MX-5/Miata is as follows:

No transmission mounts in the MX-5/Miata.
Only two differential mountings in the MX-5/Miata, instead of three.
Powerplant and drivetrain are tied by a PPF in the MX-5/Miata.

Whereas the RX-7 powerplant was mounted to the front and rear

crossmembers with a total of seven rubber mounts, the MX-5/Miata had a much simpler mounting system. This enabled us to:

Reduce the time lag between throttle application and acceleration, thus providing a sense of directness.
Keep the angle of propshaft universal joints constant, and thus eliminate coupling vibration.
Reduce gearlever vibration and improve the directness of the gearshift.

PPF structure

When a car accelerates, a reaction force from wheel torque tries to turn the differential case in the opposite direction to the wheel, raising the front of the casing. Only after all possible movement is taken up is the traction fully transmitted to the ground: this movement causes a small time lag between application of the throttle and the start of acceleration. Likewise, when using engine braking, the same thing happens in the opposite direction, giving a

similar time lag. In a car with a conventional structure and no PPF, the fore and aft mounting span of the differential case is very short, whereas, in a car using a PPF, the effective mounting span becomes very long, almost as long as the wheelbase.

In comparison with a conventional structure, the effective differential gear mounting span increases by six times, or roughly equal to 38 times the spring constant. Fig.21 shows differential case rotation during acceleration for a conventional structure and for one with the PPF.

PPF development

The PPF was new to Mazda, and there were no preceding designs which could be followed. The following describes the problems we encountered in the development process and our various countermeasures:

Vibration and noise: by joining the powerplant to the differential, there may be a new vibration mode.
Joint structure design: necessity to design strong joint structures to cope with the force from sudden acceleration.
Weight consideration: since the PPF structure is long, weight will be a problem.
Assembly sequence: no experience of installing such a long object on the assembly line.

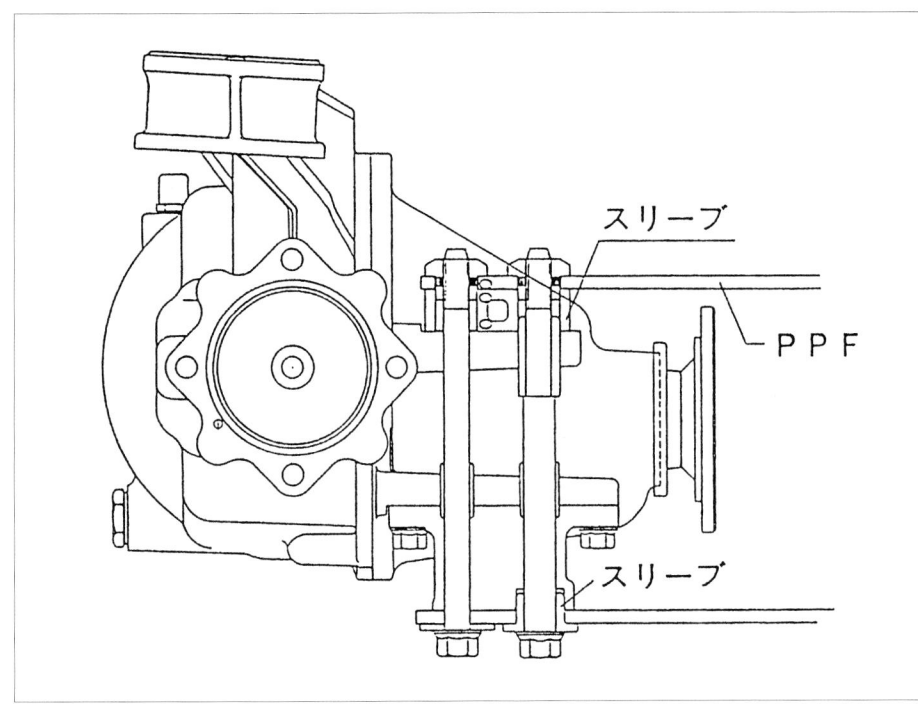

Fig.23: Drawing of the differential casing, showing the attachment points for the PPF.

スリーブ

P P F

スリーブ

In response to the above, we concluded that a rigidly connected powertrain would have different vibrations to those of a conventional structure. Normally in a powerplant system, there is a vibration called powerplant bending, which is the primary resonance node of the system. Fig.22 compares the vibration node of a PPF-equipped car and that of a conventional vehicle. As shown in the illustration, a PPF-equipped car has additional resonance nodes, one of which is a two nodal bending resonance that occurs at 43Hz, which is within the normal operational range of the engine. As a countermeasure, the mounting location for the engine and differential gear case were chosen to coincide with the vibration node where vibration is near zero. Such mounting positions would reduce vibration transmission to the body to a minimum.

Regarding the joint structure, the PPF has an open box cross-section, and its top and bottom surfaces have bolt holes for attachment to the differential gear case via long bolts. In the event of hard acceleration, the mating surfaces receive a sliding force in the shear direction of the mounting bolts. Any movement in this part would reduce the effectiveness of the PPF. So, in order to avoid any slippage, both the upper and lower front bolt holes were sleeved to eliminate slippage, while the rear bolt holes were made oblong to allow for assembly tolerance. Fig.23 shows a cross-section of the connection.

Even though the effect of the PPF is beneficial for an LWS, it must be light in weight. We chose aluminium A6061 for the PPF, with numerous lightening holes and heat treatment (T6) to secure sufficient strength. The resulting weight of the PPF came out to be 4.3kg (9.5lb) net and 4.9kg (10.8lb) with bolts and nuts. A steel PPF would have weighed 9kg (19.8lb), at least. Despite the additional weight of the PPF, we were able to avoid any weight increase compared with conventional structures through the reduction of mounting rubber, elimination of a transmission member, and a differential case front bracket.

As for the assembly sequence, Mazda's assembly line is designed to install the front suspension and engine, and rear suspension and differential case from under the body. Originally, we were planning to assemble the PPF before mounting the suspension to the body, because there was concern that later assembly of the PPF would make it difficult to locate the mounting holes. However, we found out that such a sequence would necessitate a complete change in the assembly line, and make it impossible to mix the roadster with other models. It was necessary, then, to assemble the PPF after the suspension assembly was attached to the body, and to facilitate this operation, special jigs to locate the transmission at the exact location both vertically and horizontally were developed along with other changes to make assembly easier. Thus, it became

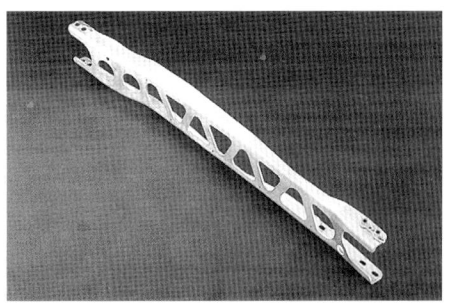

possible to produce the MX-5/Miata on the same line as other models.

We were ultimately able to achieve quick and controllable handling, a responsive throttle feel, a precise and crisp gearshift, and a number of other factors in the roadster to an extent that both we – and the consumers – were satisfied with. This success was made possible through the untiring efforts of the project members, although the PPF is only one of the new technologies we deployed in order to achieve the complete product concept.

Untold stories about chassis development

Double-wishbone suspension

One day during the development of the MX-5/Miata, Hirai called me and said: "Senior management is asking why the double-wishbone suspension cannot be replaced by a strut-type suspension. We need to explain why."

The management thought that the strut-type suspension would be lighter and cheaper than the one we had selected, and, to make the roadster affordable, the former should be chosen. Hirai, of course, knew the answer, but he wanted us to explain with passion why we chose that system. We kept ignoring the request for we believed that we would be defeated if we were to explain the merits and demerits of each suspension

system to the management using data and figures. Hirai was desperate and he was begging us, but we still declined to answer the question.

Finally, Hirai gave up, and explained by himself. We felt very sorry for him, and remember this incident very clearly to this day because of our stubborn and unhelpful attitude. Hirai, however, later said he did not remember the incident because he had too many other concerns at that time. Anyway, when we heard that the double-wishbone system was finally approved, we were more determined than ever to design a suspension that was comparable in cost and weight to the strut-type system.

PPF structure

Immediate response is one of the most important elements of a sports car. As with the handling performance of the chassis, traction response is very important. In particular, handling and traction response during cornering are the most important elements in enhancing the fun of driving.

The reason we chose an FR layout was to control the car, the front wheels via the steering wheel, and the rear wheels through traction. However, the distance between the engine and rear axle is long in an FR arrangement, and an FF layout normally has the edge on response time to the

driver's throttle control. The PPF was invented to cure this problem by rigidly connecting the transmission and differential gear case, thus providing more direct response to the throttle.

The request for a PPF was made by those of us who were responsible for designing the chassis, yet the PPF belonged in the domain of the powertrain system, and, as such, it should have been developed by the people in that section. However, they declined, saying they were not confident, and Hirai could not convince them to change their minds. Furthermore, they claimed that the proposed PPF system had a critical problem of resonance vibration at 1300rpm according to their analysis, and therefore suggested we abandon the system.

After several months, Ito, our Manager, said the PPF could be developed by us in the Chassis Design Department. Our immediate response was positive, but we saw problems ahead. It was like preparing a new dish in the kitchen of a stranger, although structural analysis was our specialty. Due to the lack of resources, we made a prototype using an old RX-7 with a PPF. The makeshift prototype had shown good driving response and with more people experiencing the driving, a stronger consensus was formed in favour of the system giving us a great sense of relief. At this time the MX-5/Miata still had no engine assigned and the prototype had a rotary engine, which had quite different vibration characteristics to a reciprocating engine.

Another problem arose on the production line. We found that the factory where production was planned, the Ujina Plant, had no space available for the assembly of the PPF except, concurrently, on the propshaft assembly line. Since the transmission mount was eliminated, both the propeller shaft and PPF had to be assembled simultaneously, almost requiring God-like hands. In order to facilitate ease of assembly, our designers invented a special jig, but we have never worked so hard with the production line people to solve such a problem. When we finally found a solution and they agreed to perform the work, we were so happy and grateful. We realized once again that when we are doing what we really want to do, a special energy somehow becomes available to make things happen.

Engineers from the UK

With limited manpower available for the LWS project, it was only a matter of time before we would be short of people. When we were beginning the detailed layout design, the manpower shortage became critical, and we had to recruit engineers from abroad to help us. We asked for two engineers, and these joined us from the UK. They were experienced in pressing and manufacturing, but it must have been very difficult and stressful for them to work in Japan, for we spoke little English.

There was one memorable incident in dealing with these engineers. Among Japanese engineers, we often turn over a job before it is completely finished expecting to have to do some changes later. This often happens when we are trying to share a concept or when timing is critical. It happened when we released the suspension geometry to begin the design of a suspension crossmember. When the outline of the crossmember was nearly complete, we had to make a change in its attachment points. When we asked for a change in our broken English, they reluctantly accepted it. A few days later, another change had to be made to the same area. Their reaction was one of outrage, and they went back to their hotel immediately. These kind of changes often happened in Mazda, so no-one was ridiculing the engineers or causing problems deliberately, but they did not understand. We were very confused as to what to do, but after a few days, they came back to work and continued to meet our requests.

Despite these incidents, which were thankfully rare, we enjoyed working and drinking with the British engineers. We have a saying: "Good friends eat from the same kettle," and we often went for a drink in Hiroshima after work. By the time they left, we quite missed them. They also showed us a difference in design culture, as their design method for a pressed component was completely different to ours. At Mazda, when we design a pressed steel component bent to 90 degrees, for instance, our design drawing is drawn with 90 degrees, but theirs show more than 90 degrees, taking in consideration of the buckling of the steel plate. While we know that there will be some buckling to the steel plate, we do not show it on the drawing. This sort of steel plate deformation is regarded as manufacturing know-how at Mazda. Since they were experts in manufacturing technology, it was natural for them to express their knowledge in their drawings, but we asked them to follow Mazda practice and revise their drawings. Similarly, they always accounted for some steel thinning after press operation in their drawing, which we did not in ours. It was, after all, a very good experience for us to learn their ways.

In closing, I would like to thank Fumitaka Ando, a member of the MX-5/Miata project, for recovering reams of old material for my text.

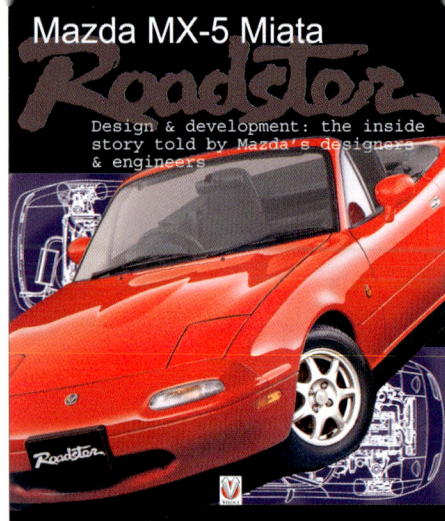

8

Powertrain development
by **Sadao Isomura**

Isomura was in charge of MX-5/Miata engine development, which started with a statement from the Division Manager: "Do only enough work to convert the transverse-mounted 323 engine for longitudinal layout, no more." But the group worked with a passion under Ohira, then Department Manager. Isomura and his team worked away, disregarding weekends to do the prohibited extra work without spending money, armed only with ideas and sweat. The day of the design drawing release finally came, revealing the result of all their hard work.

T. Hirai

The powertrain installed in the MX-5/Miata is based on the B6 type DOHC engine of the Mazda 323 model, and was renamed B6ZE (RS). This 1600cc DOHC (double overhead camshaft) unit was mated with a short stroke five-speed gearbox that was based on the M-type transmission for the 929 model. The following describes the focus of development, major features, major specifications, an outline of the new technology which was introduced, and the background to the development. The photo opposite shows the outline of the B6ZE (RS) type 1600cc DOHC engine and its five-speed manual transmission.

Focus of development

There were two targets we wanted to achieve in the development of this powertrain. The first objective was to provide a stimulating response for the driver, for that was the key target in the development of the roadster. The areas in which the powertrain could contribute in creating a stimulating feel were: quick response and free-revving performance with high torque, a crisp exhaust note typical of a LWS, a quick gearchange that gives the feeling of unity, light weight and compactness.

The second target was to create a functional beauty for this powerplant, with all the latest technology but in step with the traditional LWS concept. We aimed to design the engine and its compartment in such a way that its owner would wish to polish the power-unit and the engine bay.

Major features of the engine development

Table 1 shows engine specifications and Table 2 shows those of the transmission. Graph 1 shows the performance characteristics of the engine. Maximum bhp is 120PS at 6500rpm, while peak torque is 14.0kgm at 5500rpm. The torque curve is linear from 1500rpm to 5500rpm without stress, and the engine produces 90% of its maximum torque between 4000rpm to 6700rpm.

The MX-5/Miata powertrain, designed to give excellent driving characteristics and an air of functional beauty.

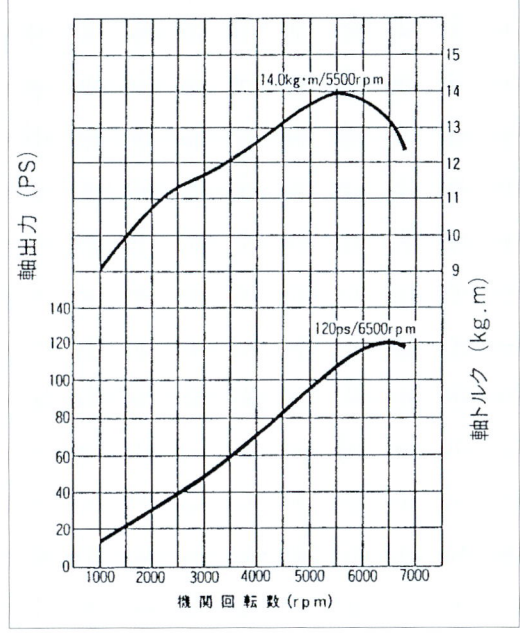

Graph 1: The engine's linear power and torque curves.

Table 1: The heart of the car was the B6-ZE (RS) type 1600cc dohc engine. These are the main specifications.

Engine	B6-ZE (RS)
Cylinders	Four, in-line
Bore & Stroke	78.0 X 83.6 mm
Capacity	1597cc
Fuel System	EFI
Valve System	Dohc 16v
Combustion Chamber	Pentroof type
Compression ratio	9.4
Max power	120PS/6500rpm
Max Torque	14.0kgm/ 5500rpm
Dimensions	620 X 580 X 615
Valve Timing:	
Intake	Open 5° BTDC Close 51° ABDC
Exhaust	Open 53° BBDC Close 15° ATDC

Transmission	Type M
Type	Five-speed manual
1st	3.136
2nd	1.888
3rd	1.330
4th	1.000
5th	0.814
Reverse	3.758
Final-drive	4.300
Clutch	Single dry plate

Table 2: The transmission ratios of the five-speed manual gearbox.

Engine for achieving "unity between man and horse"

The group in charge of the powerplant for the MX-5/Miata was a small one with only 30 engineers in total. The section manager and his deputy were primarily responsible for powertrain development on small cars such as the 323 and the 121. At that time, there were five variations of the 323 engine for the domestic market, in addition to a racing engine with a turbocharger and intercooler for World Rally Championship application. There was also a project for a 1300cc DOHC engine for the 121 undergoing concurrent development with the aforesaid manpower. On top of all that came the roadster project, and there was no way to set up a special group just for it.

Expecting a great deal of work, I assigned a development team led by Tsunetoshi Yokokura to work on the LWS engine alongside the other projects. The management had clearly stated at the beginning that the only work to be done was in converting the engine from transverse to longitudinal application. We were given no funds, and no resources for any work beyond this.

Despite such a negative environment, the spirits of the team members were very high. They were ready to give up their weekends if necessary, charged up by the desire to create a powerplant that would meet with their own approval. This sort of passion was not easily accepted within the company at first. We had to approach this problem with a calculated strategy. Our strategy was to accomplish our target, without formal approval; then, armed with accumulated facts and deeds, to force our message through.

The engineers were beginning to get excited and proposed numerous ideas to achieve the aforementioned objectives. A new camshaft cover design to give the impression of an LWS of yore, and a lightweight stainless steel exhaust manifold were examples. These special engine components for the MX-5/Miata were produced in secrecy with the agreement of the PPM and designers, and we brought them out one by one for approval when the management was in a good mood. The management gradually accepted our passion and approved these

extras in time. This sort of strategy would be difficult to carry out today, but we did it, and were successful in getting the engine we wanted.

Engine displacement
With respect to the displacement of 1600cc, there were comments among the R&D management that it was too small for a body that weighed nearly one ton and still be able to call the vehicle a sports car. There were outsider comments recommending the addition of a turbocharger, but our team had a firm belief that an engine with natural aspiration and linear output, which is more in tune with human feelings, should be used in the LWS. There was, of course, a thought in our mind that an 1800cc engine might be a better choice, but we were fully aware of the restrictions we had from the beginning, and the PPM had accepted these. As such, he was determined to develop a car that best matched the given 1600cc unit. There was no doubt that with an 1800cc engine, its performance would improve, but there were no successful precedence to this type of car and no-one was really sure of the sales potential. Because of limited resources, it was unthinkable to have an option in engine size. The PPM's determination united our thoughts, and we focused on the 1600cc unit from the 323.

Main technologies in intake and exhaust
Once the direction was set, we were very quick to attack the basic engine, modify it to provide "optimum fun and driving feel," and endow it with desirable torque characteristics and a free-revving nature.

Cylinder head
The cylinder head for the MX-5/Miata engine is based on the 323's head with a modification to reverse coolant flow direction in order to match its longitudinal engine location. Leading specifications of the engine are: DOHC with 16 valves 50 degrees apart, a pentroof-type combustion chamber with a central sparkplug, and a 9.4:1 compression ratio. The intake port was of oval cross-section equivalent to 34mm (1.34in.) diameter, with a trumpet throat of 1.3 times this cross-section ratio for smoother airflow into the cylinders. Exhaust throat area is 75% of intake throat with an equal diameter to the intake port for expansion of the exhaust gas and its smooth exit.

Improvement of rpm limit
The original 323 engine had its red zone (fuel cut-off zone) at 7000rpm, but for the MX-5/Miata, the zone was raised to 7200rpm via the following changes: the intake valve mechanism, which deals with higher levels of inertia, employed springs with a lemon shaped cross-

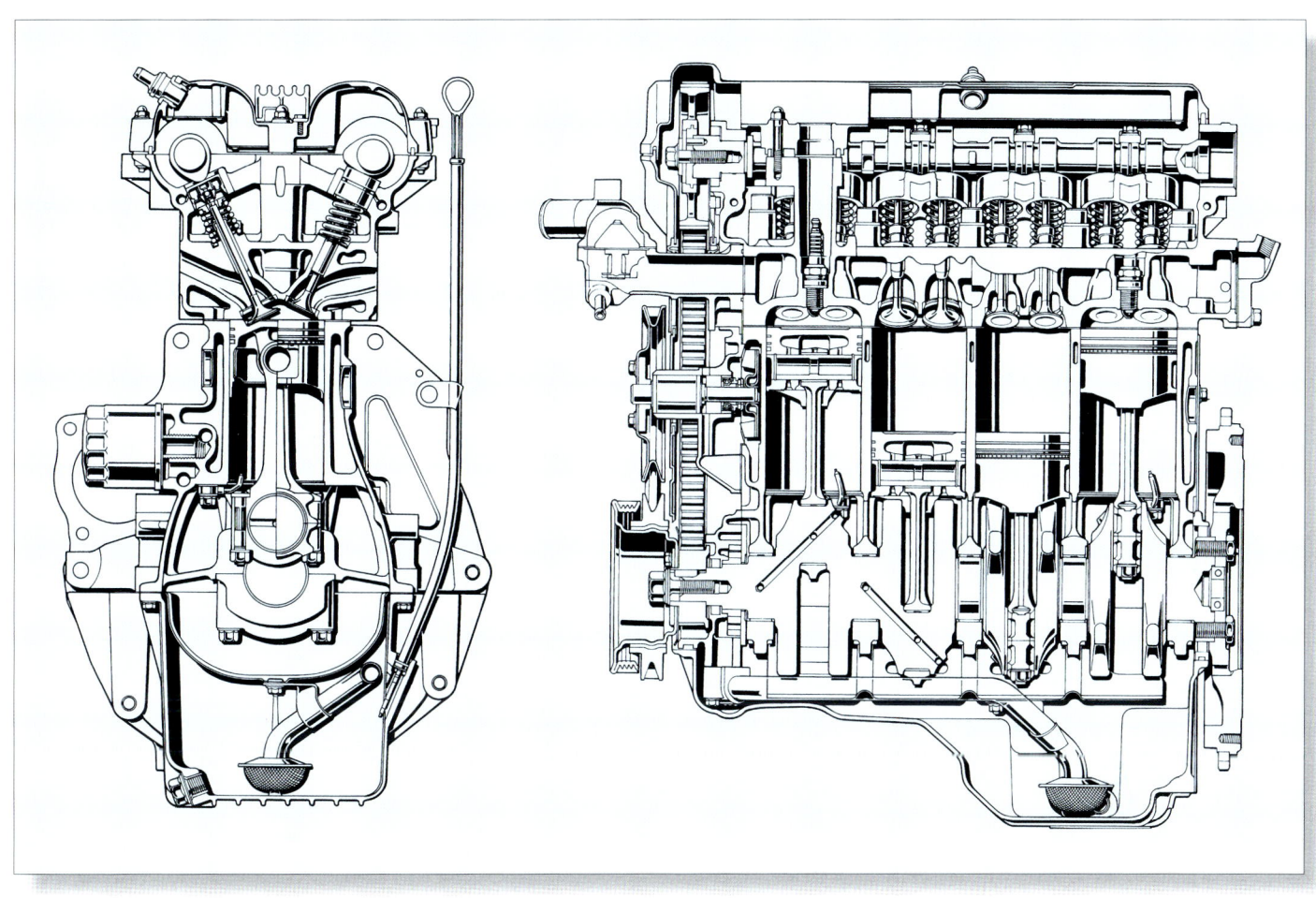

Diagram 1: Cross-section drawing of the responsive, high-revving power unit.

section for a higher spring rate within a limited space. The exhaust valve springs were of round cross-section with a matching spring rate to the intake valve springs for an equal revolution limit. A fully balanced crankshaft was adopted, with its web designed using FEM (Finite Element Analysis Method) for optimum rigidity. Connecting rods were also fully analyzed with FEM for optimum lightness. The engine oil pan (sump) was equipped with a large baffle plate to eliminate oil stirring (windage) by the connecting rods and crankshaft because this causes oil loss and reduces power at high speed. The top piston rings were of the internal bevel type to avoid fluttering and the associated blow-by and

breakage. Diagram 1 shows the engine cross-section.

Intake system and valve timing

In designing the intake system, including the selection of valve timing, computer simulation was fully utilized. A circular cross-section intake surge tank design was chosen for smooth torque characteristics, and the intake manifold was integrated for smooth power delivery at high rpm. Intake ports were tapered and the valve timing was set with an overlap of 20 degrees to allow smooth acceleration. The combination of these characteristics gave the engine stable idling and smooth, stress free torque characteristics, too.

Masa Harada, the engineer in charge of engine intake design, utilized a supercomputer for intake port simulation and arrived at an optimum design for the intake port taper. It was 40mm (1.57in.) diameter at the surge tank side and 34mm (1.34in.) at the cylinder head side, 285mm (11.2in.) long and with a surge tank volume of 1.23 litres. During the simulation, the supercomputer broke down and he received complaints from the data system people about the volume of work he was processing. To avoid this trouble, he resorted to running his calculations at night and collecting the results in the morning. With today's much-advanced supercomputers, this kind of effort is unthinkable.

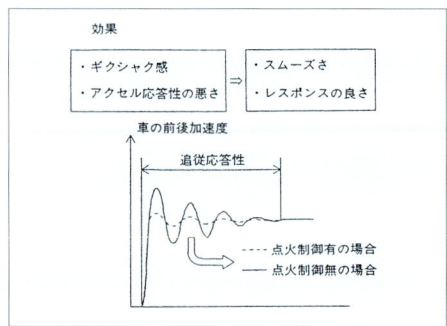

Graph 2: A graph showing body vibration caused by sudden torque input. The new ignition system endowed the car with smooth acceleration.

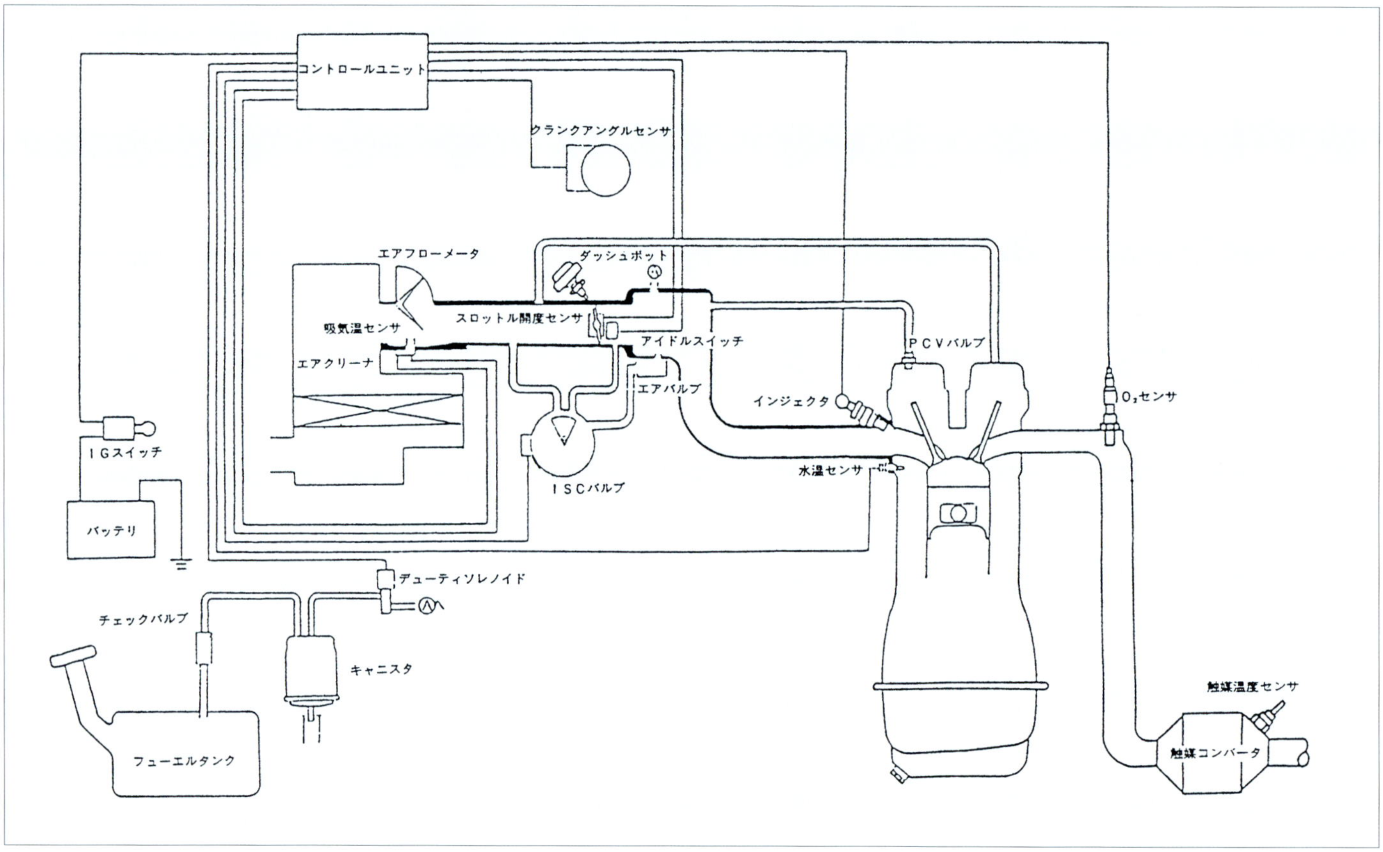

Diagram 2: The fuel and exhaust control system.

Control system

An electronic gas (fuel) injection system (EGI or EFI) was employed with an airflow meter to control the injection rate. The electronic control system employed a one chip 8-bit microcomputer with learning capability for precise air to fuel ratio control.

The ignition system was a computer controlled distributor-less system with two ignition coils installed behind the cylinder head. In addition, a new ignition timing control system was employed. This enabled the control of ignition timing to vary with engine speed changes for smooth acceleration and a vibration-free ride. Graph 2 shows the effect of the system and Dia.2 shows its control system.

The original standard 1600cc 323 engine had good low rpm torque for this displacement class, and 115PS maximum output. This performance was not sufficient for use in an LWS, however, and the improvements already described were added to achieve higher torque at higher rpm, with up to 120PS maximum bhp. We had succeeded in developing the heart

116

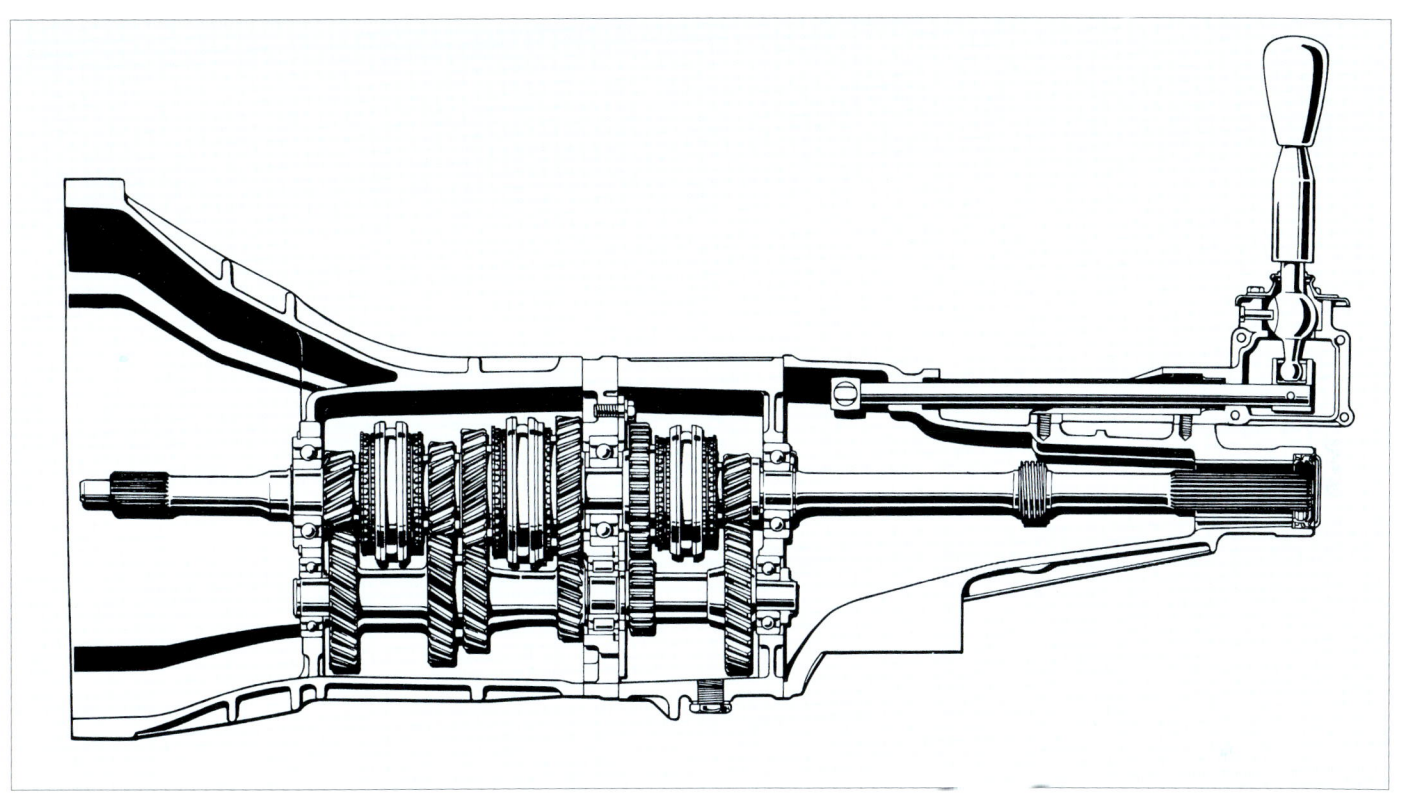

Cross-section of the five-speed manual gearbox.

of the roadster that would give it the quick and exciting performance the PPM had in mind.

Exhaust note tuning

For better exhaust efficiency, the main silencer was given an 11.6 litre capacity. However, the most important design consideration for the silencer was its exhaust note tuning! A low exhaust note is generally accepted as a sports car sound, while a rotary engine has its own characteristic high-pitched exhaust note. We wanted to give the MX-5/Miata a special exhaust note of its own. It had to pass all appropriate regulations and we could not focus on the low frequency note alone. What constitutes a pleasant exhaust note is somewhat dependent on an individual's taste, and may not appeal to everyone. This was quite a challenge, but we enjoyed a new research process!

We first took samples of exhaust notes from many cars and tried to analyze what a 'pleasant' exhaust note was. What kind of exhaust note is pleasing to the ears and how to match it to the roadster was our quest, so we did a comprehensive analysis. The test result was broken into frequency ranges, and different combinations of frequency ranges were tested. The resulting note that was pleasing to the ears and stimulating to the heart was one that had a good balance of low and high frequency notes without too much suppression but without undue noise or booming.

We then fed the data into a simulation system and established the frequency characteristics of the target exhaust note. Based on these characteristics, we designed the internal structure of the silencer with a large capacity. Although it may not be universally accepted as a pleasing exhaust note, we were able to design an exhaust system that is uniquely pleasant and compatible with all the various noise regulations of different countries.

Transmission system main technology

With the transmission for the MX-5/Miata, we wanted to provide optimum gear ratios and a direct gearchange in order to use the full potential of its engine, promoting the fun of driving and the "unity" we desired. Matsugasako, a young engineer, was assigned this task.

For optimum gearing, we designed the transmission to have close gear ratios and increased the ratio for the final-drive. Two pictures show the gearlever, to which we devoted a lot of attention to give a precise shift feeling. For that to happen, a light shift effort and rigid shift feel were sought.

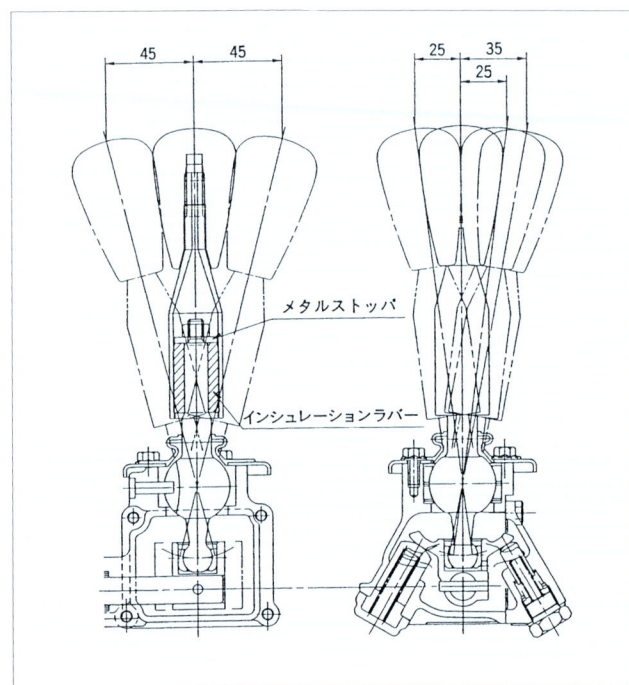

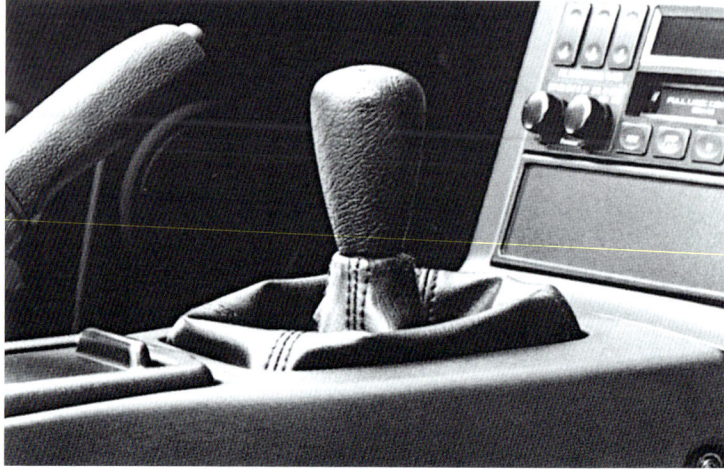

The gearknob was designed in such a way that however the driver held the lever, the shift feel would be transmitted in a pleasing manner.

Details of the gearlever, designed for short throws, and light operation combined with a precise feel.

Rigid change feel

In order to increase the taut feel of the gearchange, a direct shift mechanism was chosen. The shift rod was provided with stoppers (detents) for a precise and crisp feel, and insulation rubber was used within the shift lever body to reduce vibration and noise. The transmission's gearlever exit position was extended rearward to be near the driver's hand to provide a direct shift feel along with a short, straight shift lever.

Light shift effort

In order to reduce the shifting effort necessary to change gears, a low inertia clutch disc and large diameter synchronizing cones were chosen. The locking ball groove cross-section was changed for better matching of the synchronizing load and locking ball load, and a new transmission oil of 75W-90 grade with better friction coefficient in the static and dynamic state were developed to avoid a double action feeling. The shift stroke was set at 45mm (1.8in.), which was the shortest stroke found in any Japanese car. A special gearknob was designed also to transmit the driver's intent to the transmission precisely. All these fine adjustments created a transmission that snaps into gears and is great fun to shift.

Low weight and compactness

"An LWS must be light" was the policy dictated by our PPM, and we did all we could to reduce the weight of the powertrain. The oil pan was made from aluminum and unitized with the clutch housing, adding to the stiffness of the entire powertrain and reducing noise, vibration and harshness (NVH) levels. The exhaust manifold and exhaust downpipe were made in stainless steel, and the radiator in aluminium, all in the name of lightness.

A small sealed-type battery was chosen for the first time at Mazda, and it was placed in the trunk (boot) compartment for better weight distribution. The final-drive unit was also newly developed with reduced weight in mind. A differential case with wide span arms was adopted, and further strengthened by shot peening, material change and a thicker gear that would withstand the load of sports driving. As already discussed, many new ideas were incorporated into the MX-5/Miata in order to achieve compactness and light weight. The following episodes illustrate some of them.

Exhaust system

The PPM declared: "I'll take care of the cost, just make the exhaust the lightest in any Mazda!" Niihama, a second-year rookie, responded to this and made the entire exhaust piping out of stainless steel, whereas a traditional design used aluminum clad steel piping, only using stainless steel where it was hottest in the exhaust system. He also did away with a pre-silencer, which was traditional, and made the entire system 5kg (11lb) lighter to fulfill Hirai's request.

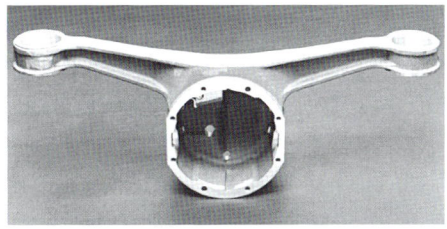

Stainless tubing was used to make the exhaust manifold. This was difficult to perfect, with cracks appearing in many of the early prototypes.

The aluminum alloy differential case with its wide-span arms.

Exhaust manifold

A traditional exhaust manifold is a piece of cast-iron, but we decided to fabricate one out of stainless steel pipe. While we were wondering how to approach the design, one of the engineers brought a Honda CB400 Four motorcycle into the design room. We were all impressed with the beautiful stainless steel exhaust manifold of the motorcycle, and made it a reference for our design. We also wanted to make all of the exhaust manifold pipes of equal length, as per the practice for racing engines, but mass production restrictions made this impossible.

Takashi Tanaka of the engine design team insisted on a semi-equal length exhaust manifold, and designed one with two of the pipes being equal in length. The fabrication of this manifold, however, was fraught with problems. The major one was cracking in the pipe gathering area, and we came close to abandoning the idea of a stainless steel manifold. But, again, the team insisted on continuing, and by changing the shape of the joint, weld rod material and the manufacturing process, we were eventually successful.

The resulting exhaust manifold was 44% lighter than a traditional cast iron design! In addition to the low weight, due to the small mass in the system, the exhaust gas temperature in the catalyst rose much faster and helped suppress the cold emissions from the exhaust system. Because of this discovery, a stainless steel pipe exhaust manifold became Mazda's trump card in cold emission control for other cars to come.

Battery

Another difficult subject was the battery. A battery is normally located in the engine compartment, but the MX-5/Miata has it in the trunk. This location was chosen partly to achieve the best weight distribution possible, and partly due to a lack of space in the engine compartment. A battery located in the trunk had to be light, as well as free from corrosive acid. Yamamoto, who was in charge, was under pressure both from his boss and the PPM, but he did his part by choosing a battery never before used in an automobile. There were some anxieties, but as time passed, other manufacturers wanted to use the same battery for their designs. The anxiety slowly flowed away and turned into a firm belief that we had done a fine job.

Designing an engine bay for a sports car

We wanted to give a functional beauty to the components in the engine compartment. The camshaft cover was newly designed to emphasize the twin camshafts, and the Mazda logo was engraved over the cast surface; its securing bolts were chrome-plated. Other accessories and wiring were also designed to express the functional beauty typical of light weight sports car.

The camshaft cover for the 323 engine, which formed the basis for the MX-5/Miata unit, was a black square box that lacked any sporty feeling. The DOHC mechanism was traditionally regarded as a symbol of high performance, and for this reason, it was chosen for the roadster. We, therefore, wanted to make the head cover look like that of a sports car, and make it symbolic under the hood (bonnet).

Sasada, a member of the engine design team led by Yoshi Tanaka, worked hard to design a

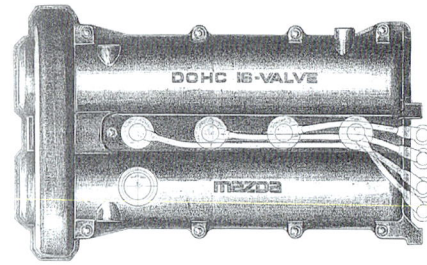

The camshaft cover design clearly alluded to the fact that two camshafts resided underneath, and is reminiscent of classic Alfa Romeo and Lotus engines.

camshaft cover with two semi-cylindrical bulges to emphasize the camshafts under the cover. He purposely left the cover unpainted so that the owner could polish it later with a polishing compound, and a 'Mazda DOHC 16 VALVE' logo was sunk into it. (This was changed a few years later and the logo stood proud of the surface of the cover, increasing production efficiency, but much to our chagrin.) As an option, the surface of the head cover was polished with cut-wire to give a surface similar to a buffed finish. Again, this approach was made with no authorization at the beginning, but we got it approved after a demonstration of how fine it was compared to the conventional paint or shot-blasted finish.

In the middle of development, a problem was found with the camshaft cover. A ventilation pipe attached to it and feeding upstream of the throttle body picked up some oil. The location of the vent had to be changed to cure the problem, but this would alter the vent hose route, and the new one proposed would spoil the beautiful sight of the head cover. To counter this problem, we had to design a formed pipe at additional cost. The new vent pipe gave the engine compartment a new definition line, and looked even better as a result.

The MX-5/Miata's unique camshaft cover, and the ventilation piping added at the last moment, dominated the view under the bonnet.

Looking back

The above summarizes the development of the powertrain system for the original MX-5/Miata. Our design target to give the car a special driving feel, rather than ultimate power output, was achieved, and it was a very memorable experience. After the roadster became a success, I had a chance to talk to the team members. Their response may be summarized with the following statement: "When we were faced with the development of the MX-5/Miata, we honestly felt extreme pressure. But developing a car that we really wanted to drive for fun and to own, which was also affordable, was a great experience, and we enjoyed it a lot."

When I was asked to contribute to this book, I had a chance to talk to Yokokura. He said: "Although the work was going to be hard, I felt it was worth doing. I wanted to

make a truly traditional roadster mine, and started saving money the day I was called in."

Sasada, who designed the camshaft cover, said: "During the development, I always went home very late and gave my family a hard time, but after the car was released for sale, I took one out on the winding roads of Namitakiji, and felt all of my previous worldly thoughts literally wash away. I felt a sense of deep satisfaction."

These comments prove how important it is to have a clear target and a condition where one's ideas have a chance to be appreciated. The MX-5/Miata has kept maturing with age, and it now has an 1800cc engine and an automatic transmission option. I sincerely hope the roadster and its powertrain will be supported by users all over the world, and long into the future.

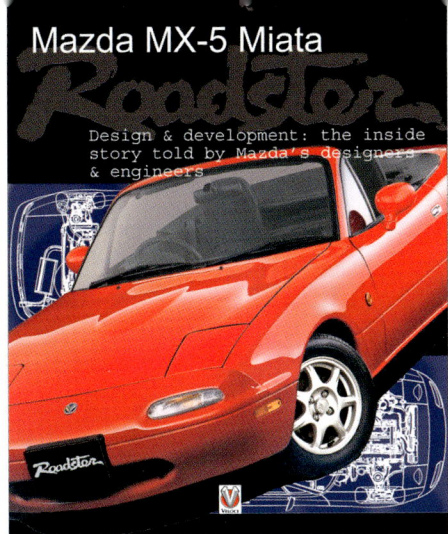

Mazda MX-5 Miata
Roadster
Design & development: the inside story told by Mazda's designers & engineers

9

Development of the body
by **Yutaka Imura**

When the project started with virtually no manpower, Imura joined the team despite his other assignments. How he was able to do this without getting into trouble with his boss remains a mystery to this day. He often went totally against my direction, but somehow got my point and made the body to my satisfaction.

T. Hirai

The roadster is an open bodied two-seater that was becoming increasingly rare in the 1980s. In order to achieve the ideal "unity between horse and rider," feel the fresh air rushing by and, generally, get closer to nature, there is no better arrangement than an open body. To develop an open body design exclusively for the MX-5/ Miata was the best approach to achieve the performance requirements for a sports car, as it eliminated the many restrictions otherwise applicable for a closed body development evolving an open body design. This section describes the fundamental requirements we established for the basic body design, and our approach to achieving these requirements through some personal recollections.

Requirements for body development
From the very beginning of development, we groped around for the specifications that are necessary to achieve the feel of "unity between horse and rider" in the roadster. Fig.1 illustrates the four major sensations that we thought would make up this "unity" – speed, directness, tautness and man-machine communication. Through the process of breaking down the target concept, we confirmed that no matter how good an engine or a suspension system is, the target of "unity" could not be achieved without a rigid, lightweight open body design.

Importance of a rigid body
The body is the foundation of an automobile, playing host to all the various components, and providing space for the driver and passenger.

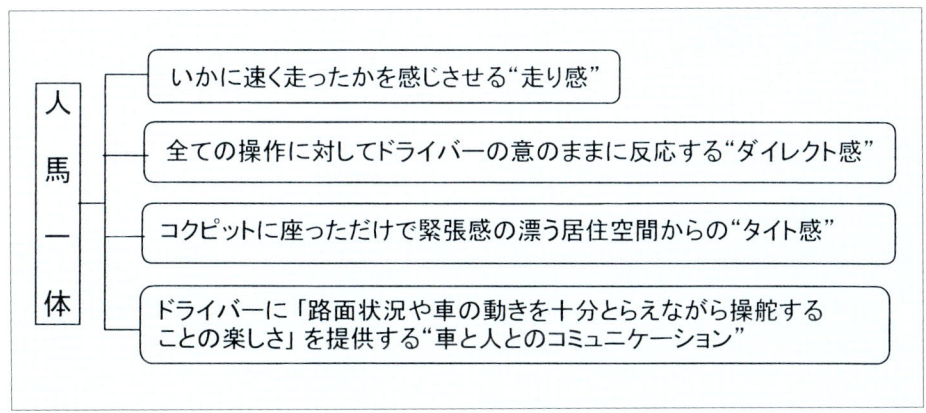

Fig.1: Chart showing the four main factors necessary in producing a car that gives a feeling of 'oneness between horse and rider.' High rigidity and light weight were regarded as the key elements.

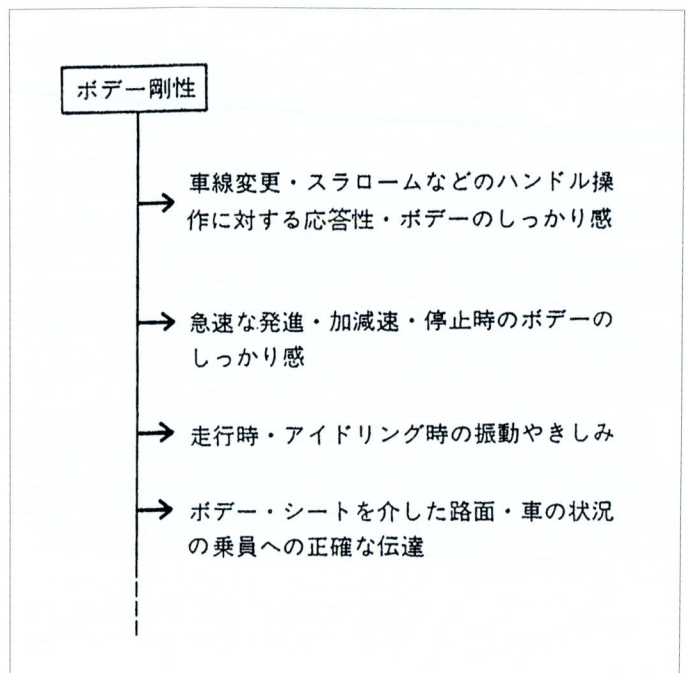

ボデー剛性

→ 車線変更・スラロームなどのハンドル操作に対する応答性・ボデーのしっかり感

→ 急速な発進・加減速・停止時のボデーのしっかり感

→ 走行時・アイドリング時の振動やきしみ

→ ボデー・シートを介した路面・車の状況の乗員への正確な伝達

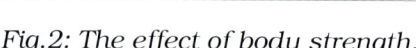

Fig.2: The effect of body strength.

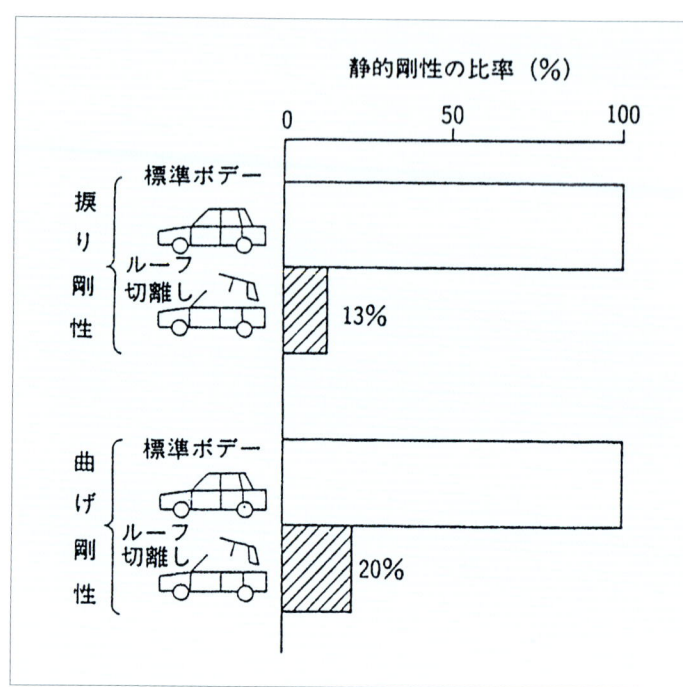

静的剛性の比率 （%）

捩り剛性 — 標準ボデー / ルーフ切離し — 13%

曲げ剛性 — 標準ボデー / ルーフ切離し — 20%

Fig.3: A chart showing how weak a structure becomes after simply cutting the roof off a sedan or coupé in order to make a convertible.

The rigidity of a body, therefore, affects the performance and driving feel of the car, as shown in Fig.2. If the roof is simply cut off a closed body, the rigidity of the remaining open body falls dramatically, in fact, to less than one-fifth of the original closed body (Fig.3). If the rigidity of the body is insufficient, the undesirable effects described in the following text can be experienced.

Suspension and steering units are designed for a highly rigid body. No matter how good their design may be, they cannot demonstrate their potential on a poorly designed body. Such units installed in a closed body may demonstrate quick handling and sharp response, but if the body's roof is cut off, it will not have enough rigidity, and the car will no longer have the original handling qualities. We had a Porsche 911 Cabriolet as a reference vehicle, and we were quite impressed with its body design, as it displayed rigidity comparable with that of a closed body.

The vibration and noise that arise from a lack of rigidity make the driver and passenger feel uneasy. This spoils the fun of driving, at the very least, and the targeted "unity" is then extremely hard to achieve. Body rigidity can be classified into many elements, such as torsional rigidity, bending rigidity, cabin rigidity, rear body rigidity, and other local areas of rigidity. Among these, the most important factor is the torsional rigidity of the entire body. As shown in Fig.3, cutting the roof off a sedan results in a drastic change in torsional and bending rigidity, and its resonance frequency in torsional motion gets down to the lower frequency range, as shown in Fig.4, affecting the people in the car, as they will feel this torsional vibration.

Importance of lightness

The weight of a car affects the 'footwork' of the car whilst running, turning and stopping. An LWS that boasts "unity between horse and rider" must be made light in weight via all means possible, but it must also display a high level of rigidity.

Significance of exclusive open body design

An open body that evolved from a closed body design requires many reinforcements in the body. Thicker steel, increased structural members, and double and triple reinforcements are commonly applied. The resulting weight of this type of evolved design, even though the roof is missing, tends to be heavier than the original by about 30%.

The rigidity of a body depends on the location of the main structural members, their cross-section shape and size, and the

122

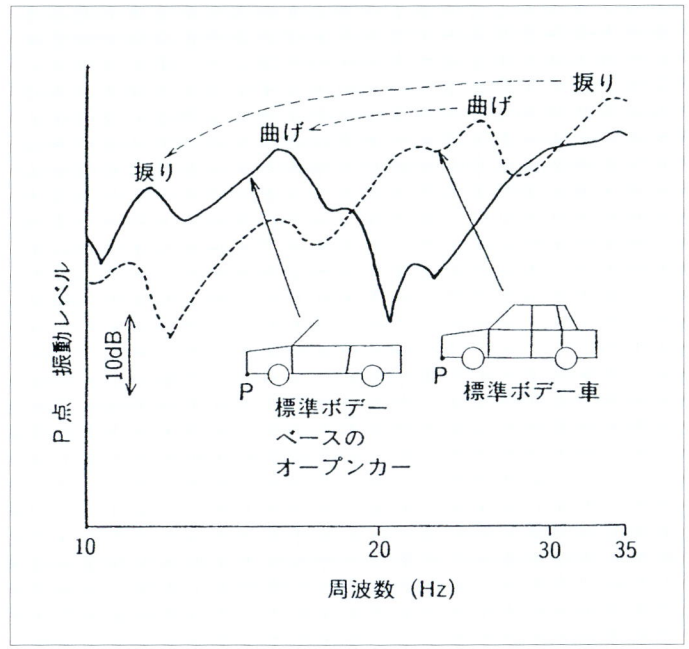

Fig.4: Vibration patterns in closed and open bodies.

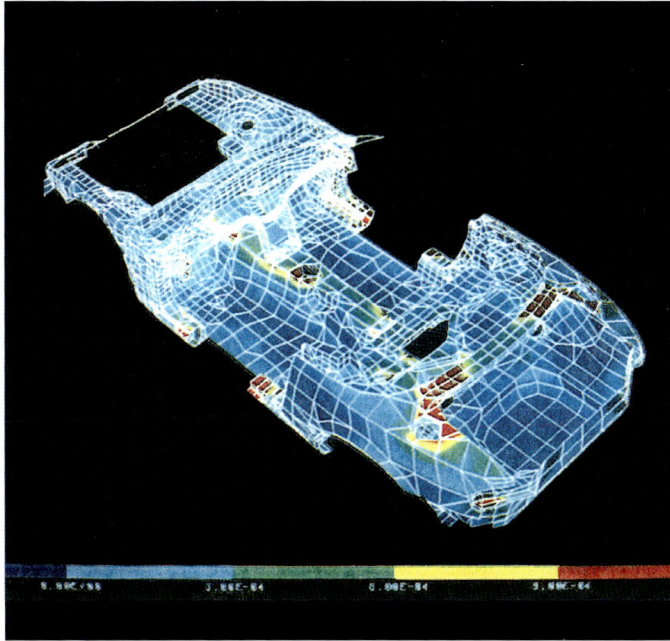

Computer simulation of the MX-5/Miata body under torsional load.

stiffness of their joints. It is, therefore, simply not logical to evolve an open body design from a closed body, because a weight increase is unavoidable if such a route is taken. In order to achieve a highly rigid and lightweight open body design, a fresh start is necessary.

Body structure features

In view of the foregoing factors, we started the design from the question: "What structure should an open body have?" rather than "How do we reinforce a weakened body." However, at the beginning, we were very short of manpower due to ongoing main product development, and we eagerly awaited the pre-prototype being developed in the UK by a consulting firm.

However, the pre-prototype design was not suitable for mass production, and we made up a design team with five young engineers. The pre-prototype test results demonstrated poor body

rigidity. Ironically, this negative environment actually raised our spirits. We were determined that we would design a modern lightweight sports car with an open body that would be acceptable in the 21st century.

There was not much comment from our Testing and Research Department prior to pre-prototype testing, but as the results of pre-prototype tests became available, they voiced many suggestions for design improvement. Accepting all of their suggestions would have added too much weight to the body, so we resorted heavily to computer analysis. Our design was analyzed repeatedly for strength, rigidity, and vibrational characteristics via the extensive use of CAE (computer aided engineering) in order to find the most effective reinforcement structure.

During the internal design review session, opinions were expressed by the head of body testing that our design still lacked

sufficient rigidity, but the PPM insisted we go on with the current design on the condition that a total redesign would be performed if the prototype did not attain target rigidity. With this provisional approval, we were able to release the design drawings. If the body design had to be completely redone, it would cause at least six months' delay in the schedules, and make a big dent in the corporate business plan. However, the PPM showed his determination to follow the design through, and we were most impressed by his vision and personal capacity.

During fabrication of the prototype, a foreman in the prototype shop told me that, from his experience, the roadster prototype felt far more rigid than any preceding open-bodied prototype. The body design had its share of concerns and troubles, but this was a great relief for us all and I quickly informed the PPM, who must have been the most concerned.

123

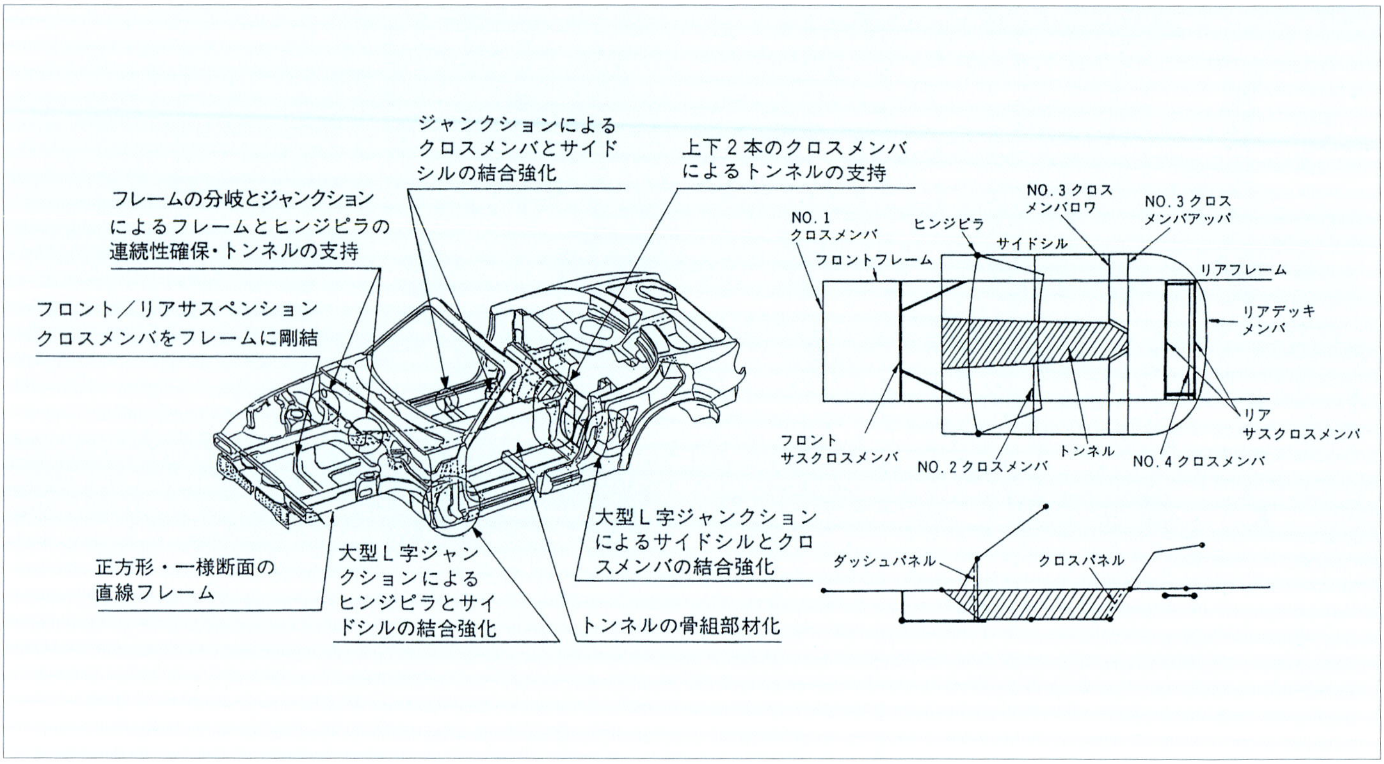

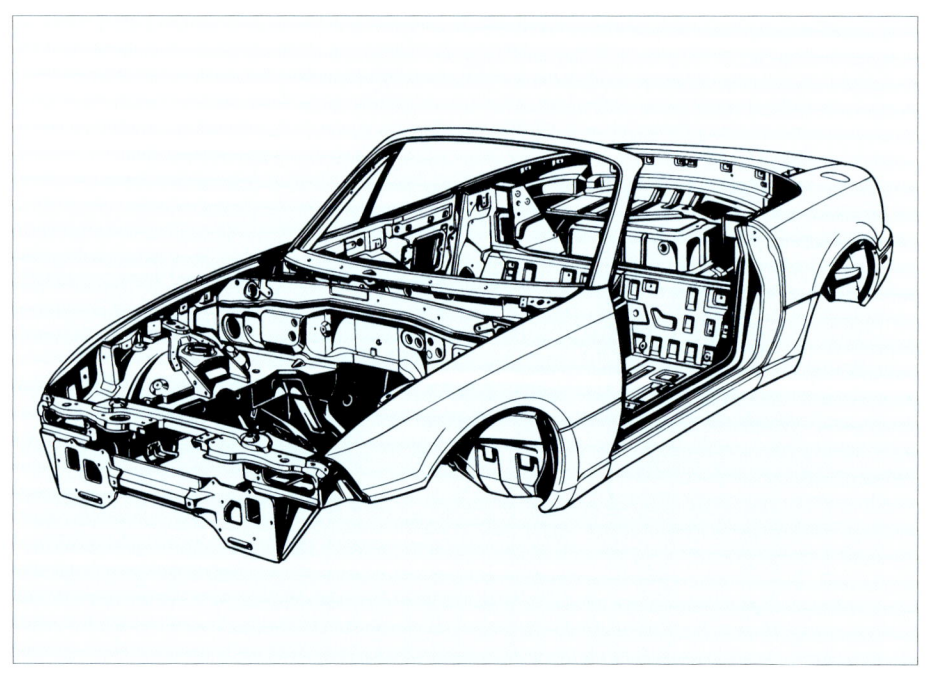

ジャンクションによる
クロスメンバとサイド
シルの結合強化

上下2本のクロスメンバ
によるトンネルの支持

フレームの分岐とジャンクション
によるフレームとヒンジピラの
連続性確保・トンネルの支持

フロント／リアサスペンション
クロスメンバをフレームに剛結

正方形・一様断面の
直線フレーム

大型L字ジャン
クションによる
ヒンジピラとサイ
ドシルの結合強化

大型L字ジャンクション
によるサイドシルとクロ
スメンバの結合強化

トンネルの骨組部材化

NO.1 クロスメンバ　ヒンジピラ　NO.3クロスメンバロワ　NO.3クロスメンバアッパ
フロントフレーム　サイドシル　リアフレーム　リアデッキメンバ
フロントサスクロスメンバ　NO.2クロスメンバ　トンネル　NO.4クロスメンバ　リアサスクロスメンバ

ダッシュパネル　クロスパネル

Fig.5: The body structure in detail. Frame components were made as straight as possible using metal of the same section to give strong joints. The shaded tunnel area played a major role in the car's rigidity, and allowed a simple, thinner floorpan.

The monocoque body structure.

Continuous lattice structure

The skeleton structure of the body is a combination of longitudinal and transverse lattice structure as shown in Fig.5, and looks like a ladder frame when seen from above. This is to distribute the deformation load to the whole structure to achieve a sufficient level of body rigidity. In order to form this continuous lattice structure, the following measures were taken:

Multiple branching skeleton: The back end of the frames in the engine compartment and the front end of the trunk (boot) frames were branched horizontally as well as downward to continue to the floor tunnel, door pillars and side sills.

Backbone frame tunnel: We adopted the concept of a backbone

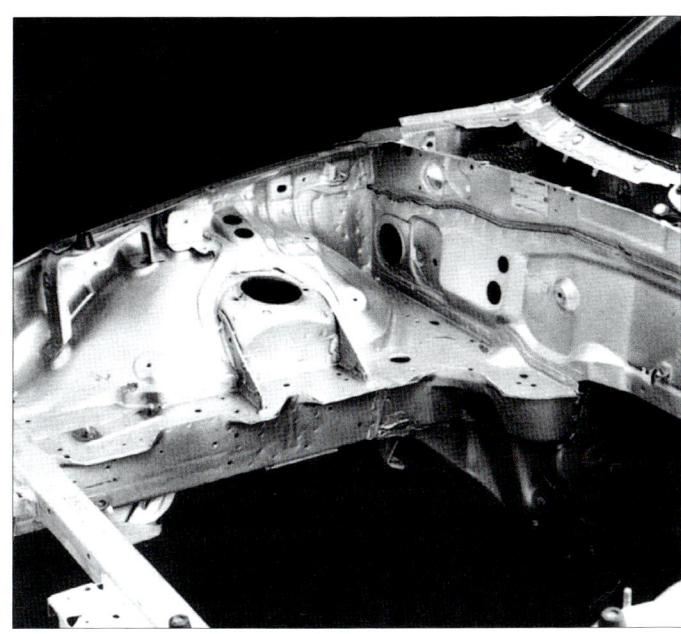

Front frame, this picture showing the inner wings and bulkhead.

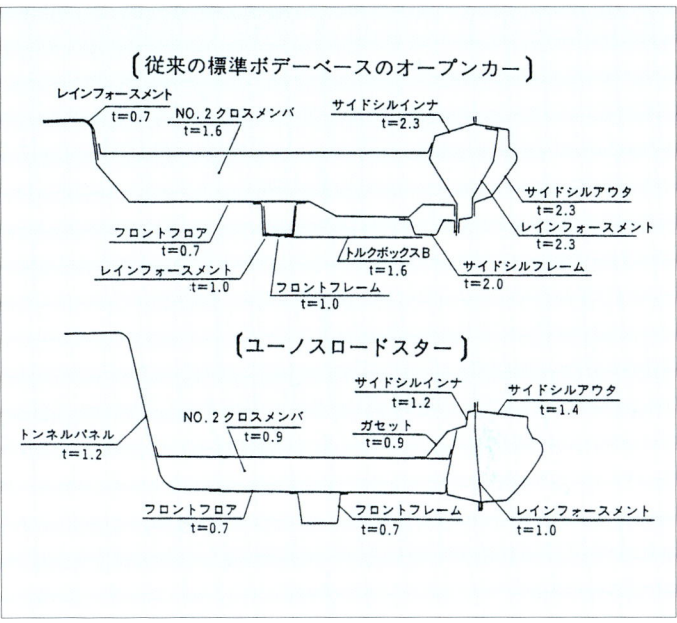

Fig.6: Cross-section of the simplified floorpan (below), compared to that of a traditional open car. Reinforcement was only necessary in the side sill, and thinner gauge metal could be used elsewhere.

frame structure, as used in a plastic-bodied car. In order for the floor tunnel to function as a backbone, the front and rear end of the tunnel was joined to the horizontal crossmembers with junction plates. With this approach, load to the side sills was lessened, and no additional thickness or reinforcements were required.

Effective use of suspension crossmembers: The crossmembers for the front and rear suspension systems require a high level of strength and rigidity. These crossmembers were rigidly joined to the body frame to function as part of the body structure. As an added bonus, rigidity of the suspension arm attachment was increased, which resulted in crisper handling for the roadster.

Efficient shaping of components

In order to achieve a rigid framework without a weight penalty, the following measures were taken in the design of frame components: All structural components were designed with uniform cross-sections and with straight lines to the greatest extent possible. This was to avoid local weak spots due to unnecessary bends and narrowing. Square cross-sectional shapes were chosen as much as possible for components that were subjected to bending and twisting forces from multiple directions. For those components that were directly related to interior space and could therefore not adopt a wide cross-section, vertical height was increased.

Efficient joints

In order to obtain strong joints, each member was designed to avoid offset to the greatest extent possible. Furthermore, for major joints, such as fore and aft of the side sills, a large junction structure was adopted with overlapping connections, while other junctions were reinforced with gussets and trumpet shaped joints. Where conventional welding was not sufficient to give the desired strength, we chose a new welding technique in order to obtain it.

Fig.6 is a comparison of floor panel cross-sections. In comparison with the cross-section from a conventional open car derived from a closed body, the MX-5/Miata had a simpler structure using thinner steel sheets.

The LWS with an open body left its mark in history in the 1960s and 1970s. While the MX-5/Miata continued the traditional layout of these sports cars, its design evolved through the utilization of advanced computers as a design tool. In our section, we utilized these computers in design, testing and analysis, with successful development ultimately being achieved through our past design experience with the 323 and RX-7 Cabriolet.

Mazda MX-5 Miata
Roadster
Design & development: the inside story told by Mazda's designers & engineers

10

Computer simulation
by **Youichi Shibuta**

The design review came to a standstill for two weeks when the testing and research group voiced strong opposition over the body design. After a thorough explanation, they still insisted that computer analysis is not always reliable. Shibuta's eyes shone with confidence upon hearing this, and both departments reluctantly agreed to continue work with the condition that all design work would be redone if the original design proved unacceptable. No redesign was necessary, and I still remember those bright eyes.

T. Hirai

An open body
An open car should be lighter than a closed car because of the lack of a roof. Many people think this way, but it is not so. Unless all sorts of design considerations are made, an open body will often come out much heavier than a closed body. In Japan, where the climate is variable with rain, snow and sunshine, and with its shorter history of automobile production than Europe or America, there were few examples of open bodied cars. In the design of the MX-5/Miata, we faced many challenges and surprises that an experienced Western automaker might have cleared without fuss.

Background
In order to appreciate the difficulty of open body development, it is necessary to go back to the mid-1980s, when Mazda was designing its first cabriolet for the 323. From the three-door hatchback design of the 323, we started to take off its roof and door pillars for the initial drophead design. The roofless body showed one-fifth of bending rigidity and one-tenth of torsional rigidity compared with the original body. This made the car almost too dangerous to be driven. Even with some reinforcements, the car showed unpleasant vibrations and terrible ride quality in the 25-38mph (40-60kph) range, the normal city driving speed in Japan. No matter what other attributes were excellent on the car, such structural weakness made it terribly unattractive. A roof is not only to protect the driver and its passenger from rain, wind and sunshine, but it is also one of the most important structural elements of a car's body.

In reality, it is not surprising that a roofless body shows a drastic reduction in rigidity. A closed body is a three-dimensional structure, but, without its roof, it is reduced to a two-dimensional structure, and its floor is the only member that resists bending and twisting forces applied to the body. In the 323 Cabriolet, many reinforcements were added to secure body rigidity. Such reinforcements must be made

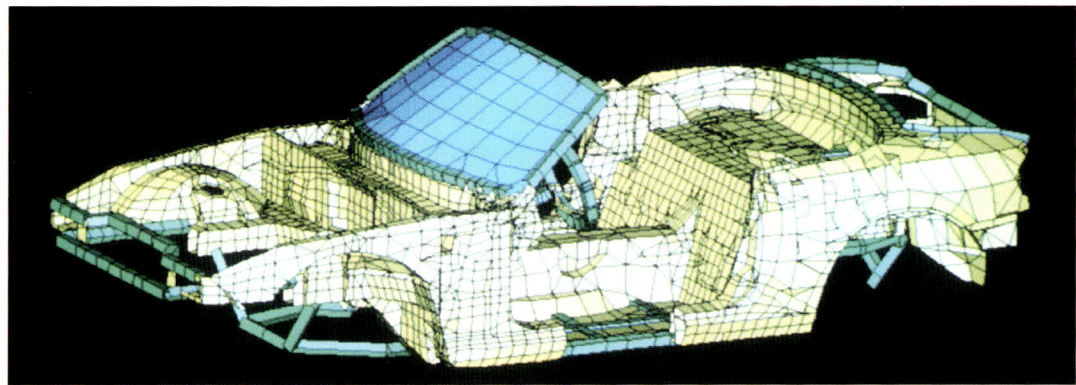

without sacrificing the space, function and utility of the cabin for its driver and passengers. Considerations for productivity are also very important. After days and nights of hard work, the total weight of additional reinforcements for the 323 added up to about 80kg (176lb). This far outweighed the roof and pillars that were removed.

In respect of changing closed cars into open ones, there was no exception for European cars. Some manufacturers reinforced the floor with a second floor panel and some completely covered the propshaft tunnel from beneath to achieve the necessary rigidity. Such design considerations often resulted in increased cost and reduced productivity or serviceability. Mazda's second open body challenge was the RX-7 Cabriolet. After the experience of the 323, know-how and technology were greatly advanced. We achieved good success, especially in the US market. But even then, much effort was needed to reinforce the body once the roof was removed.

Design of a roadster
The MX-5/Miata was to be an LWS and not a luxury or a fashionable car. The PPM requested that we design the bodyshell to be less than 200kg (440lb). Other open body frames, including that of the 323, exceeded the target weight by quite some margin, and we all felt

that it was a very difficult goal to achieve. We had to start with a new design concept and our past closed body derived experience had no place in the development of the roadster. Many of the open bodied cars produced in Europe or in the US were limited production models, and complicated reinforcements were possible because of the small numbers involved. But the MX-5/Miata had a production target of 5000 units per month.

We were all appalled by the weight target. If this number of cars was to be produced, the design must be optimized for mass-production.

With respect to LWS culture, the PPM told us that in a traditional US family, when a boy leaves home for college, his father would give him an LWS as a last gift. This story, along with other stories the PPM told us about LWS culture, left me shaking with excitement. The PPM did not use any material. He just spoke softly about the background of the LWS, and although no clear image of one was available, I had a vision in my mind.

The computer & automobile development
The use of computers in automobile development is widespread, but the benefits of such utilization are directly linked to the technical capability of the automaker. Full

utilization of these computer systems occurred only during the 1990s.

In calculating the rigidity, strength and vibration of a body structure, there are generally two approaches. A classic method would use a mathematical formula based on physics. This technique dates back to Newton's age, but its importance is still recognized.

Another method is generally called "computer simulation," where computers are used extensively. The difficulty and complexity of a car body design must surpass that of a supertanker, largely due to the complex shapes involved in a car body. Most of the components in a car have no clear geometrical shape, and the body itself can be very complex. By comparison, a supertanker can be broken down into components with rather simple geometrical shapes. In a classical method, the formula to analyze the behavior of simple geometrical shapes under load may be constructed fairly easily, but is nearly impossible for complex structures. When it comes to a complicated calculation, the classical method is very limited in its application.

New method
Structural analysis with computer simulation was developed to break through the limitations in the classic method of body design, and it is called the "Finite Element

Method" (FEM). While it may be impossible to construct a formula to analyze a complex shape, a simple triangle or a square structure can be analyzed via simple formulae. By breaking a complex shape into small triangles and squares, and considering the body as a combination of these simple elements, a series of simultaneous equations can be formulated for them. Since there are thousands of these small elements, there will be hundreds, or even thousands, of simultaneous equations to be solved. It is humanly impossible to do this, and computer usage becomes essential.

In order to describe the body of an automobile as a series of squares and triangles, a very fine breakdown must be carried out: just as the digital cameras of today use many millions of individual picture elements to present a clearer complete picture. The capacity requirement for the computer increases proportionally with the square of such fine breakdown elements. This is the scale of computer simulation.

The automobile industry was one of the first industries to introduce computers in the field of design. Mazda was one of the pioneers in the industry regarding the introduction of computers, but in the 1970s, even the largest of computers was still not capable of running a simulation with very fine elements. It was, therefore, common to have small scale simulation for trial use only.

During the 1980s, computer capacity increased dramatically and much finer analysis, that roughly simulated a body shape, became possible. Because of the sheer size involved, ship and aircraft design utilized such computer simulation extensively, but for automobiles, because of the ease of making and testing real size prototypes, computer simulation was still in its infancy. By and large, automobile engineers were still designing cars with *Kan* (senses), *Keiken* (experience) and *Dokyo* (guts), and this method was, sarcastically, called KKD development.

Many older engineers and managers openly told simulation engineers that it was a waste of time, and that a car can be designed without such technology. Some of them even challenged us to design a car only with simulation. However, the design of an open body was beyond the reach of the KKD method. Because of a lack of experience, even older engineers had nothing to support their gut feelings. Because it was an exclusive design, there was no way to test it by cutting off a roof from a base car. With this background situation, everyone, whether they believed in computer technology or not, had high expectations for our work. Everyone knew, however, how difficult it was to design an open body from our past encounter with the 323 and RX-7, and most of them were already very busy with major production projects. That left me - with very little experience - to do the simulation. I was given one young assistant.

Although a lot relied on the computer simulation, my assistant and I were all the manpower that was allocated to it, clearly showing that, at that time, car design utilizing computer simulation was not a recognized approach. There was, thankfully, supporting technology available that was developed during the creation of past convertible designs, established methods for testing and simulation procedures and, just as importantly, structural performance requirements for the open car.

The start of simulation

The first simulation was performed on the pre-prototype from the consulting firm in the UK. In performing a computer simulation, there is always a bottleneck in the computer capacity caused by the sheer volume of data to be input. If a body is broken into 1000 elements, the number of individual inputs will be about 60,000, with half of them being 3-D coordinate data. Since body curvature is not simple, no coordinate data is a combination of simple numbers. The vast majority of them are in

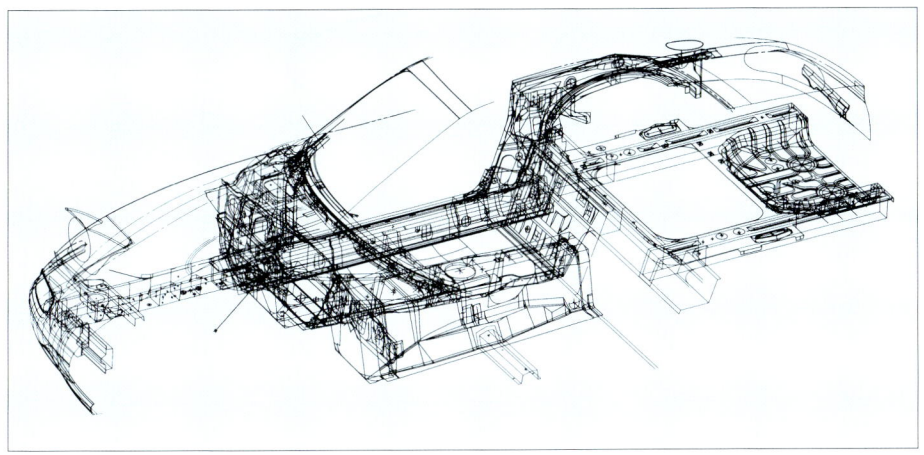

six to seven digits. And for every cross point, called a node, an identification number is allocated to avoid a double count. For each triangle or square, relevant node numbers are allocated, and each such combined element was given another ID number. The thickness of each element was also given as input, as was the weight of major components, such as the powerplant, doors, hood, and seats. Any single mistake would give a wrong output or no output at all. If the design data is all in digital form, this is not hard work but, at that time, all design data was on sheets of paper. Today, all design work is performed on computer, and is called "Computer Aided Design" or "CAD." But at the time of the roadster's development, CAD was still in its development stage. The designs made by the British consulting firm were all in the form of large, actual size drawings, and all data points had to be read off from them. The work was like battling with a giant serpent!

Structural characteristics

An open body is fundamentally a two-dimensional structure, and decidedly weaker than the three-dimensional structure of a closed body. It is, therefore, most important to make the two-dimensional structure as close to

a three-dimensional structure as we can. We did not have enough know-how when we developed the 323 and RX-7 Cabriolet, we only realized this simple truth with the MX-5/Miata design. The roadster body structure features three-dimensional structures in the following areas:

A step-up from the cabin (cockpit) floor to the rear floor that forms the seatback bulkhead; the rear floor is located in the middle of the body height, and the drop to the cabin floor forms a rear bulkhead for the cabin. The rear bulkhead also functions as body side structure, supporting the door pillars.

The front side frames are located high to correlate with the rear side frames and create a large drop to the floor. A structural member behind the dash panel reinforces the drop area and also supports the front door pillars at the same time.

A large floor (transmission) tunnel. The front and rear bulkheads are similar to the hipbone and shoulder/ collar bones of a human body, but they only stiffen the front and rear of the car. The floor tunnel in the center, with its wide trapezoidal cross-section, connects the two bulkheads and functions as a backbone. The height of the floor

tunnel together with the floor panel creates a large, three-dimensional structure.

The scale of computer simulation performed on the pre-prototype was 1100 elements with 1200 nodes. This is a very simple simulation by today's standards, but this scale was generally acceptable at the time of the LWS development. My assistant and I fought with the large drawings for three full weeks to make the input data. While we were struggling with the pre-prototype, the design of the true prototype was proceeding concurrently. The upper body of the pre-prototype was made of plastic, while that of the new prototype was made of steel, and the scale of simulation increased to 1600 nodes and 1500 elements.

First simulation result

The first computer simulation results showed that the pre-prototype design had better rigidity and vibrational characteristics than those of the 323 Cabriolet and the RX-7 Cabriolet. Its body structure had proven to be effective in that distorting energy was evenly distributed over the body, and there was no excess material in the design. Our own prototype design showed even better results.

Some of the experienced testing and research engineers

129

had a dim view of the pre-prototype, commenting that it would not be able to withstand a series of physical tests, and when the tests began the result proved them right. After one or two hours in a durability test, its body started to crack. This crack was repaired, but another one started at another location and, after a few hours, the test was terminated.

At that time, our computer simulation findings were regarded as a complete failure. There was only a month left before the release of the prototype design drawings. We did not have a suitable explanation for such a dramatic difference between the simulation and the physical test results. We worked hard with a designer for an effective design improvement. Fortunately for me, the designer understood the necessity of simulation, and was not one to abandon it after a failure. We worked hard to find answers.

The necessity of higher resolution
I did not think there was a critical mistake in the basic structure design of the car. Rather, I thought that it was a well thought out design that could be improved. Computed results, drawings, past experience, and knowledge of structural engineering were all put together to evaluate the simulations validity.

A good basic skeleton layout is a prerequisite of a strong structural design, otherwise no amount of modification can make it into a good structure. But even a good basic layout can only provide the potential for a good structure.

If there is no specific problem with the structure, the junctions between the individual structural elements will be the key to making it a truly good structure. The problem with the pre-prototype stemmed from poor joints, and that was where the failures occurred. Unlike the engineers and designers that had cast doubt on the pre-prototype, due to a lack of experience, I could not forsee this problem.

There was one other simulation which we did for the 323 and the RX-7 Cabriolet, but the MX-5/Miata design had not undertaken as yet. It was a large scale simulation involving 8000 elements or more. Because of the smaller elements and higher resolution, smaller parts of the body could be focused on, giving the simulation more accurate results. A smaller simulation with 1500 elements is suitable for determining major structural layout and rigidity distribution but, due to the inherent low resolution, it is not suitable for finding local weak spots. The focus was now on structural bonding, and a large scale simulation with high resolution was absolutely necessary. As a trial, input data for the pre-prototype was modified to give a high resolution in local areas. Its simulation result supported my thoughts. In order to perform a large scale simulation, we needed input data from detailed design drawings, however. For the 323 and RX-7 Cabriolets, we had detailed drawings from their original closed body design, but none existed for the MX-5/Miata. But by this time, prototype design had progressed, and detailed drawings were slowly becoming available.

Large input data
The biggest problem left was to secure sufficient manpower to generate the input data necessary for such a large scale simulation. It had taken two of us three weeks to prepare a set of data for a small scale simulation. If we had no more manpower, there was no way to finish making the input data before the date of drawing release. All other simulation engineers were kept busy with their own projects, and thus, no extra help was available from that quarter. Fortunately, the body design group offered to send a few engineers to help us generate the data. I was then afraid, that while such help was appreciated, the design work would be late. But I gratefully accepted the offer and started the task with these engineers. They were slow at first, but within a week, they were generating accurate data in large quantities.

Wheelhouse design

My assistant was a young woman in her early twenties. She was working hard generating input data, although there were many design details still missing. One of them was the rear wheel housing design. We could not create our own wheelhouse design, but there was no time to wait for the drawings to arrive. Feeling the pinch, she called up the designer, and asked him to draw a line indicating the missing wheelhouse. Although there were no drawings available, its design must have been clear in his head, and with a trembling hand, the designer drew the line. It was doubtful that this line had been accurately drawn, but that was all we had. Silently, my assistant read off the coordinates and entered the numbers as CAD data input.

A few days later, the design of the wheelhouse became available as CAD data, and, upon comparison, we were astonished by the accuracy of the freehand line drawn by the designer and the numbers my assistant read off from it. They were within 2mm (0.08in.) of each other!

Although we had extra help in generating the huge input data necessary for the simulation, she was the one who put all of it together to simulate the whole roadster. This assistant was not an engineer by training, nor had she any training as a computer simulator. This unsung heroine was a home economics graduate at a junior college!

Mounting pressure

After the pre-prototype test failure, physical test engineers became more vocal in their opposition day by day, and said they couldn't wait for the results of the large scale simulation ... I attended a daily meeting to give various modification proposals based upon the simulation results from the pre-prototype. The vibration test department had a new simulation method derived from their test results, and presented their own modification proposals. The problems with the pre-prototype had caught the attention of the heads of the engineering design department, and they voiced their concerns. Proposed modifications varied. Some were easy, with little effect, and some were unrealistic even though effective. Some were feasible and effective, but added too much weight; others were effective at the sacrifice of ride comfort. There was no good modification proposal agreeable to all involved in the project. As the day of design drawing release got closer, the pressure mounted, especially within the testing department, bringing into doubt the entire development schedule. The pressure was just as great for us. With all this data that had no decisive direction, the designers kept silent but must have sensed an impending disaster.

Prototype in a mesh drawing

Meanwhile, the input data for the large scale simulation was nearly complete. The input data was just a collection of numbers, but when it was displayed on a computer screen, it showed the body structure in a large mesh. Normally, we grasp the body design through CAD data and paper drawings first, and then generate the input data, but due to the tight schedule, I did not have time to view the structure of the car in detail. And, because of that, the first chance I had to view the basic structure of the prototype was as a meshed image on a screen. By removing parts one by one from this image, the basic body structure and major assemblies became clear, almost like viewing the instruction sheet of a plastic model kit.

Checking everything bit by bit, I saw in front of my eyes a highly sophisticated basic structure. Where the structural members came together, they were finely joined with minimal gussets and junctions, as if they were from an old temple where no nails were used to join wooden beams, yet they created a tough and durable structure. Where two structural members overlapped they created a thick section, and some sections seemed like a knot in a bamboo

Chart showing the necessary computer simulations as a project develops.

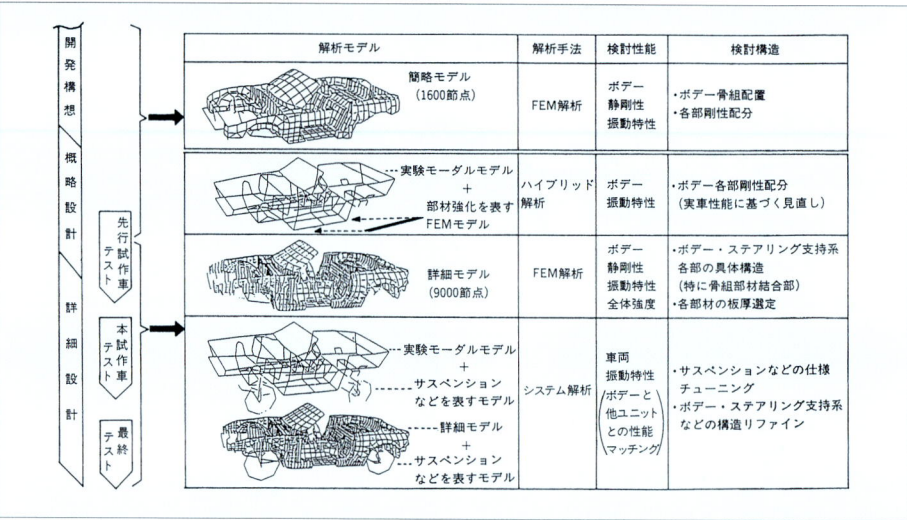

	解析モデル	解析手法	検討性能	検討構造
簡略モデル (1600節点)		FEM解析	ボデー 静剛性 振動特性	・ボデー骨組配置 ・各部剛性配分
実験モーダルモデル + 部材強化を表す FEMモデル		ハイブリッド解析	ボデー 振動特性	・ボデー各部剛性配分 (実車性能に基づく見直し)
詳細モデル (9000節点)		FEM解析	ボデー 静剛性 振動特性 全体強度	・ボデー・ステアリング支持系 各部の具体構造 (特に骨組部材結合部) ・各部材の板厚選定
実験モーダルモデル + サスペンション などを表すモデル 詳細モデル + サスペンション などを表すモデル		システム解析	車両 振動特性 (ボデーと 他ユニット との性能 マッチング)	・サスペンションなどの仕様 チューニング ・ボデー・ステアリング支持系 などの構造リファイン

開発構想 概略設計 詳細設計 先行試作車テスト 本試作車テスト 最終テスト

cane for added strength. Other structural elements made a gentle transition to another structural element, making the load distribution smooth and even. It was apparent how each structural element was assigned a function within the framework. All this seemed like a completely new and rational arrangement of structural members.

While the design retained most of the frame arrangement of the pre-prototype, its total rigidity and strength greatly exceeded that of the original. The sophistication of design was also apparent in the upper body steel structure. The rear deck member located between the trunk space and soft-top storage area was originally a fragile design, but now it was beefed up with ten times the cross-section of the original. This rear deck member not only tied both sides of the upper body, it held pillars behind the two doors, while enclosing the soft-top storage space. A major structural skeleton was given to the upper body of the roadster by this means.

This will make it!

Our designers had provided a very sophisticated structure. They were studying and discussing my analysis results: after thoroughly checking the structure, I called up one designer and told him how splendid the design was. His reply was: "Perhaps, we overdid it?"

No matter how good a structure looks, we must have confirmation with numbers to make it a viable design. And at that moment, my computer simulation was the only way to prove it. It was around 9pm that the PPM came in to check on the results. After a moment of silence, he asked me: "How is it? Do you think it will get through?" He must have had confidence in the design, but I understood how he felt. I really wanted to tell him: "Sure, it will," but I had to be a little more conservative. I said: "If you ask me to bet on yes or no, I'll bet on yes."

A big question remaining at the time was how long would it take to calculate the results? At that time, one simulation run took about a day: two days if there were other calculations to be done. We had only two weeks left before the drawing release. We not only wanted the results, but we needed the input data to be perfect. Also, after the expected results were released, we might still have to make minor corrections to the design before releasing the final design with the consensus of all related parties. Since everybody was aware of the problem we had had with the pre-prototype, they were keenly watching our results,

and no time was allowed for a second try … I just had to pray that the computer would run without trouble.

We got the results the next morning, and hurriedly confirmed them from every direction possible. All the results were positive and affirmative. The rigidity and vibrational characteristics of the body surpassed everything in its class. All the stress loads were distributed to the whole body, and wherever load concentration occurred, there was sufficient reinforcement. The load concentration on the prototype was reduced to between one-fifth to a half of that of the pre-prototype.

Project meeting

The night before the day of design release, a project meeting was held. In the meeting, I presented the simulation results and concluded that the planned release target was achievable. The designers also explained how they had reinforced the original design to achieve such good simulation results. But the Testing & Research Department stubbornly rejected our explanation. They maintained that more reinforcements were needed in the underbody. They insisted that the side sill should be made deeper for better torsional rigidity, even at the cost of driver ingress and egress. When I told them that such necessary reinforcements had already been realized within the steel upper body, some even said that they didn't give any credability to computer simulation. Although it was humiliating for me, their worries were understandable: they were the ones who faced the hardest time in the event that a production prototype was found to have many problems. Our computer simulation technology had a short track record for everyone to fully believe in it and, after all, we'd failed miserably during the simulation of the pre-prototype model ...

The PPM finally opened his mouth: "Let's not keep going on about the pre-prototype, rather let's look at the drawings in front of us. From my experience of seeing many cars and their structures, this design looks like a winner. While I understand the concerns expressed by the Testing & Research Department, I would like to bet on the simulation results being good. If this proves to be a failure, I'll take all the responsibility and let you completely re-design the car."

The disgruntled engineers finally gave in. The moment of silence felt like a solemn moment to me. After the meeting was over,

one experienced test engineer came over to me and said: "Although my boss was very negative back there, I think the upper body design will be quite effective in providing the necessary rigidity. Let's hope for the best."

Reward

After the routine drawing check was over, my simulation work was largely finished. A few days later, I, along with other staff members, were called by the Division Manager of R&D to make a presentation on the structural performance of the roadster. The Division Manager was also interested in the future outlook for the MX-5/Miata, the third open-bodied model for Mazda, but its first exclusive open body design. After my presentation was over, the PPM commented to the Manager: "The design release couldn't have been possible without the simulation." This was the first word of praise I had heard! The Manager replied: "I look forward to the test ..." The comment made by the PPM was not 100% accurate, though. The project's fast progress was not simply down to the simulation, but also because the PPM had committed to the design as an act of faith. All we did was to boost his morale and confidence in the cars design with our positive numerical demonstration.

Prototype test

A prototype based on the design plans was completed within a couple of months. This was the first time for everyone to see the real MX-5/Miata that they had been dreamt of. The first test drive was conducted on a small test course at the Ujina Plant. Real performance tests would be at the Miyoshi Proving Ground, but it was possible to see a glimpse of the roadster's performance even on this small test course. In reality, if it didn't shine here, it would never shine anywhere.

In a bus heading for the test course, my boss told us: "If the MX-5/Miata is a failure, we'll all be fired! Remember that." We all took turns in test driving the prototype. My turn came. The first time around was a gentle one, while the second lap was a little faster. The roadster felt solid, like a closed car. In the third lap the car felt more solid than any of other open bodied cars I'd driven. However, I was not a professional test driver. I needed to know how the professionals and the PPM felt about the car. When I asked one testing engineer, who had earlier been very critical of the design, he gave a little smile and walked away. If there was any problem, he would have made a harsh comment, but he didn't. Finally I asked my boss: "Are we all going to stay at Mazda?" He said: "Sure, no problem."

Durability test

Durability testing of the prototype began, and we remembered that the pre-prototype failed within a few hours. Four hours after the test had begun, I visited the test stand and asked the manager in charge, who was a strong proponent of a redesign, how things were going? He replied with a smile on his face, "Oh, it wouldn't be good if it failed so soon."

Ultimately, there was no damage to the body after two days of testing. The prototype was bouncing off the test roller with all sorts of fierce shocks that cannot be found even on a rough road. But its behavior was clearly different from that of the pre-prototype. The pre-prototype was twisting, wriggling almost, as it was bouncing. But this prototype was different. It was bouncing with no obvious twist, and its suspension seemed to absorb all of the road shocks. After a few days, the durability test was over. It was not stopped at any point and ended as scheduled. There were some minor failures, but none were critical.

Another test measured the car's bending and torsional rigidity. The results showed that the prototype demonstrated 40% more rigidity than Mazda's previous open bodied models, which had evolved from a closed body design, and with the exception of some speciality cars with a much higher selling price, the figure was among the best. In a vibration test, the prototype recorded an overall resonance frequency of around 20Hz. Most of the cars previously tested had 16Hz of lower resonance frequency, and it proved that its dynamic strength was also quite high. This was the moment that the 200kg (440lb) body of the LWS with its exclusive design was openly recognized as being superior. Later, the Vibration Test Manager told me: "Your simulation worked well this time."

Human power

After the development of the MX-5/Miata, many people told me that this was a victory for computer simulation. But the true victors were the designers and engineers who realized the body, and the PPM who believed in that design. Simulation can tell if the structure in question is feasible or not, and where the problem might exist, but it does not tell you how to remedy a problem. Today, computer simulation is widely recognized as a powerful tool, but it is only one of many, and its usefulness depends on people. No matter how complex a simulation is performed, it must be correctly interpreted, and appropriate feedback must be delivered in order to achieve a more rational structure design.

When we were working on the pre-prototype with incomplete data, the designers were working to evolve an unprecedented design based on lessons learnt. The PPM believed in the design. Test engineers worked hard to collect experimental data necessary for the simulation, although they showed a tough attitude towards the technology they doubted. What happened during the development of the MX-5/Miata clearly demonstrates that the human element is still the most important for success.

Since the time of the LWS design, computer capacity has dramatically improved and the original large scale computers have been replaced by supercomputers. In 2002 the capacity of Mazda's computer was roughly 1000 times that of 1988, and the scale of simulation is exceeding 500,000 elements and 600,000 nodes. Mazda's simulation engineering has undergone changes also, but the fact remains that it is always the people who do the real work.

It is interesting to note that, nowadays, what was a large scale simulation of 8000 elements and 9000 nodes can be performed on a common PC within minutes without any special techniques. As I think back, it is indeed very interesting that the fate of this project once hung on the capability of what, in today's terms, was a poorly equipped computer, though only for a short time.

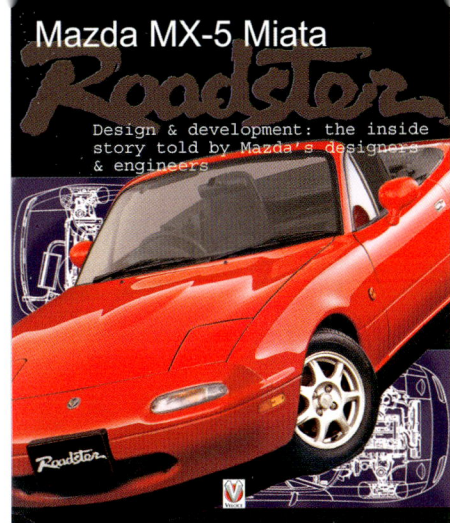

Mazda MX-5 Miata

Roadster

Design & development: the inside story told by Mazda's designers & engineers

11

Development of the soft-top
by **Sadamu Nishiguchi**

A French engineer, who spoke only French, and a Japanese engineer, who spoke only Japanese, worked together day and night, and, given this communication problem, it seemed unlikely that they would ever produce a satisfactory soft-top design. However, starting from a simple sketch, they progressed to a model, and then to CAD to check the frame linkage. Finally, a full-scale mock-up was made, along with a full set of drawings. When the Frenchman left Japan, the two engineers parted without words in French or Japanese, yet their work told me that they must have communicated well. Despite the fact that some water leakage in a soft-top is considered excusable in this industry, Nishiguchi and his French partner provided us with a truly waterproof hood.

T. Hirai

In order to realize an open bodied lightweight sports car, a manually operated, retractable soft-top with a vinyl covering was to be developed. I was assigned to design a soft-top that was both light and beautiful. My experience in this field was limited only to the 323's soft-top, but I had the assistance of an experienced French engineer dispatched by a British consulting firm. He only spoke French, of which I had no

knowledge, and communication was a problem at first. But soon it became possible to work together and jointly design a soft-top that was suitable for mass production. Through such work, I was able to learn that there are no borders in technology, and it is possible to work together with someone, even though there is a language barrier.

Design targets
We established the following targets in order to realize a true LWS:

Light weight: Although light weight was an important target, we also designed the soft-top to have the equivalent strength of a steel roof against snowfall, and to suffer no deformation from a sidewind force of up to 30kg (66lb).

Operation: The soft-top was to be opened or closed from the driver's seat, and its locking mechanism operated with only light force.

Appearance: We wanted to give it a racy look without sacrificing cabin comfort, and to make it as compact as possible when retracted so that it could be stored below the beltline of the roadster.

Water tightness: While it may not be possible to guarantee the same level of water tightness as that of

The soft-top was designed to fold smoothly, with the mechanism and cloth top folding neatly below the beltline.

In the closed position, the frame was laid out in such a way as to give the car a good profile.

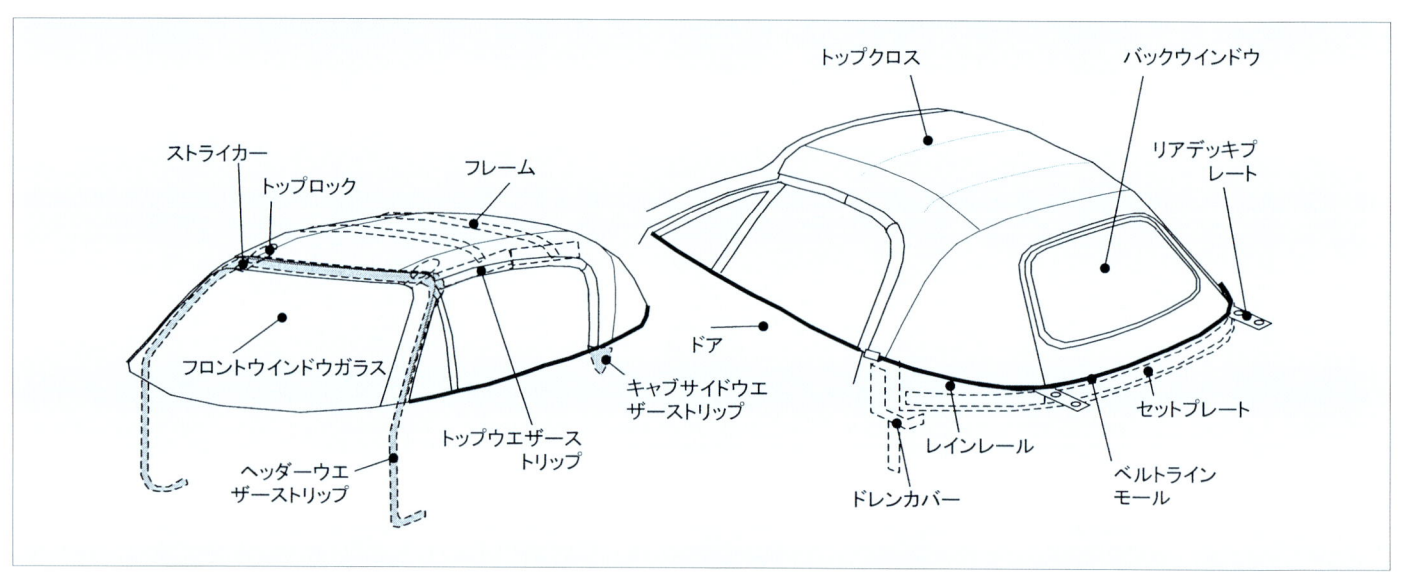

トップクロス　　　　バックウインドウ

ストライカー　　　　フレーム　　　　　　　　　　　　　　リアデッキプ
　　トップロック　　　　　　　　　　　　　　　　　　　　レート

フロントウインドウガラス　　　　　　　　　　　ドア

ヘッダーウエ　　　トップウエザース　　キャブサイドウエ　　　レインレール　　セットプレート
ザーストリップ　　　トリップ　　　　　ザーストリップ

ドレンカバー　　　ベルトライン
　　　　　　　　　モール

An overview of the soft-top.

a fixed roof, we aimed to achieve minimum leakage into the cabin. With the exception of a concentrated water jet from below, the soft-top would satisfy this requirement.

Ease of production: We designed the soft-top so that it would be possible to assemble the MX-5/ Miata on a production line mixed with other cars. The existing shower testing equipment was adjusted in order to be able to inspect leak tightness on the same test line as closed cars.

Structure of the soft-top and its development process

In order to make a soft-top manually operable, the frame structure has to be light, and its geometry has to allow smooth operation. Also, when the soft-top is retracted, there has to be sufficient space between its linkages to avoid any damage to the top fabric.

The link structure was designed with eight joints that were made from thick steel plate. The header part was made from

pressed steel sheet for rigidity, and the roof members were made from tubing for stiffness to resist the weight of accumulated snow. The seal retainer was made with stamped thin steel in order to attach the weather strips.

The most difficult part of the design was the frame layout. In order not to disturb a beautiful beltline, the top, when retracted, had to store below the beltline. But the question was how to store the linkage and fabric within a restricted space? Even though the

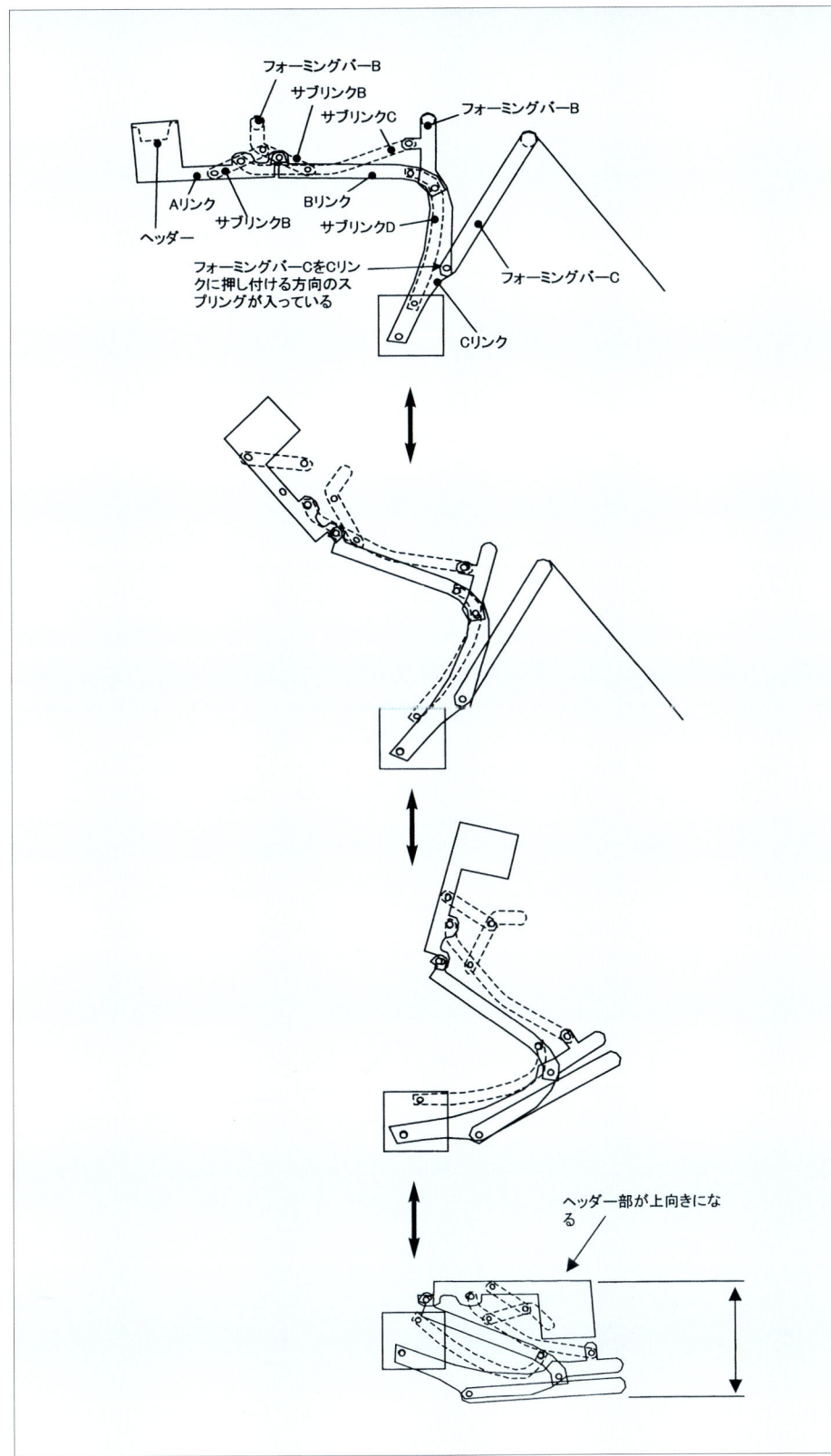

フォーミングバーB
サブリンクB
サブリンクC
フォーミングバーB
Aリンク
Bリンク
ヘッダー
サブリンクB
サブリンクD
フォーミングバーCをCリンクに押し付ける方向のスプリングが入っている
フォーミングバーC
Cリンク

ヘッダー部が上向きになる

space was limited, the top fabric and rear vinyl window had to be protected from tearing and/or wrinkling. In order to achieve that, we had to provide ample spacing between the frames. To obtain more headroom when the top is up, the soft-top would inevitably require longer frames that would lessen the trunk space, which was minimal already. And in order to be manually operable, human engineering factors had to be incorporated in the design too.

In order to satisfy these sometimes conflicting requirements, we worked hard on the drawing board, as well as with many prototype models. The accumulation of repeated design, trial and error, finally resulted in success, but it did not come easily. The only relief from this difficult situation was a comment the PPM made about the soft-top. He said: "Design priority for a soft-top is when it is retracted; don't worry so much about its looks when it's up." With this priority in mind, we worked together to design a soft-top that was light in weight and easy to operate, and it would be an added bonus if it looked good when erected.

Fabric selection

The soft-top's fabric material must be durable, not susceptible to weather, and must possess the appearance of quality. We eventually chose a material made

The MX-5/Miata in profile with the top down and its soft-top cover in place. From this angle, it is easy to see that the beautiful beltline was unaffected by the soft-top.

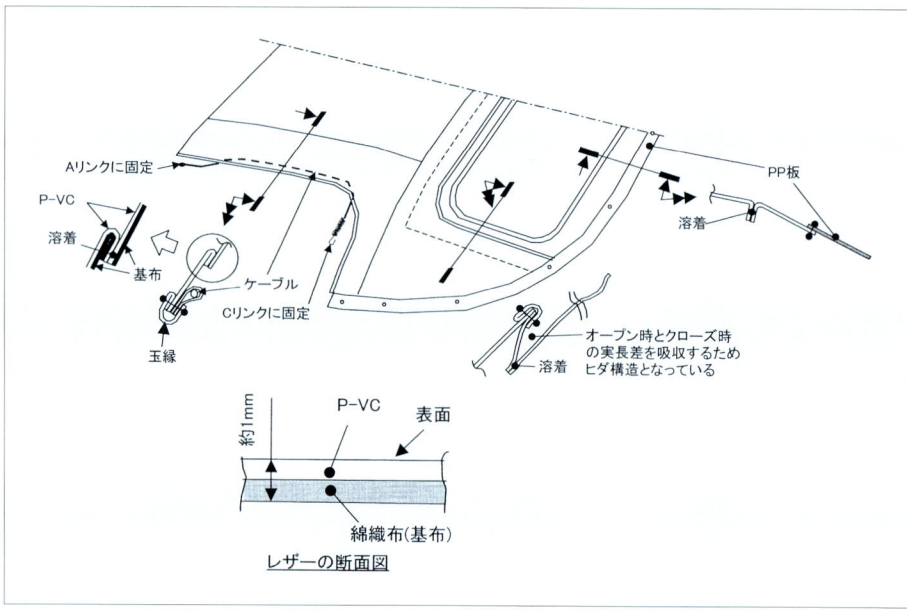

Aリンクに固定
P-VC
溶着
基布
ケーブル
Cリンクに固定
玉縁
PP板
溶着
オープン時とクローズ時の実長差を吸収するためヒダ構造となっている
溶着
約1mm
P-VC
表面
綿織布(基布)
レザーの断面図

Trial and error was the only way to achieve the perfect soft-top design. Some parts were stitched, others fused, and great care was taken to avoid the top crinkling.

by a German supplier that had an established record. This fabric would have no backing and the back window was made semi-detachable via a zip fastener to allow the soft-top to retract to a minimum stack height without crumpling the window. Its attachment to the rear deck was via a plastic rain rail for water drainage. Before deciding on the German material, we tested various fabrics for durability and cost, and went as far afield as California for weather testing.

A problem to overcome with the fabric was how to achieve an optimum tightness of the cloth when the hood was erect? It is easy to say that the cloth should be on the small side, so that it is stretched to achieve the optimum tension, but it is not that easy ... Depending on the driving conditions, the fabric or the back window would flutter if not taut enough. A delicate balance between the stiffness of the frame linkage, transverse tension of the top cloth and the tension created by the locking mechanism was the solution. However, to achieve such a delicate balance on the mass production line was another trial, calling for close coordination with the production engineering chief (Nakagaki) to achieve such precise production control.

Back window structure

For expediency, the back window was made from clear plastic. Its material had to meet high standards of durability and weather resistance, so the PPM insisted that we use the best material available. After thorough testing of materials from various suppliers, the clear plastic chosen was from a Swiss supplier.

Locking mechanism

The locking mechanism of the soft-top had to be secure against thieves, safe and easy to operate. Two die-cast locking mechanisms were deployed on the front header rail for crisp locking and ease of use. The locks were common with those employed on the detachable hardtop.

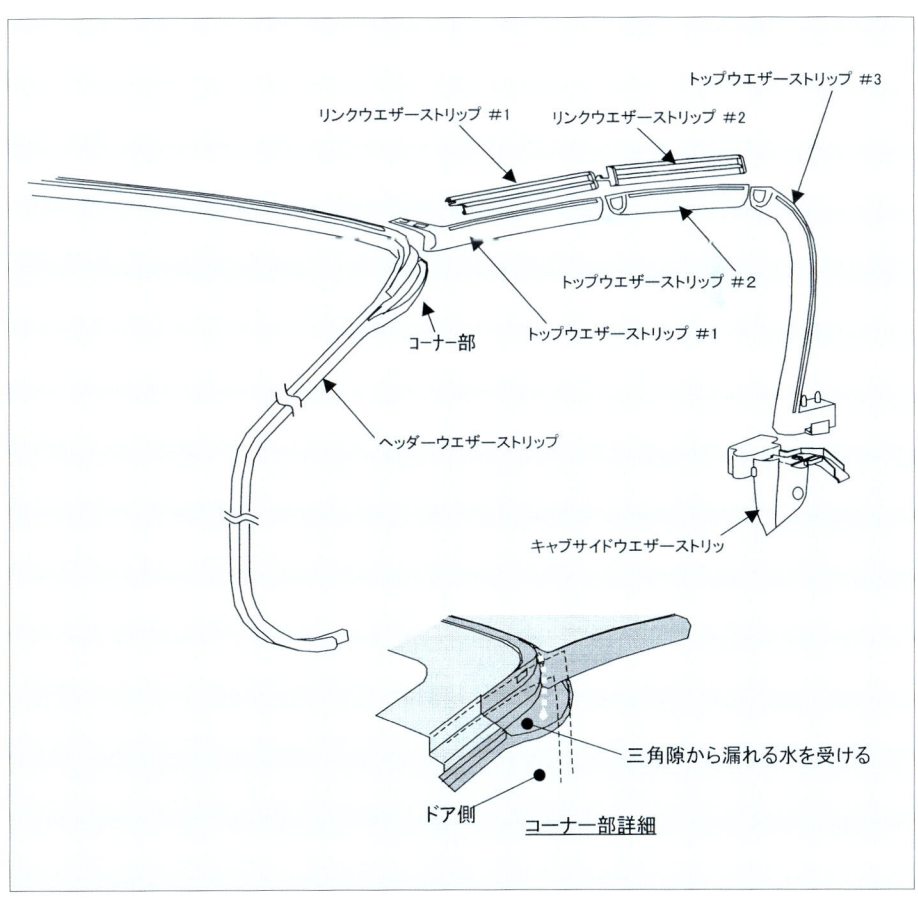

The top lock and striker mechanism.

ロックフックの逃がし
ストライカー
キャップ
本体
リンク
スクリュウ
ロックフック
ロックレバー
ロック解除ボタン（解除位置）
ロック解除ボタン（ロック位置）

Weather seal

I have been told that common sense prevailed during an earlier open sports car era: "Don't forget your bath towel when you take a ride in the rain." While it may have been true and accepted in the 1970s, that idea would not wash (forgive the pun) in Japan as we headed for the 21st century. We had to provide the car with appropriate weather sealing.

In consideration of wind noise and leakage protection, the front header was equipped with double sealing, while the side windows were sealed with a hollow weather strip of large cross-section. The triangular area between the front window, side window and top side of the soft-top was the most difficult part to seal against water. The soft-top comes in from above and the side window closes sideways, but there is no order established for which happens first. Considering these difficulties, we designed a special weather strip with a provision to collect and drain water. L-shaped plastic weather strips were provided between the front frame and the fabric top's sides to seal off water.

With respect to the rear deck, although it was much easier to attach the fabric above the top

リンクウエザーストリップ #1
リンクウエザーストリップ #2
トップウエザーストリップ #3
トップウエザーストリップ #2
トップウエザーストリップ #1
コーナー部
ヘッダーウエザーストリップ
キャブサイドウエザーストリッ
三角隙から漏れる水を受ける
ドア側
コーナー部詳細

The weather strip in detail. The joint at the top corner of the windshield was the most difficult to design, as three seals meet at that one point. The fact that the seals moved more often, and in different directions compared to a regular sedan, also had to be taken into consideration, along with manufacturing time and costs.

139

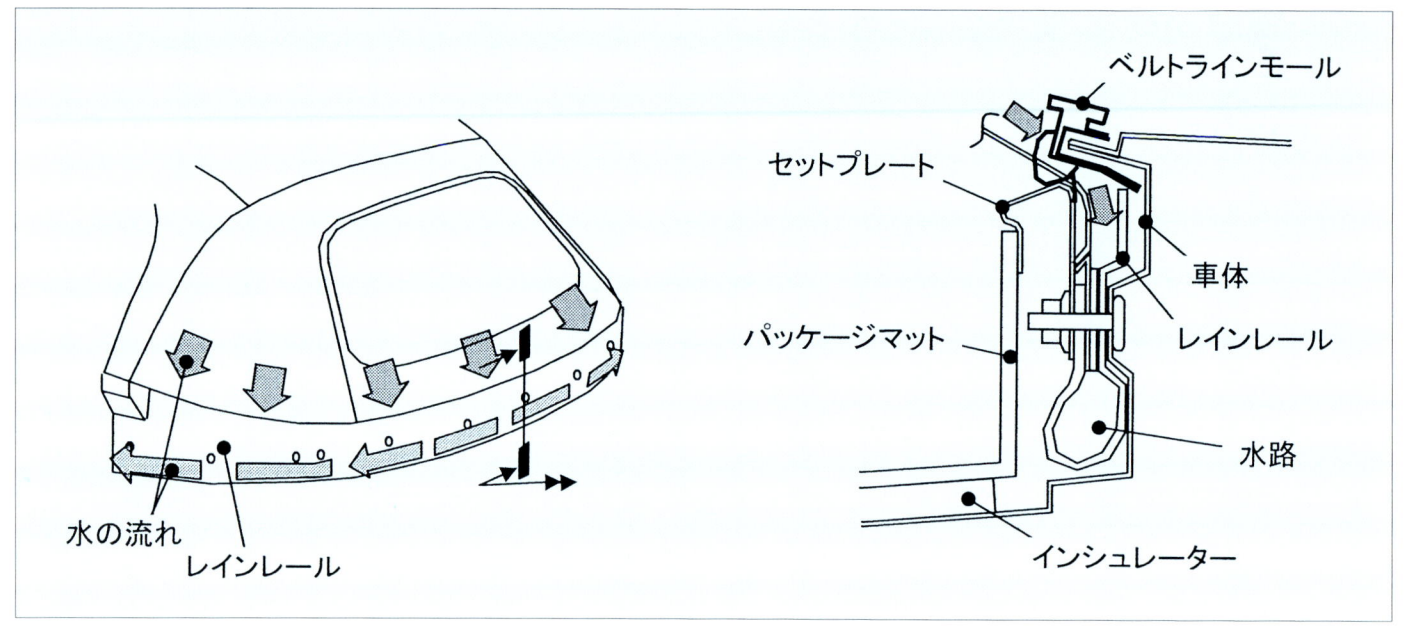

ベルトラインモール
セットプレート
車体
パッケージマット
レインレール
水路
水の流れ
レインレール
インシュレーター

Detail drawings of the rain rail fitted at the base of the soft-top.

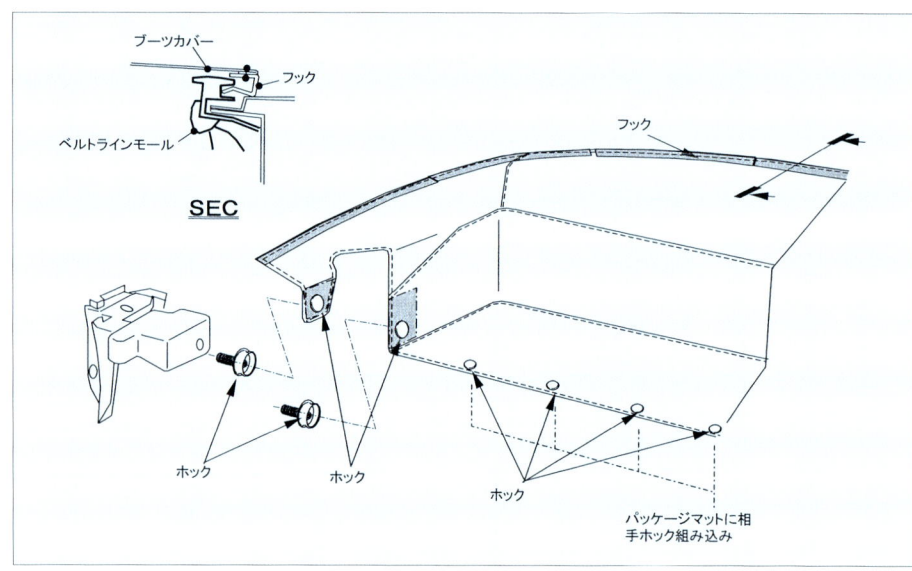

ブーツカバー
フック
ベルトラインモール
SEC
フック
ホック
ホック
ホック
パッケージマットに相
手ホック組み込み

The soft-top cover had to be designed to be as light as possible, but it also had to be tight, hence the rear of the cover was hooked in place, and there were a large number of fixing points on the leading edge.

I thought, and I designed a special attachment and water passage. The water passage was supported by the package shelf mat bracket to facilitate later assembly on the production line.

Boot cover

A boot cover is a cover for the soft-top when it is folded down. In order to give it good looks, it was attached to the rear deck with a full hooking mechanism around its periphery. The rear deck attachment doubled as sealing material for the detachable hardtop.

Although Mazda had had two previous experiences with a soft-top, this was the first time we had developed a lightweight soft-top. At the time I was assigned for the job, I had little confidence. However, with the help of a French engineer, project members and subcontractors, we were able to develop a first class soft-top for the MX-5/Miata. Every time I see one go by, the memory of those hours I spent working on the soft-top design comes back as a fond memory.

deck for leakage protection, we chose to attach it from inside to make the top invisible when folded down. This internal attachment would, of course, make it difficult to drain water that collected between the deck and top cloth, and a special provision had to be made. At that time, only Alfa Romeo had this sort of attachment, and it used a U-shaped steel sheet as a water passage with sealant at its attachment. This system would not guarantee good sealing quality,

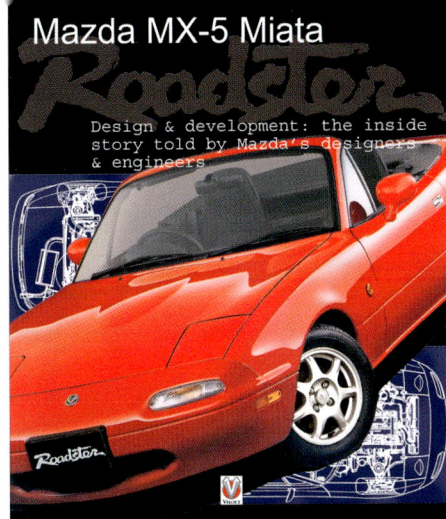

Mazda MX-5 Miata

Roadster

Design & development: the inside
story told by Mazda's designers
& engineers

12

Development of the detachable hardtop
by **Seiichi Omoto**

Omoto immediately went to Europe upon hearing of his assignment. He went there to learn from European predecessors, including BMW and VW, and came back full of ideas. As a result, he had Nishiguchi design a soft-top that would not leak during a typhoon, while he himself concentrated on the design of a detachable hardtop. He achieved excellent results in both these fields, far exceeding our expectations. He is now PPM for the Mazda 6 and having a busy time.

T. Hirai

The detachable hardtop (DHT) for the roadster determined its third body styling. We were able to design and fabricate a DHT using a sheet molding compound (SMC) process to produce a light and tough hardtop that could not be made with a steel stamping.

There are DHTs that are made with polyester resin and glassfibre laid up over a mold, but utilization of the SMC process for DHT manufacturing was a world first. The process made it possible to fabricate a complex inner structure with a uniform outer thickness for a light, strong and beautiful DHT.

In designing a DHT, crash resistance and weight reduction are conflicting aims, and we tried many different combinations of inner and outer thicknesses in search of the best balance. At that time, material data for SMC was not available and we started with the measurement of test pieces to accumulate a database for design analysis. With CAE (computer aided engineering) analysis and various prototype tests, we arrived at the best combination of panel thickness and structure to give us optimum strength and light weight. The final design was a two-piece bonded structure with an outer panel of 2.3mm (0.09in.) thickness tightly bonded with epoxy resin to an inner panel. In order to clear fabrication limitations, the inner panel was made in two parts. The rear window glass was made with

With the soft-top down, it was possible to fit the optional detachable hardtop. The DHT gave the car a completely different character.

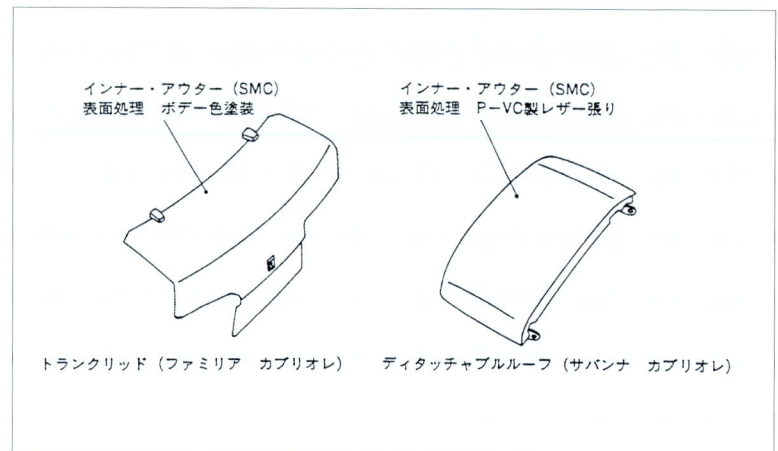

インナー・アウター（SMC）
表面処理　ボデー色塗装

インナー・アウター（SMC）
表面処理　P-VC製レザー張り

トランクリッド（ファミリア　カブリオレ）

ディタッチャブルルーフ（サバンナ　カブリオレ）

Early SMC car parts, such as the 323 Cabriolet trunk lid and detachable roof panel from the RX-7 Cabriolet.

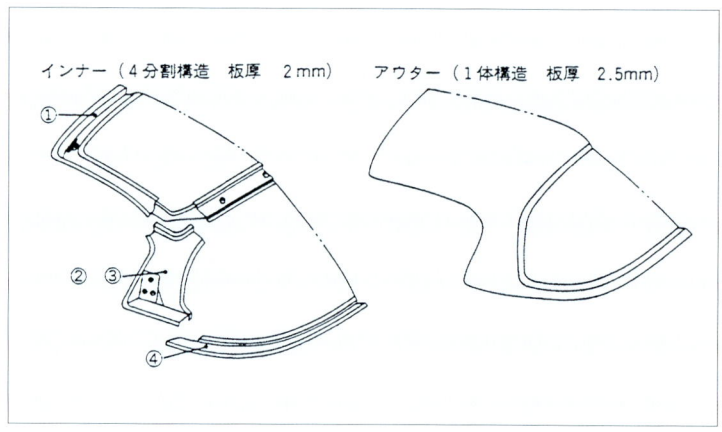

アウター

インナー

オンリー成形

接着アッシー治具

The inner and outer panels, and how they are mated.

インナー（4分割構造　板厚　2mm）

アウター（1体構造　板厚　2.5mm）

①
②
③
④

The DHT structure #1.

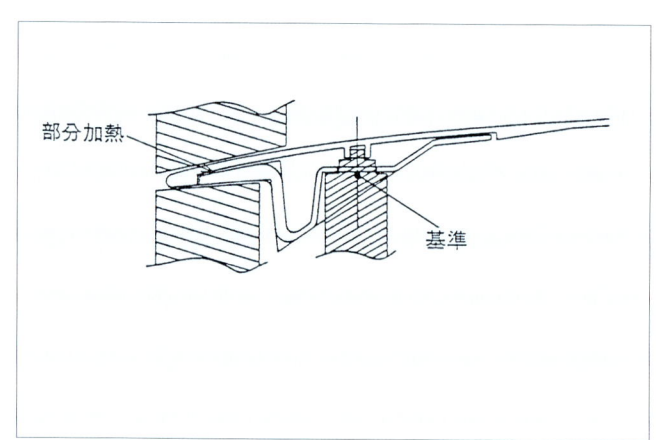

部分加熱

基準

The DHT assembly in detail.

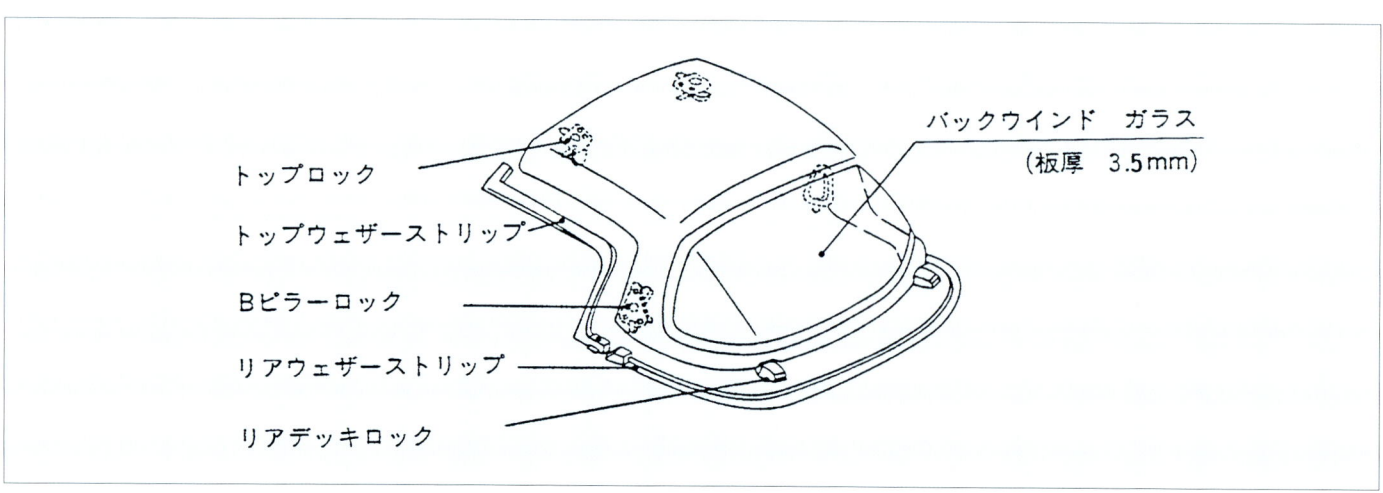

バックウインド　ガラス
（板厚　3.5mm）

トップロック

トップウェザーストリップ

Bピラーロック

リアウェザーストリップ

リアデッキロック

The DHT structure #2.

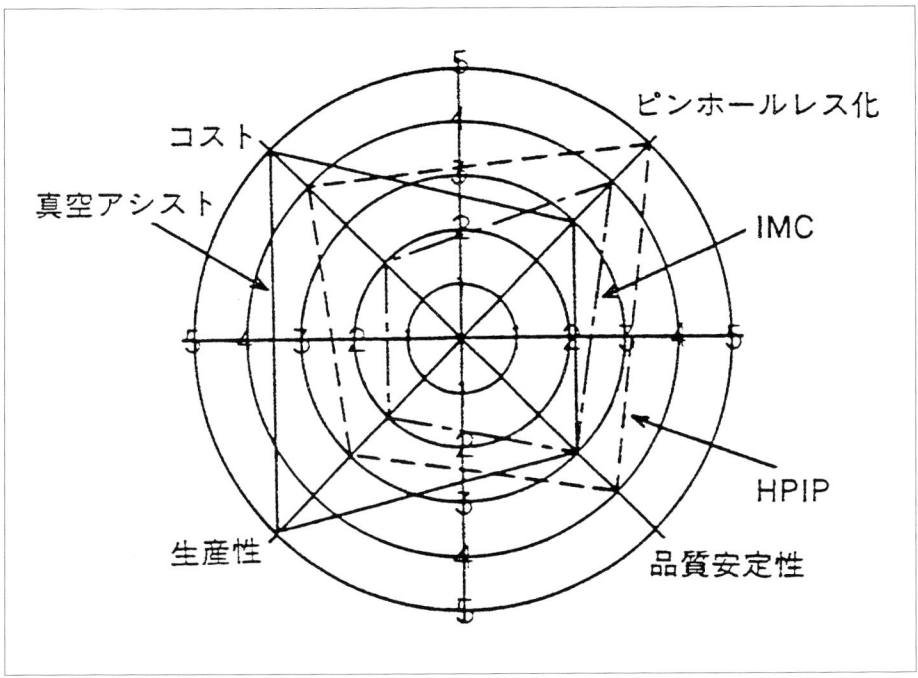

Chart drawn up to balance techniques and cost in production of the DHT. The elimination of pinholes after painting was a prime consideration.

maximum curvature for a wide rear view and the good looks that contributed to the overall success of the DHT.

Earlier experiences with the 323 and the RX-7

The SMC process was once under the focus of attention as an alternative to steel construction for body panels. I first dealt with this technology three years before the MX-5/Miata's development. At that time I was assigned to the 323 Cabriolet project, and one of my jobs was to study, with the members of the Technical Center, the SMC process for its suitability to produce outer body panels. The trunk (boot) lid of the 323 Cabriolet was to be fabricated using the SMC process, and I was engaged with its design. Since there was a great deal of risk in the fledgling SMC process, a steel lid design was also pursued as a backup.

Although the trunk lid employing the SMC process passed all the design requirements and came close to mass production, its use on the 323 was postponed due to a lack of experience and time to assure quality. About 200 SMC trunk lids for the 323 Cabriolet were produced for a field test, and its advantages, including its resistance to corrosion, were later confirmed. My next project was the RX-7 Cabriolet, which employed a top section made via the SMC process as an extension of the earlier development for the 323. This background led to the success of the DHT for the MX-5/Miata.

First obstacle: precision

The biggest obstacle in the development of the DHT using the SMC process was control over precision. In order to make a roof detachable from the body, air sealing and water sealing provisions are necessary. For one body employing both a soft-top and a DHT, precise accuracy control was necessary in production. In prototype production, no such problem arose, for each part was hand fitted, but in the mass production stage, accuracy control became a

big problem after the inner and outer shells were glued together.

With the start of mass production getting closer, I was forced to take corrective action very quickly, and I was starting to feel desperate. It was at this time that Nakagaki, who was in charge of production engineering, asked me, rather forcibly, to join him for a visit to the supplier who was responsible for the DHT.

Nakagaki had already prepared a remedy in his mind. Similar to the spot welding of sheet metals, he had the supplier establish reference points for the inner and outer panels, and had both panels clamped together as the glue was curing, while reference points were matched to a standard surface. Other components were adjusted according to the clamped down position. Based on his rich background with sheet metal work, Nakagaki instructed precisely where to clamp the DHT for precise control. This resolved the accuracy problem like a charm. On the way back from the supplier, it started to snow over a narrow winding road to Hiroshima. The snow got thicker as the time passed, and we eventually realized that we were going the wrong way. After wandering around lost for several hours in the dark snowy night, we finally got to a major highway which was congested with cars due to all the accidents.

The wraparound rear screen gave good rear visibility, while the SMC top provided good weather protection in the winter months.

Second obstacle: pinholes

The second major obstacle we faced in the development of the DHT was the formation of pinholes on the painted surface. The quality standard for outer surface painting is very severely controlled at Mazda, and SMC resin was susceptible to having minute pinholes after formation. In small scale production, such holes can be removed by thick under coating and hand rubbing, but that was not feasible in our case. With the addition of a vacuum to the inner panel die, pinhole occurrence was reduced but it was not eradicated.

In a quality control meeting before mass production, we faced a difficult decision. At that time it

was provisionally decided that it was only acceptable to produce the DHT with a black matt finish to conceal the pinholes. We were not satisfied with the decision, as we all wanted to match the color of the DHT with the body color. If we produced a matt black DHT only, there would surely be aftermarket DHTs with original body colors, drastically reducing the market value of the genuine item. We had to make it possible to produce a DHT in original colors. After thorough investigation of all possible avenues, we tried various forming methods, and finally found a way to control the occurence of pinholes, enabling mass production to go ahead.

During development, we faced

many problems, but once the MX-5/Miata was made available to the public and seen on the road, the difficult times we'd had faded away into insignificance.

The DHT for the MX-5/Miata was made possible by the combination of production expertise, advanced technology, and the passion of the engineers involved. The design of the DHT is still unchanged to this day, yet, by any standards, it does not look old fashioned. It is still modern and in step with current fashion. I believe that the ageless appearance was made possible because of the design flexibility inherent in the SMC process, something that cannot be found in steel fabrication.

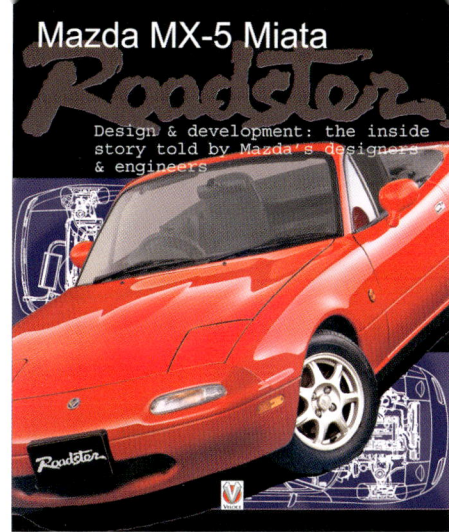

Mazda MX-5 Miata
Roadster
Design & development: the inside story told by Mazda's designers & engineers

13

Development of lightweight bumpers
by **Sumiaki Mizunaga**

Mizunaga joined Mazda after a spell with Honda. He is an excellent trumpet player and a foremost artist within the team. He understood the importance of a bumper system that greatly contributed towards achieving the "unity of horse and rider." In an event commemorating the birth of the roadster, there was said to be present a silent trumpeter in tears ...

T. Hirai

In the development of the MX-5/ Miata, a blow molded bumper beam was adopted for its lightness, contributing to the overall lightness of the LWS in order to produce the "unity between horse and rider" feel. This system absorbs the shock from a collision by deformation and bending of the bumper beam, which is completely different to a conventional shock absorbing system. The production system enabled the bumper beams to be 8kg (18lb) lighter than a conventional system, resulting in the lower yaw moment of inertia that helps to give the MX-5/Miata its fun-to-drive quality.

Blow molding
This is a method of forming a thermoplastic with an empty inner space. Nowadays, this technique is commonly used to form plastic drink bottles, large liquid containers, and even plastic boats.

A molten resin placed in an open metal die is inflated with air after the die is closed, forcing the resin against the inner surface of the die to reproduce the required shape. The wall thickness is controllable to produce products with differing specifications. This production method enabled us to make a closed hollow structure that was light and simple.

When I visited the Riverside Hotel as a member of the team after my assignment to design the bumper system, the PPM told me that he had high expectations for the roadster's bumpers and explained the reasons why. Upon hearing such passionate words, I felt a bit tense but, at the same time, felt my spirit rising up to meet the challenge.

Bumpers are located furthest from the car's center of gravity and directly affect the cornering ability of the vehicle. A short bat can be swung fast, but a long bamboo pole of the same weight cannot be swung as fast because its yaw moment of inertia is larger than that of the short bat. In an automobile, lightweight bumpers make a great contribution in achieving a responsive, quick handling car.

System selection
At the time of MX-5/Miata development, there were many types of bumper systems available to choose from. Using US collision

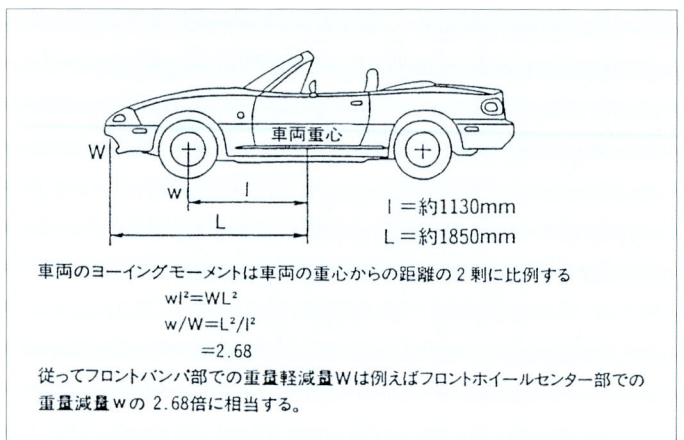

車両重心

W

w ← l →

← L →

l =約1130mm
L =約1850mm

車両のヨーイングモーメントは車両の重心からの距離の2剰に比例する

$$wl^2 = WL^2$$
$$w/W = L^2/l^2$$
$$= 2.68$$

従ってフロントバンパ部での重量軽減量Wは例えばフロントホイールセンター部での重量減量wの2.68倍に相当する。

The theory behind yaw moment of inertia.

エネルギ吸収体

バンパビーム
(ex.steel)

ブロー成形バンパビーム

バンパフェイシャー

スカート

バンパフェイシャー

スカート

Comparing standard bumper construction (left) with that of the MX-5/Miata.

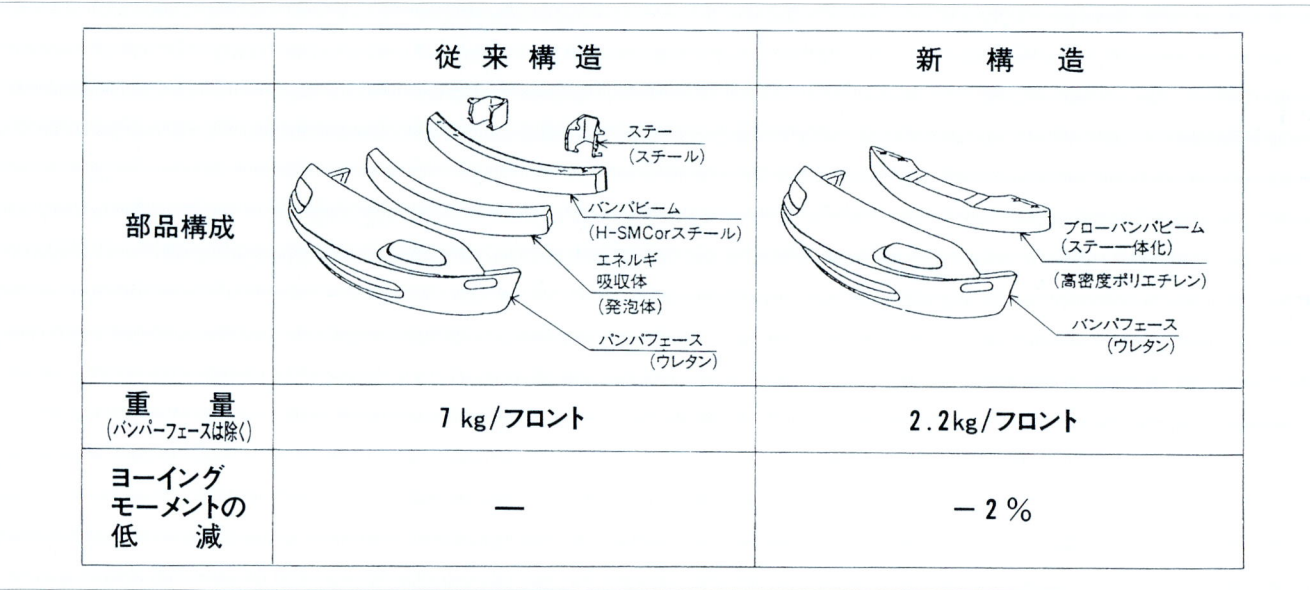

部品構成	従来構造	新構造
	ステー（スチール） バンパビーム（H-SMCorスチール） エネルギ吸収体（発泡体） バンパフェース（ウレタン）	ブローバンパビーム（ステー一体化） （高密度ポリエチレン） バンパフェース（ウレタン）
重量（バンパーフェースは除く）	7 kg/フロント	2.2kg/フロント
ヨーイングモーメントの低減	—	−2%

An illustration showing the weight saved by adopting new production techniques for the bumpers.

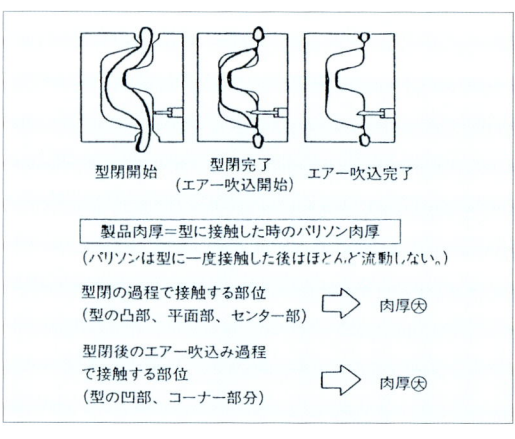

型閉開始

型閉完了（エアー吹込開始）

エアー吹込完了

製品肉厚＝型に接触した時のパリソン肉厚

（パリソンは型に一度接触した後はほとんど流動しない。）

型閉の過程で接触する部位（型の凸部、平面部、センター部）⇒ 肉厚大

型閉後のエアー吹込み過程で接触する部位（型の凹部、コーナー部分）⇒ 肉厚小

The problems of unequal thickness after blow-moulding caused many headaches that had to be cured before production could start.

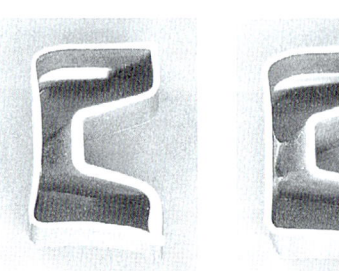

Bumper beams before and after the manufacturing technique was perfected.

146

Systems devised to control parison dimensions.

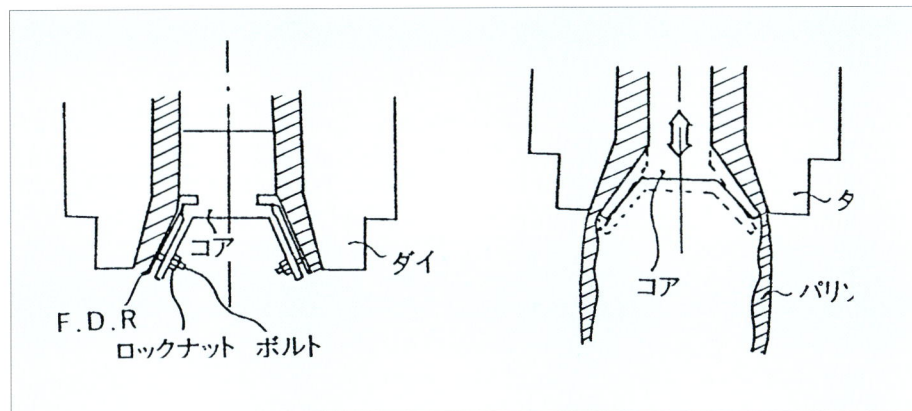

requirements as the basic starting point, I compared various systems, listing their individual merits and demerits. This research clearly indicated that blow molding was the only way to go. But since this was the first case of the processes' use for bumpers in the industry, there was naturally opposition to selecting such a system.

I found a test piece made several years back as an exterior component of a bumper that was later abandoned. I brought out the component from a warehouse and tested it with regard to the assumed weight of the new roadster. The results indicated that the system was promising, and this experiment gave me a lot of confidence in my later work.

Internal co-operation

In order to adopt a new system for the MX-5/Miata, I made a development plan and looked for supporting information from our past experience, explaining my choice to the various departments concerned with a comparison table. For the production department, this must have been a welcome move, for they had been making fuel tanks by this method, and the addition of bumper beam production would increase the utilization of their facility. In the development plan, I built in several decision points at which we could switch either to a conventional system of manufacture or start

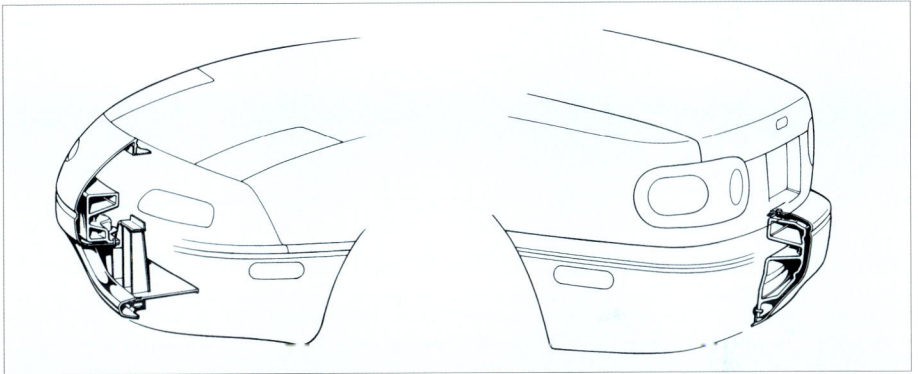

Cutaway drawing of the lightweight bumper system. The bumpers made a massive contribution towards achieving 'oneness between horse and rider' because of their lightness.

using stronger materials to overcome a potential problem. But I was determined not to go back to the conventional system with its inherent weight penalty, and vowed to make the blow molding method work.

Failure after failure

Work began with the design of a mechanical prototype vehicle to conduct advance testing of the bumper system. Its design drawings were completed with the help of production engineers, but this was the beginning of a big problem. After a prototype die was made, I heard numerous negative comments from the production engineers. They said that they couldn't make the form as they'd planned. When I visited their trial production shop, the place was filled with deformed bumper beams. Even though they were hollow plastic products, they resembled huge loaves of bread imperfectly baked and discarded on the floor. Production and test engineers voiced their discontent with the technology. "This can't possibly succeed." "We can't make products using this technology." "How do you expect us to test the mechanical prototype?" "We can't wait until we can start making *decent* bumpers!" These were only some of the comments, I was on a bed of nails!

While we were making these ugly, mishapen plastic objects, the day for making a final decision on production method was drawing closer ...

In order to make a prototype fit for testing, I had to remake the die, but that was not planned and there was no budget. However, just at that time there was a company-wide campaign for weight reduction in components. I went to the task leader of the campaign and asked for some of his budget to be made available for my work. I was successful in obtaining funds, and then went to the subcontractor with our team members to gather information on the technology. Since I took so many people to the subcontractor's facility, they must have thought that this was a critical mission, and provided us with masses of information. With the help of this intensive meeting with the subcontractor, we were able to gain more confidence in the technology and predict the outcome on a design drawing.

The revised die produced a beautiful prototype product. There were still some imperfections in thickness and dimensional tolerance, but we were much closer to reaching our target. My next job was to test the bumper under light collision conditions and this, too, was cleared without incident. We were ready for mass production.

Further improvements

For a large object such as a bumper beam, the parison (the resin material) is also large and stretches by its own weight: this is called "draw down." Also, during the blow molding process, the lower part of the parison tends to get thicker, while the upper part of the component had a thinner cross-section. A local thin spot and uneven thickness would:

Cause stress concentration on the thin spot and make the part unsuitable as a load carrying member.
Necessitate more resin to achieve the specified strength, and thereby make the part heavier.
Cause deformation of the product as it cools, causing low productivity.

To counter these thickness variationsand achive a more uniform section thickness: we implemented two types of parison control:

Circumferential parison control: This was to control the thickness of the parison as it was injected into the die.
Vertical parison control: At the time of withdrawing the parison, a metallic core was used to control the flow of parison so as to give the final product even thickness.

These two controls worked perfectly and resulted in products that were 0.6kg (1.3lb) lighter on average. The die cooling time to achieve dimensional accuracy was also reduced by 25%. In addition, a special die was made to form two bumper beams at once, thus raising productivity further. These improvements not only achieved the design objectives, but also helped enhance productivity in line with the increased production volume of the MX-5/Miata.

In 1990, I made a presentation at an SAE conference on blow molded bumper development. As I think back, this project gave birth to a great deal of new technology on the back of a very simple design principle – a light and compact body on a simple frame directly connected to bumper beams. Because of the light body requirement, the bumper beams had to be lighter, which resulted in improved technology. I was so very proud to hear from other LWS project members that my bumpers made a great contribution towards making the car handle so well.

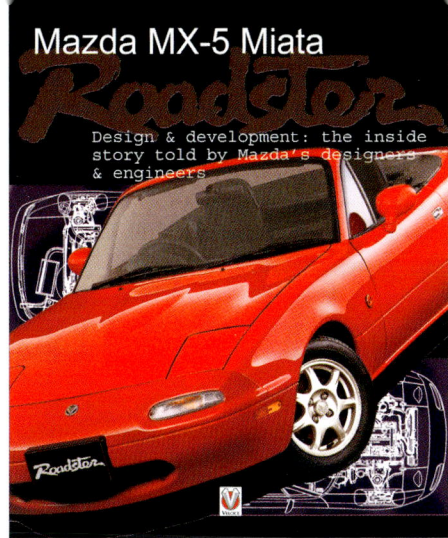

Mazda MX-5 Miata
Design & development: the inside story told by Mazda's designers & engineers

14

Testing & the M2 story
by **Hirotaka Tachibana**

Tachibana-san was born with Castrol R in his blood. His love of old sportscars (he adores Jaguars of the 1960s) is equalled only by his passion for racing vintage motorcycles. As a true enthusiast, he was an obvious choice to become involved with the M2 project.

B. Long

In new car development at Mazda, there has long been a saying that the Product Planning Division (PPD) makes the skeleton, the Engineering Design Division (EDD) makes the gut, and the Testing & Research Division (TRD) makes the vehicle's blood run.

The work of the PPD is to create a car concept that is in tune with the times, and to establish the basic design layout in order to allow the concept to materialize. The design layout includes exterior and interior dimensions, drivetrain, and the suspension system – in other words, the vital components necessary to achieve the performance and functions of the original concept. This is indeed the skeleton of an automobile. The EDD designs the chassis, body, interior and exterior to achieve the targeted performance and functions of the car. Engineering design work is closely related to cost and weight, balancing these elements against performance and function. Finally, the duty of the TRD is to make the car come alive. How to bring the car to life and keep its blood running is the subject of this chapter.

The TRD in Mazda

The TRD was subdivided into more than ten groups, including Chassis Testing, Vibration Testing, Aerodynamics Testing, Marketability Testing, Strength Testing, Safety Testing, Equipment Testing, Climate Testing, Reliability & Durability Testing, and a few others, with roughly 800 engineers involved.

In the TRD was an organization called TR Planning, where testing and research work on all of the Mazda cars was co-ordinated. This organization consisted of many veterans, and had the function of giving each Mazda vehicle its planned performance, making

them ready for the marketplace. This work was all about "making the blood run in a car."

Until I was transferred to M2, which I'll explain later, I worked in TR Planning for many years, and led testing and research efforts on the first generation FF 323 (later chosen as Japan Car of the Year), the 626, the RX-7 (also voted Car of the Year) and the MX-5/Miata.

The reason that customers regard Mazda as a maker of fun-to-drive cars, I believe, stems from the fact that each R&D division has a clear philosophy with regard to automobile building, and their product is then seasoned by a group of specialists in the TRD team.

Birth of the MX-5/Miata

During the 1980s, Mazda had a special, so-called 'off-line' project group. Its members were charged with proposing new car concepts for the future, away from the prevailing market environment and the then-current production range. While I was a member of TRD, I was also engaged in this project, and spent many enjoyable days with the young engineers to formulate concept cars of the future. This group was basically the predecessor of "M2 Corporation," which will be discussed later, and covered a broad spectrum of vehicles, including a 4WD buggy, a mini-sized sports car, and space utility model. However, an LWS was to become its major project.

At the same time, Bob Hall, a Product Planner at MRA (Mazda Research and Development of North America, earlier known as MANA), was working on a small lightweight sports car concept, and sent a proposal to us. His concept was based on an old rear-wheel drive 323 design, and to give it greater feasibility, he emphasized the utilization of existing components. As for myself, I was looking for an LWS, a sort of MGB-like sports car using current technology, and by a mere coincidence, Bob's proposal matched with mine.

There were only ten or so members in the off-line project, and the team worked on three types of LWS layout. The first one utilized the platform of the front-wheel drive 323 for an FF sports coupe. The second one was a closed body car having a midship location of the powertrain, again borrowed from the FF 323. The third one was an FR car, and Bob Hall, Tom Matano and I all agreed that this project had to be an open roadster.

Tom Matano was the chief designer at MRA, having worked for Opel, Holden and BMW – a designer of international renown. Tom took the lead in developing the FR design, while the FF and MR designs were tackled in Japan.

While we had the open-bodied FR model down as the favorite, the fact that this design would have to be an all-new vehicle made it the most expensive choice among the three, and it would also have the longest development time for the same reason.

Although the concept had these obvious disadvantages, in September 1984, Mazda approved the further development of the roadster concept. The degree of completeness of the FR concept was much higher than the other two, and when all three models were shown in a presentation room, that was the one that attracted the most attention. We were all convinced that this was the car to go for, and such strong conviction must have moved the management.

However, the marketing people had a very pessimistic view, predicting a global sales target of just 2000 cars per month, with domestic sales prospects of only 100 units per month ... Once the MX-5/Miata hit the market, the sales target was multiplied for many years, both in Japan and the oversea markets. By 2004, 15 years after its introduction, the total production figure reached 700,000 units!

Grease monkeys do the work

After the decision, in September of 1984, to create an open two-seater prototype model, a running

prototype was made by a British automobile consulting firm. The basic layout design was Mazda's original, but its detail design and fabrication was done by the British firm due to a lack of manpower within Mazda.

I had the chance to visit the firm in England many times during this period, and one day I asked the Chairman if I could test a few lightweight sports cars. He said that it could be easily arranged, and the next day I was shown a collection of nearly ten lightweight sports cars, including an MGB, Triumph Spitfire and Lotus Elan, all owned by his employees. After test-driving these cars, we talked about sports cars, and I learnt that he was an enthusiastic collector of MGs. He showed me his collection, and told me how much work he'd put into restoring the cars. While it's true that England was the birthplace of the LWS, it was still a touch strange to see employees and employer enjoying driving 1960s LWSs to work in the 1980s!

A year passed before the pre-prototype arrived. It was painted in BRG, and was a charming little car. The work of TRD really began from this day. We subjected the pre-prototype to a series of tests. The first job was to measure the body in detail to check if it was made to the design drawings, and then the car was turned over to the Vibration Testing Group and the Strength Testing Group to evaluate torsional strength and scuttle shake – critical factors in an open roadster.

The body was clamped to a table and its deflection measured with many instruments under various loading conditions. For a one-off prototype, these measurements showed reasonable values. With respect to scuttle shake, the car was put on a vibration table, and its body vibration measured while the suspension was moved up and down with varying load. The test car showed a number of vibrational problems that had to be resolved.

The test car was then taken to the Chassis Testing Group for measurement of suspension geometry, and to evaluate its on-road potential. The potential for maneuverability lies in a combination of many elements, including yaw moment of inertia, roll centre, suspension stiffness and so on, and it forms the basis of lively performance for the final product. The pre-prototype was created to test each of these elements, to arrange them in the desired combination, and to measure the resulting potential in sports car terms. All of the results found from the series of tests were fed back to the originators of the design drawings.

Since the start of an off-line project in 1982, it had taken three years for the concept to get provisional approval to move into a production program. In 1986, the P-729 code name was given, and the prototype design work formally started.

In the prototype factory, about 20 first-stage prototype cars were fabricated for testing purposes. Because of the keen interest among the engineers, which added a sort of silent energy, these test vehicles were completed in record time. Prototypes started running on the Miyoshi test course as well as various test benches, and there was a sudden surge of enthusiasm within the company.

The Global Road Circuit was completed within Miyoshi Proving Ground in 1985. This 2.1-mile (3.4km) special test course simulated typical road conditions from all over the world, faithfully recreating mountain roads from the Monte Carlo Rally, Belgian pave road, and American freeway from LA. P-729 prototypes completed many hundreds and thousands of laps at this circuit, and various other test courses within Miyoshi.

At the same time, one P-729 prototype was sent to Brussels, Belgium, with a truck-full of spare parts for European testing. Although it was normal to test a prototype with a reference car for comparison, there was no such car available. The lonely prototype, supported by a service vehicle loaded with spares, was tested on

人馬一体

the back streets of Europe for 2500 miles (4000km).

In Belgium, there was a special combination of roads about 13 miles (20km) in length that we used for evaluation. The test course consisted of freeway-type (motorway-type) roads and twisty stretches, enabling us to evaluate the suspension system of the prototype. One day, as we were changing suspension parts, we spotted a person in a car watching us through a telephoto lens. We hurried up the work and drove into the woods to get away from the spy. By driving hard on the mountain road we were finally able to shake off the camera man but, by that time, we were completely lost! For this type of road testing, we give the car dull paint and remove all emblems, but the cute little MX5/Miata seemed to attract people's eyes wherever we went.

Belgian highways are paved with a coarse grained surface to clear water quicker, but it causes annoying high frequency road noise. Yet in town, there are roads with smooth cobblestones from the Middle Ages that are very slippery. This combination of Belgian roads gave us a very hard time when it came to making a good tyre selection.

Although a great deal of testing was done in Europe, several prototypes were also sent to the US for test purposes, as this was to be the main market for the roadster. They were tested around Los Angeles on freeways and highways, on city streets with cracks, and on Mulholland Drive, where James Dean is said to have crashed his Porsche causing his untimely death. In LA, our favorite test course stretched for about ten miles, and consisted of a section of freeway and a tight winding road with various undulations. During these tests, we were able to prove that our little MX-5/Miata prototype had greater potential than many other sports cars of the time.

While it was normal for a sports car to travel a winding road quickly, our prototype showed no signs of tricky handling over bumpy and undulating roads. When a car goes over a bump at speed, all four suspension springs stretch to the limit and tyres become momentarily airborne; the next moment the springs become fully compressed and squeeze the bump stops, but there was no wandering in this situation and the car continued as if nothing had happened, straight as an arrow. This fantastic stability was achieved by the double-wishbone suspension system on all four wheels. A sports car with semi-trailing link suspension would have lost directional control after it landed hard after such a bump. This is because such systems cause a greater suspension geometry change compared to the double-wishbones used in the MX-5/Miata.

The purpose of overseas prototype testing is to fine-tune the design with respect to handling, braking, driving stability, road noise, ride quality, etc. Because of the time difference with Japan, we were able to test very efficiently, because we'd receive the analysis of our test results the next morning from head office.

Meanwhile, the TRD team in Hiroshima was slaving away on less attractive, but equally important test work. The Strength Testing Group had a prototype on a shaker table for vibration tests that would go on for 24 hours a day to see if any cracking occured in the body structure. The Reliability & Durability Testing Group would test the car, on a three-shift basis, 365 days, come rain or shine at a given driving mode, to verify the reliability and durability of the prototypes. The Safety Testing Group was in charge of crash testing the car to comply with the global safety requirements that were getting stricter with each passing year. While it was necessary to crash test many expensive prototypes, we tried to computer simulate to reduce the number of real tests in order to make a saving on the total cost of development. This effort still continues to this day. However, in the 1980s, when we did the development work on the roadster, much was still done by human hands rather than PCs.

"A sports car is still a sports car, even at 40kph"

I've loved motor vehicles since my childhood, and have owned more than 90 motorcycles and cars so far. About half of them were four-wheelers, including Nissan Fairlady SP, MGB, Porsche 911, Austin-Healey Sprite, Jaguar E-type and others, most of which were sports cars. Even so, I'd been wondering from the beginning of MX-5/Miata development, exactly what is a sports car? The answer did not come easily, but I concluded there is no way to determine a sports car by measurements or by specifications alone. It required the heart and sense of the person making the vehicle to give it a sports car character and, as such, there was no theory, and no way to imitate someone else's design.

It takes a long time to generate and nurture a sports car philosophy, and each designer/producer uses his/their own philosophy to create a distinctive world – the world of Ferrari, Aston Martin, and Renault-Alpine, for instance. The Austin-Healey Sprite was powered by a feeble 997cc engine, but it still managed to create a distinctive and delightful aura. Thus, a sports car cannot be classified as a high-performance car, or a stylish and sleek vehicle. A sports car is a sports car, even

when it is slowly cruising down a city street. With this in mind, we created a slogan: "A sports car is a sports car, even at 40kph."

Needless to say, the car must be controllable not only at 25mph (40kph), but all the way up to its maximum speed. This is not easy, however. In order to achieve direct and linear steering, stiffer springs, dampers and bushings are normally required, resulting in a harsh ride and high road noise. To avoid such negative affects, the basic potential of the roadster was made high to start with, including wheel print (wheelbase and track), the centre of gravity, and the roll center. Body rigidity, including the stiffness of the suspension attachment points, was also important to achieve linear handling and good ride quality. Based on a high potential body structure, our testing groups evaluated a great number of combinations of springs, dampers, stabilizers and bushings to find the best combination of driving and ride qualities for the roadster. Last, but not the least, was tyre development. A tyre with high grip would negatively affect gas mileage, and a fuel-efficient tyre would not only give insufficient grip, but also result in high road noise and poor performance in the wet. Careful improvements in every aspect of the car worked together to create the "unity of horse and rider" feel we wanted for the MX-5/Miata.

When we invited a few journalists to test drive the roadster at Miyoshi Proving Ground, they were fascinated by the linear handling of the car, much like that of a go-kart, and they soon were cornering it with its tail out: it became a sort of drift contest. After thoroughly enjoying the drive, they came back to me and asked me to show how well I could drive the car. Apparently, they wanted to see me go through a winding section of the test course drifting all of the four wheels. Since I had tested the car on the test course so many times, I was able to demonstrate going through the courses esses on full opposite lock: this ability meant that the roadster was exceptionally controllable.

The Renault-Alpine A110 of the 1960s was a great car. Its engine was only 1300cc, but the directness of its driving feel was so enjoyable that it was not only fun to drive at low speeds, but also controllable at its limit with the help of its B-pillar holding the driver's shoulder. The MX-5/Miata re-created the best qualities of the Renault and combined them with a better ride, more suited to the 1990s.

Another traditional element we could not omit was the small, and often cramped, entrance to a sports car. It is like a ritual that must be observed to enter into their world, just as we Japanese

The M2-1001 was the first M2 project, making its debut in December 1991.

enter a shrine after a few steps and then through a gate into a sacred world. Small doors on an open sports car are necessary in order to retain sufficient stiffness in the body, but they are also part of the unwritten law that has to be followed. There are other rules for the interior design: The leather seats of an open roadster must use real leather on the seat cushion and the seatback only, as the material on the seat backs must be of a waterproof material because, when folded, it will protect the seats from sudden rain or direct sunlight while the car is parked with the hood down. In addition to improving overall performance, these basic sports car requirements were developed over many years, and provide the driver with a special feel that is unique to a real sports car.

MX-5 has a pleasant rhythm

The most important element in creating that special sports car feel is the rhythm of the car that stems from its dynamic performance. Although a car may be designed by a computer and made by robots, it can become a splendid vehicle – or a bad one – through its tuning. All great sports cars have their own rhythm, and by proper tuning of the dynamic performance areas, a wonderful driving feel can be created.

The RX-7 and the MX-5/Miata have very distinct rhythms. The RX-7 extracts the full potential of the rotary engine, while the MX-5/Miata is built around a light reciprocating piston unit, giving the car a different character. However, the pick up of its engine, its steering response, shifting with the throttle wide open, the feel of the road – indeed, every aspect of the car – was finely tuned to give a pleasant rhythm for the driver.

Generally speaking, a Mercedes-Benz has a more tolerant and easy rhythm, while that of BMW is more up-tempo. Citroen has a broader embracing feel - the 2CV was so light, and the slow pace of its engine response was a perfect match with the character of the car.

Another element of a great car may be characterized by its apparel-like quality. For example, when you have a slight headache from drinking too much the night before, a change into light sportswear often makes you feel better. When you wear a high quality tweed jacket, your behavior will tend to reflect the garment. Furthermore, when you are in a tuxedo or a formal kimono, your

The classic steering wheel and instrument panel of the M2-1001.

spine will be straight and you behave formally. People become more active in a red shirt or a sweater. This is also applicable to a car.

I have often heard that once someone has driven an MX-5/Miata, they'll never forget the feeling. This does not come from the absolute performance of the car, but the result of its finely tuned dynamic rhythm and its apparel-like quality. Together, they create a refreshing, pleasant feeling, one that I think will allow the little Mazda roadster to go down in history as one of the all-time greats.

The M2 Corporation

The M2 Corporation was created to further polish the MX-5/Miata concept, and other cars in the Mazda line-up. M2 stood for second Mazda, and was described internally as the "Tokyo Software Development and Experimental Workshop." The company was formed in November 1990 to gather automobile infrastructure information for Mazda headquarters and, at the same time, increase the marque's presence in the eyes of the general public. In order to achieve this target, development engineers of the M2 Corporation were charged with planning, developing and selling specialized vehicles to fulfill the niche market demands of car enthusiasts.

M2 was located in Tokyo in a modern facility that was built at a cost of 5.5 billion yen. M2 lasted less than five years and its staff was only 30 strong, but within this period, no fewer than 30 cars were developed, and various proposals were made on behalf of Mazda through the many events and forums held at the M2 offices.

There were two types of proposals we were expected to make at M2. The first one was to think up and then provide the public with unique hardware, and to seek their reactions. As such, our projects became a communication tool between Mazda and enthusiasts. The second type was addressed directly to Mazda headquarters, and involved putting forward proposals for new models, as well as pointing out an emerging category of automobile concepts for the future. The latter function resulted in several unique proposals, including vehicles for physically handicapped people and a minibus for the youth market named the Panorama Tall Boy. These cars are now more common, but we were considering such projects more than ten years ago.

The specialty cars produced by M2 were simply given consecutive numbers, starting from 1001 and ending with 1030. Of these, seven models were based on or around the MX-5/Miata, three of were which being sold to the public. However, I would like to cover all seven of them here.

M2 1001

The first model, 1001, was also referred to as the "Clubman," and had extensive tuning in its engine and suspension systems. Its camshafts were changed to a high-lift type, the intake ports were polished, the pistons were changed to give a higher compression ratio, and the exhaust system employed a 4-2-1 configuration. The resultant power increase was only 10PS, but its torque output increased by 2kgm, and there was an improvement in fuel consumption along with more performance.

The suspension modifications included a change of springs, bump stops and bushes, along with tyres that were two sizes bigger. The oversize tyres (195/50-15) were jointly developed with Dunlop and named M2. In order to obtain a better balance of aerodynamic forces over the body, a front airdam and a ducktail rear spoiler were fitted.

M2-1001.

155

An aluminum roll bar was fitted to increase the stiffness of the body, while a large cooling duct was placed under the body to cool the engine oil and disc brakes so that the car would perform well on a circuit.

In order to make these modifications stand out, aluminum parts were used inside and outside the car. The speedometer and tachometer were fitted with chrome rings on a crystal painted aluminum panel. Other details included leather trimming on the door, and a sporty interior. The seats were replaced with a more tight-fitting design made exclusively for 1001, covered with a buckskin-like material for better grip and support.

Only one color was available – blue-black with a hint of red, which gave a purplish hue on vertical surfaces. The price for the car was twice the standard model at 3,400,000 yen, but because of the extensive modifications, its profit margin was very tight, especially as model approval limited production to only 300 units.

As soon as the 1001 was announced, enthusiasts rushed in to get the car and we had to resort to a raffle to choose the customers,

which was unthinkable at the beginning. Discounting the fact that Japan was at the height of its economic bubble (great prosperity) at the time this car was made available, there can be no doubt that the 1001 appealed to the hearts of many sports car drivers. and remains the most memorable car in my career as an automobile engineer.

M2 1002

The next model, 1002, was named "Vintage." The seats were covered with ivory leather, with the floormats and door trim in the same color. Aluminum parts from the 1001 design were fitted on a Navy-blue instrument panel (made from a buckskin-like material). The soft top was made with a beige-colored canvas instead of standard black to match the interior.

While its suspension set-up remained unchanged, larger tyres of 185/55-15 section were fitted on all four corners. Both 1001 and 1002 employed a manual steering rack, by the way.

The front valance was changed to give it a sharper look, and the contrast between the milky white interior and blue-black exterior finish was comparable with some

of the great historic cars of the world. In my opinion, the car exhibited the kind of beauty that was first witnessed in the Lancia Lambda of 1927, the Facel Vega of the 1960s, and nowadays in the Rolls-Royce. A total of 100 of these vehicles were sold to the public.

M2 1003

Model 1003 was a simplified and affordable version of the roadster named the "Junior." Similar to the Austin-Healey Sprite, it was put forward as a proposal to Mazda headquarters.

M2-1006.

The M2-1006 concept study model was powered by a V6 engine.

The M2-1028 was the final M2 project.

M2 1006

Model 1006 was a Mazda version of the Shelby Cobra, with a three-litre V6 engine fitted under the hood and a rear subframe transplanted from the RX-7 for added strength. The front tyres were 225/50-16s and the rear ones were 245/45-16, fitted under bulging fenders. The market reaction to this car was very good, but because there were too many modifications from the standard design, we finally gave up on any ideas of putting it into production.

M2 1007

Model 1007 was a stillborn four-door sport sedan to capture the post-MX-5/Miata market. We proposed a full-size layout and a one-fifth model to Mazda.

M2 1008

Model 1008 was a coupe with refined aerodynamics and a more rigid body design. I did the exterior design of this car with its truncated rear and a combination of crisp surfaces. Although more than ten years have passed since I did the design, I believe it should still fare well against more modern auto designs. We modified the chassis and engine for the car, and then built a running prototype for presentation.

M2 1028

The last model was numbered 1028 and called the "Clubman 2." It was a lightweight affordable model, slightly different to the 1001 but with some engine and suspension tuning added. We sold 300 of them in a limited production run.

The total number of cars sold by M2 amounts to only 800 units (700 were based on the MX-5/Miata, and 100 on the AZ-1), but even though ten years have passed, there still exists an active M2 Fan Club. The members of the club are not only M2 enthusiasts, but also very eager Mazda fans, and we produce special parts that are otherwise not available for them.

M2's activities were not limited to the creation of special cars, and its contribution to automobile culture, I believe, was significant because of the various social events and cultural forums held by the organization. Among them was a forum named the "Automobile Industry Horizontal Club" where engineers of competing automobile makers had a chance to see and communicate with each other on their mutual problems and the future of the industry. This sort of activity, proposed by M2, was accepted by the trade as a new approach to market development, and provided the stimulus for Toyota's creation of the Amlux showroom in later years.

The activities of M2 also gave sufficient stimulus to the Japanese Ministry of Transportation (as it was then) to relax vehicle regulations so that aftermarket parts could be fitted without special permits, and the subtitution of certain parts, such as tyres and mufflers, would be legally accepted.

However, perhaps the most important achievement of M2 was the internal development of the 30 staff members. I had the role of leading its technical activities, and had to leave the organization earlier than I would have liked, but the friendship and level of human communication that was created during the short time M2 existed was the greatest treasure, one that could not have been achieved otherwise.

M2-1028.

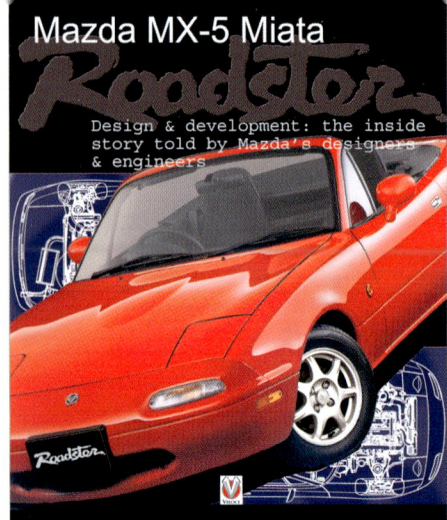

Mazda MX-5 Miata

Roadster

Design & development: the inside story told by Mazda's designers & engineers

Roadster

15

Production history
by **Brian Long**

Born and brought up in Coventry, Britain's motor city, Long has been surrounded by automobiles all his life. Coming from an engineering background, he has written more than 30 books, including a number on Japanese marques. In fact, he is regarded as a leading authority in this field, having covered various models from Mazda, Nissan, Toyota (and Lexus), Subaru, and Mitsubishi. His passion for recording motoring history, from a worldwide perspective, is equalled only by his love for mechanical watches and Nikon cameras. As a former MX-5 owner (he replaced it with an RX-7), he was the perfect person to write this chapter.

K. Kobayashi
(Publisher Japanese edition)

The Mazda Miata MX-5 was finally unveiled at the 1989 Chicago Auto Show in America, which opened on 10 February. However, this was still something of a preview, as sales did not begin until the summer of that year.

The American market was given the familiar 1.6 liter twin-cam engine, linked to a five-speed manual gearbox. Introduced at $13,800, one of the few concessions to modernity was the standard fitment of a driver's-side airbag.

A number of options were available for the Miata, including two packages: Package A, priced at $1145, included alloy wheels, power-assisted steering, a Panasonic stereo radio/cassette, and a leather-trimmed steering wheel, while the $1730 Package B included everything in Package A, plus electric windows, cruise control, and headrest speakers.

Air conditioning, a limited-slip differential, CD player, and floormats were available as options, and a number of dealer-installed accessories were also listed, such as a detachable hardtop, front and rear spoilers, side skirts, a tonneau cover, a front mask/bra (to protect the car's nose from stone chips), a luggage rack for the bootlid, and a selection of anti-theft devices.

Body colors included Classic Red, Crystal White, and Mariner Blue, although the hardtop was only available in red initially (the other two shades followed in the spring of 1990). Yellow and British Racing Green were expected to join the line-up in the near future, but it was a silver shade (Silver Stone Metallic) that arrived first, augmenting the range in March 1990, the month in which an automatic option was first offered.

Japan's first models
The Eunos Roadster was announced on 3 July 1989 (deposits started being taken two days later), although sales did not begin until 1 September 1989. The home market had a standard 1.6

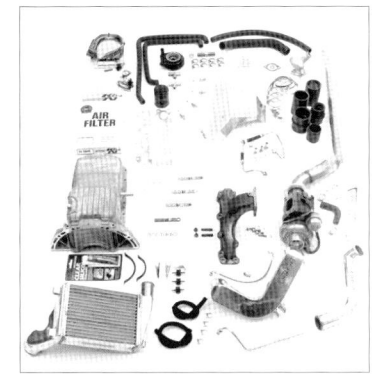

liter model, and a "Special Package" version.

The basic car (priced at just 1,748,000 Yen) was indeed basic - the epitome of the LWS concept. The Special Package model gained features like power steering, alloy wheels, electric windows and a Momo leather-trimmed steering wheel. This extra equipment added 150,000 Yen to the price of the base vehicle.

Major options included air conditioning, a detachable hardtop (in red or black for Japan, although the other shades would follow in due course), a CD player and a limited-slip differential. In addition, the familiar 5.5J x 14 seven-spoke alloy wheels were augmented by two 6J x 14 designs - a Mazdaspeed five-spoke alloy, and a 17-spoke version by SPA.

Minor items (such as polished treadplates, a front airdam skirt, rear mudflaps, projector lamps, an alloy gearshift gaiter retaining piece and handbrake handle, and door edge protection mouldings) were also available.

Other accessories mentioned at the time of the launch included a wood-rimmed Nardi steering wheel with matching gearknob and handbrake trim, a polished cam cover, chrome door mirrors, and an uprated suspension kit. There was also a range of Eunos clothing and luggage, and a TAG Heuer watch for the ultimate Roadster enthusiast.

As in America, a four-speed automatic transmission was added to the options list in March 1990. Linked to a slightly detuned engine (to bring in maximum torque at 4500rpm), it cost 40,000 Yen. From the outset, the car was available in Classic Red, Crystal White, Silver Stone Metallic or Mariner Blue in Japan.

The MX-5 in Europe

Introduced on the British market (by far the most important in Europe for Mazda's little sports car) at £14,249, the MX-5 was officially launched on 14 March 1990. It was powered by the usual 1.6 liter four (which produced 114bhp in UK trim), with drive being taken to the rear wheels through a five-speed manual gearbox.

Available in the same four colors as those listed for the home market (the interior was always finished in black on all early cars), standard features included PAS, alloy wheels, electric windows, a Momo leather-trimmed steering wheel, and a Clarion radio/cassette unit.

The official Mazda UK price list dated 5 September 1990 quoted £14,899 for the basic car (the turbocharged RX-7 coupe was £22,599 at this time). Metallic paint added £175, while air conditioning (a rarely taken option in Britain) put an extra £1259 onto the bill. A hardtop had just been

announced as well, produced in conjunction with TWR, and this cost £1145; it was available in red, blue or white, to match bodywork, or with a black grained finish.

By far the most common complaint heard in Britain related to the MX-5's relatively low power. Mazda was quick to respond: "Mazda Cars (UK) Ltd, in conjunction with Brodie Brittain Racing, are proud to present the Mazda MX-5 BBR Turbo - a superbly-designed sports package that retains the handling characteristics of the standard car."

Introduced in November 1990 and priced at £2700, the BBR conversion contained more than 140 separate components, including a Garrett T25 turbocharger, a new engine management system, and a new exhaust system. Surprisingly, the 9.4:1 compression ratio was retained, but this meant an increase in power (to 150bhp at 6500rpm), as well as enhanced torque output (up to 154lbft at 5500rpm). As a result, the 0-60mph time was cut to just 6.8 seconds, while the top speed went up to 130mph (208kph). Incidentally, to complete the package, BBR also offered an optional set of OZ alloy wheels shod with Dunlop tires, an uprated suspension kit, and a limited-slip differential.

The V Special

At the 1989 Tokyo Show, a car with a tan leather interior and BRG (British Racing Green) paintwork was exhibited to gauge public reaction. In July 1990, it joined the home market line-up as the "V Special," introduced to celebrate the first anniversary of the Eunos Roadster.

Based on the Special Package model, it had Neo Green coachwork, a tan interior (including the leather-trimmed seats) with matching soft top cover. This was complemented by a classic, wood-rimmed Nardi steering wheel, a wooden gearknob and wood handbrake trim. A CD player was included as standard, as were polished treadplates featuring the "Roadster" logo. It was available with either manual or automatic transmission, priced at 2,122,000 and 2,162,000 Yen, respectively.

The M2 project

The M2 project brought together a group of engineers and planners to develop MX-5 and other specials. The brainchild of Hirotaka Tachibana, the M2 project was established in Tokyo's Setagaya in November 1990. The main objective of this new concern was to act as a bridge between Mazda and the end-user, as well as building prototypes for test marketing. The first car - Tachibana's favorite - was the M2-1001, which was announced to the public in 1991.

Several MX-5 based specials followed before the M2 operation was closed down in April 1995.

American update

During 1990, the Miata was named *Automobile* magazine's "Automobile of the Year," and also claimed the title of "most trouble-free" sports car in the JD Power Survey. *Road & Track* named it one of the "Ten Best Cars in the World," and the best Sports/GT in its price bracket.

For the 1991 season, the Miata was now available with ABS braking as a $900 option. Other than the new ABS system, mechanical specifications and options stayed pretty much the same as those from 1990.

However, March 1991 saw the launch of the high spec Special Edition. Basically - apart from a few subtle differences (such as the steering wheel) - it was the American equivalent of the home market's V Special. Ironically, the dark green shade was known in the States as British Racing Green, but the Special Edition was undoubtedly an attractive package with its tan interior and soft top cover, leather-trimmed seats, CD player, polished treadplates, electric windows, a personalized brass plaque and real wood detailing (including a Nardi gearknob) all coming as standard; a matching hardtop was available for $1400. Listed at $19,249, all

4000 built were sold within just three months.

The UK scene

What Car? magazine voted the MX-5 "Sports Car of the Year 1991," and on 14 March 1991, Mazda UK announced the £18,249 MX-5 "Limited Edition" to celebrate the first anniversary of the car in Britain. Another variation on the V Special theme, a total of 250 were built. The BRG paintwork was set off by contrasting tan leather seats and a tan interior. It featured a wood-rimmed steering wheel, wooden gearknob and handbrake trim, unique 6.5J x 15 alloy wheels, central locking, a four-speaker radio/cassette, polished treadplates, a clock, leather-trimmed overmats, a special leather owners' wallet and keyfob, a certificate of authenticity and an engraved brass plaque mounted on the dashboard.

Following the marque's victory at Le Mans, Mazda UK launched another limited edition to commemorate the event. The MX-5 "Le Mans" was equipped with the BBR Turbo conversion, spoilers and side skirts, and an outrageous paint scheme that followed that of the winning Mazda 787B. Only 24 were produced, priced at £20,499 apiece.

A minor change

In July 1991, a minor change was announced. It was found that a

The MX-5 Le Mans, built to commemorate Mazda's victory at Le Mans in 1991. Only 24 were made available.

"performance bar" - basically a brace that connected the lower control arm pivot points on both sides - would stiffen the car and strengthen the rear suspension. Naturally, export models produced after this date received the same modification.

Sales of the revised cars began in August. The basic Eunos Roadster (now available in manual guise only) was still listed but never particularly popular. With prices starting at 1,885,000 Yen for the manual car (an automatic gearbox added 40,000 Yen), the Special Package found a great deal more favor.

The V Special continued, albeit at a slightly higher price. Neo Green paintwork was still a feature, but the V Special could now also be bought in Brilliant Black, thus becoming the first roadster on the home market to be offered with black coachwork. Polished kickplates around the door speakers were now a standard fitment on this top-of-the-range model.

At the same time, Japan's first limited edition example was announced: the 1.6 liter "J Limited," finished in a color known as "Sunburst Yellow." Based on the Special Package, features included the same Nardi steering wheel as that used on the V Special, a Nardi gearknob (on manual cars), wood trim on the handbrake, and stainless treadplates. A hardtop finished in the same color as the body was listed as an option. Only 800 were ever built, and all were sold on the first day!

For the 1992 Model Year, side-impact bars were added to the specification, and a remote bootlid release was placed alongside the fuel filler lever.

The USA's 1992 season

Changes for the 1992 Model Year had been announced in October 1991. Of course, the suspension modifications brought about in Japan during the summer of 1991 were inherited by the American cars, but more specifically for 1992, a remote bootlid release was fitted across the Miata range, and the Package B option now included an electric aerial; the optional hardtop at last came with a heated rear screen.

In March 1992, the Silver Stone Metallic body color was discontinued and two new hues joined the line-up: Sunburst Yellow and Brilliant Black. The Sunburst Yellow shade was only available with the Package A upgrade, although air conditioning, automatic transmission, a limited slip differential and a hardtop could be bought as options. Like the J Limited in Japan, which was finished in the same bright color, production was restricted, and just 1500 cars were allocated for the States.

The Brilliant Black model was not a limited edition, but had a higher specification than that of the run-of-the-mill Miata. Tan leather trim came as standard, and the soft top was finished in the same color to give a classy contrast with the coachwork. It came with alloy wheels, power steering, a radio/cassette unit, and electric windows included in the $17,050 price. For a further $1400, the black car could be specified with the newly-introduced Package C, including BBS alloy wheels, a Nardi wooden gearknob, wooden handbrake trim, stainless treadplates, cruise control, an electric aerial, and headrest speakers.

On the racing front, although rarely seen in IMSA events, the Miata could often be found competing at SCCA meetings. Indeed, the Miata took SCCA Showroom Stock C honors for the first time in 1992, a category ideally suited to the little Mazda, with Randy Pobst taking the victor's laurels.

The UK in 1992

Features for the 1992 season included a remote bootlid release, front number plate holders, and a new radio/cassette unit. Standard colors included shades of red, white, blue and silver.

Following the success of the previous Limited Edition model, in April, Mazda UK decided to offer

In America, the MX-5/Miata was very successful in SCCA racing. The car was ideally suited to grassroots motorsport.

the £17,788 MX-5 "Special Equipment." The Mazda MX-5 SE model was the first cosmetic upgrade to be offered in unlimited numbers in the British Isles, and featured Brilliant Black paintwork, tan leather seats and interior trim, a wood-rimmed steering wheel, wooden gearknob and handbrake handle, ABS braking, ten-spoke 7J x 15 polished alloys with locking wheelnuts, special 'SE' badging, chrome treadplates, an electric aerial, and an analogue clock.

Interestingly, the SE was one of the first UK models to be built in the Hofu plant (Yamaguchi Prefecture), although production would return to Hiroshima (where MX-5s had been built from day one) by the end of the year, as demand for the open car subsided. Incidentally, the 250,000th MX-5 (built at Hiroshima on 9 November 1992) went to Australia, and is now an exhibit at the Australian National Motor Museum.

Japanese Specials
Mazda celebrated the third anniversary of the Eunos Roadster with the announcement of the "S Special." Production began in August 1992 to take advantage of a scheduled minor change - side impact bars, and the option of an airbag (fitted in what for Japan was a unique four-spoke steering wheel, but was basically the same as the one found in the States) - and sales started in September.

The S Special was a distinctly sporty version of the Eunos Roadster. Available in Classic Red or Brilliant Black, it came with manual transmission only and was priced at 2,030,000 Yen. It featured an uprated suspension with Bilstein shock absorbers, a front strut brace, 6J x 14 BBS alloy wheels fitted with 185/60 tires, a Nardi three-spoke leather-trimmed steering wheel, Nardi leather gearknob, stainless treadplates and speaker grilles, and a rear spoiler. The only luxury item was the optional Mazda Sensory Sound System, priced at 220,000 Yen.

In December 1992, Mazda announced the S Limited - a run of 1000 cars based on the S Special. Finished in Brilliant Black, the model came with a red leather interior, attractive gold-coloured BBS alloys, and the aforementioned Sensory Sound System.

America's 1993 MY
For the 1993 model year, the car's suspension was refined, but the thing most people noticed was the new badge on the nose (leading to the deletion of the 'Mazda' decal on the front bumper) and the center caps on the optional alloy wheels. In addition, the steering wheel boss now had 'SRS Airbag' in place of the 'Mazda' script.

An AM/FM stereo radio/cassette with integral digital clock

became standard, having previously been part of the Package A option, and Brilliant Black was added as a standard color; the base Miata was now priced at $15,300.

The option packages were rearranged for the 1993 Model Year and included the following items: Option Package A ($1300) added power-assisted steering, a leather-wrapped steering wheel, electrically-adjustable mirrors, alloy wheels and headrest speakers to the basic model. Package B ($2000) included everything in Package A, plus cruise control, electric windows, and an automatic electric aerial. The new Package C ($2700) had all the items in Package B, plus a tan-colored interior with leather seat facings, and a tan vinyl top. This was available on all paintwork options with the exception of cars finished in Mariner Blue, which could be supplied with the standard black trim only.

Mazda's Sensory Sound System (MSSS) could be bought as a separate option, as could ABS braking, automatic transmission, a limited-slip differential (for manual cars), a hardtop, and air conditioning.

Midway through the year, the 1500-off Miata "Limited Edition" made its entrance. The American cousin of the S Limited, it was finished in Brilliant Black with a red leather interior (a red vinyl

tonneau cover was also part of the package), and came with the usual luxury touches. Power-assisted steering, ABS, a limited-slip differential, 14-inch BBS alloy wheels fitted with 185/60 tires, an uprated suspension with Bilstein shock absorbers, and front and rear spoilers were also included in the $22,000 sticker price.

Incidentally, the Miata was the SCCA Showroom Stock C class winner once again, this time courtesy of Michael Galati.

Another 'SE' for Britain
On 5 May 1993, Mazda UK announced the second MX-5 SE. This latest SE was basically the same as the original, although the 15-inch alloys were different, and the stereo unit was also changed. As the press release noted: "The Mazda MX-5 SE, priced at £18,686, is offered in black and comes with contrasting tan leather interior with extensive use of wooden mahogany trim. The specification list is impressive and includes an anti-lock braking system, electrical aerial, and seven-spoke chrome-plated alloy wheels."

By July, a number of changes had started to filter through for the next season. An electric aerial was declared standard, as was a Clarion radio/cassette unit, while on the safety front, the MX-5 now came with side-impact door protection beams. In addition, the new corporate chrome badge appeared on the nose, replacing the old 'Mazda' decal applied to front bumper.

The Australian market
Sales began in Australia in October 1989. Just one model was listed, but in an attempt to try and make the convertible more tempting, Mazda launched the $39,990 MX-5 "Classic." Finished in red with a tan leather interior, the package included BBS alloys, a CD player, a Nardi gearknob with matching handbrake trim, and even a signed picture of Toshihiko Hirai (he left the company shortly after to become a university lecturer).

Limited to 100 units (this was Australia's fourth limited edition, incidentally - the first was a Neo Green model launched at the end of 1990 and restricted to 300 examples; there were 55 produced in Malibu Gold during 1992, and another 300 in Neo Green later that year), it sold out almost immediately, despite competition from the vastly improved Ford Capri, which was built in Australia and was some $11,000 cheaper.

A new Series
In February 1993, the V Special adopted the Sensory Sound System as standard but, more importantly, in July, Mazda announced the first major facelift of the MX-5. With Hirai declaring his wish to leave the company, Shiro Yoshioka was put in charge of the project.

Complying with forthcoming regulation changes meant a sizeable gain in weight for the car. Mazda concluded the only way to keep the vehicle's performance at its current level was to increase the engine capacity. There were initially thoughts of retaining the 1.6 liter four and introducing a new two-liter unit to augment it. But instead, the 1.8 liter BP-type engine from the Familia GT was chosen, largely because it was a good compromise: some of the Roadster's edge on economy would have been lost with a two-liter lump (and it would have meant higher insurance, too), while the 1.6 would have struggled to remain sporty with the heavier body, especially when combined with an automatic transmission. Modified to give 130bhp at 6500rpm, the 1839cc unit was given the BP-ZE designation.

The body was strengthened for the arrival of the new engine, with "performance rods" added up front and in a U-shaped configuration at the back to enhance torsional rigidity. In addition, a cockpit brace bar was introduced, joining the seatbelt anchor towers to further enhance the rigidity of the shell.

The suspension settings were revised to suit, and the diameter of the brake discs was increased. A Torsen lsd came with the five-speed cars, and the optional alloy wheels were completely restyled.

人馬一体

Interestingly, despite the rim width increasing to 6J (from 5.5J), each wheel was around 1kg (2.2lb) lighter than the original design.

Although the manual gearbox ratios were untouched, the final-drive ratio was changed from 4.3:1 to 4.1:1. The optional four-speed automatic transmission was now an electronically-controlled unit with slightly different ratios, but the final-drive was actually the same as the manual cars at 4.1:1 (instead of 4.444:1, as used on the 1.6 liter automatics), signifying another important change.

The 1.6 liter cars had carried the NA6CE chassis designation, whereas the new 1.8 liter models were given the NA8C code. A useful identifying feature at the rear of the car was the "Roadster" badge, the script now being red instead of the original black. Other distinguishing features included a different number plate holder, standard rear mudflaps, and the addition of large elasticated door pockets. On the base models, Classic Red, Silver Stone Metallic and Chaste White became the extent of the standard color range, signifying the end of Crystal White and Mariner Blue.

Announced in July, sales of the 1.8 range started in September. At 1,791,000 Yen, the manual-only 1.8 liter Series I standard model served as an entry-level Eunos Roadster, but the Special Package version (available with either manual or automatic transmission) again made up the bulk of sales. Weighing in at 990kg in manual form (10kg more than the basic car), it was priced at 1,966,000 Yen, while the automatic gearbox added 30kg and 50,000 Yen.

The V Special was continued, but there was now also the "V Special Type II." The extra 100,000 Yen needed to secure one added a highly-polished finish to the seven-spoke alloy wheels, chrome door mirrors, and a tan-colored soft-top.

The line-up was completed by the manual-only S Special. Based on the Special Package model, it came in either Laguna Blue Metallic or Brilliant Black, and featured an array of tempting items: an uprated suspension with Bilstein shocks and thicker anti-roll bars, a front tower brace, rear body brace, 14-inch BBS alloy wheels, polished treadplates and kickplates (which surrounded the door speakers), and a Nardi steering wheel.

A few months later, in November, Mazda released a limited edition of just 40 cars finished in Brilliant Black with a tan hood. Known as the "Tokyo Limited," this model employed a number of interior parts from the M2-1002 run. The cream leather trim was beautiful, and the added detailing fully justified the 2,458,000 Yen price tag - even the automatic version (at 2,508,000 Yen) seemed cheap compared with the 3,000,000 asked for the M2-1002.

In December, another limited edition Eunos Roadster was announced - the "J Limited II." Based on the Special Package model, the J Limited II was finished in Sunburst Yellow, just like the original J Limited. However, the windscreen surround was finished in black on this occasion. Bucket seats with independent headrests were used, a CD player was a standard fitment, and Pirelli tires were mounted on the familiar 6J x 14 seven-spoke alloys. Limited to 800 examples, prices started at 2,030,000 Yen for the five-speed version, with automatic transmission adding 50,000 Yen.

British update
Although the SE continued to be listed at £18,686 (its original launch price), by now the cost of a standard 1.6i model had risen to a hefty £16,490. However, on 18 April 1994, Mazda UK announced two new models to supercede them - the 130bhp MX-5 "1.8i" and "1.8iS."

As well as having more power and torque, the new models also benefitted from an uprated suspension and a stiffer body (through the use of the addition bracing described earlier) to give a better ride and improve handling. Inside, the old high-backed seats

'95 is going to be a great year for Merlot.

America had a special model based on the M Edition each year from 1994. This is the 1995 version, finished in Merlot Mica.

were replaced with a new type (like those found on the J Limited II) incorporating an adjustable headrest. At the same time, door pockets replaced the armrests.

The top 1.8iS model had all the previous 1.6i features, but added ABS, a driver's-side airbag, new seven-spoke alloy wheels, a rheostat for the panel lights, electric mirrors, an electric aerial, and a detachable radio/cassette unit. It was priced at £17,395.

The 1.8i was the basic model. Some £2900 cheaper than its 1.8 liter stablemate, it came with 5.5J x 14 steel wheels, a urethane steering wheel, and a generally lower level of equipment. The base model was sold without PAS and ABS, an airbag, electric windows, internal bootlid release, and the radio/cassette unit. However, both models were fitted with an immobilizer as standard.

Going on sale from 2 May, Laguna Blue Metallic and Chaste White replaced the Mariner Blue and Crystal White shades, whilst British Racing Green and Brilliant Black became available as standard color options. Classic Red and Silver Stone Metallic made up the six-color range.

On the other side of the world, Australian sales were helped by the introduction of two new models - the "1.8" and the "Clubman."

All change in America

Of course, the biggest change for the 1994 Model Year (announced in October 1993), was the adoption of the 1.8 liter engine. In US guise, the power output was listed at 128bhp at 6500rpm (a gain of 12bhp), with maximum torque being quoted at 110lbft. Not only was this an increase of 10lbft, it was also more useable, coming in 500rpm lower down the rev range than before.

The American market naturally gained all the body modifications associated with the 1.8 liter machine (namely performance rods front and rear, and a vinyl-covered brace bar connecting the seatbelt anchor towers), as well as the Torsen lsd and restyled alloys (both in the Package A option), uprated suspension and larger brakes, all introduced with the bigger-engined Eunos Roadster in

Japan. In addition, for the US, dual airbags were made a standard fitment.

Mariner Blue was replaced with the new Laguna Blue Metallic shade, and the "Miata" script on the rear badge was now in red instead of black. At the start of the 1994 Model Year, the Miata's base price was just $16,450 but, in reality, few cars were sold without one of the option packages.

At the Chicago Auto Show, two new special Miatas were announced - the "M Edition" and the "R Package." The M Edition was a luxury model finished in Montego Blue Mica, with a tan leather interior and tan hood. Features included highly-polished seven-spoke alloys, a wooden gearknob and handbrake handle, electric windows and mirrors, central locking, and a special keyfob. It cost $21,675 - $4250 more than the base model at that time.

The R Package option was available on the basic car, priced at $1500. Stiffer springs, bushings, and Bilstein shock absorbers gave the Miata R notably sharper handling, but with a choppier ride. With its alloy wheels, Torsen lsd and front and rear spoilers, the R was a pure sports car. Items such as power-assisted steering and ABS were not available - in fact, a body stripe and air conditioning were the only options.

US sales for 1994 were almost the same as they had been in

1993, while in competition, the Miata duly took the SCCA Showroom Stock C title for the third year in a row (Michael Galati lifting the trophy); Terry McCarthy claimed the E-Production crown. Incidentally, the new 1.8 liter cars were placed in the Showroom Stock D category.

For the 1995 Model Year, it was decided to combine Package A and B to create a new option known as the "Popular Equipment Package;" Package C became known as the "Leather Package," although the R Package (still for manual Miatas only) remained unchanged. The optional ABS braking system was now lighter than before, and Montego Blue Mica could be specified on all cars in the range unless they were fitted with the R Package.

Midway through 1995, Mazda introduced another special, the Miata "M Edition." Finished in a striking Merlot Mica, it was priced at $23,530. For that, the buyer got leather trim, 15-inch BBS alloys fitted with 195/55 tires, ABS brakes, a limited-slip differential, Nardi wooden gearknob and handbrake trim, polished treadplates, M Edition floormats, a CD player, and unique badging. A nice touch was the M Edition keyfob and lapel pin.

More Limited Editions
Mazda announced the 500-off "RS Limited" in July 1994. With sales

starting in September, the 2,215,000 Yen car was based on the S Special and finished in Montego Blue Mica. Interesting features included a lightened flywheel, a 4.3:1 final-drive ratio, Bridgestone tires mounted on BBS 6J x 15 alloys, Recaro bucket seats, RS decals on the front wings, and a Nardi leather-trimmed three-spoke steering wheel.

Sales of the M Package-based "G Limited" began in January 1995. Priced at just under 1,900,000 Yen in manual guise (automatic transmission was available on this model), only 1500 were produced, all finished in Satellite Blue Mica with a dark blue hood. Low-back bucket seats (like those used in the J Limited II) were employed, along with a new-style Momo leather-covered steering wheel, seven-spoke alloy wheels, and an uprated sound system.

In the following month, the "R Limited" was introduced at 2,175,000 Yen. Based on the S Special, the R Limited came in Satellite Blue Mica or Chaste White with a red leather interior. Like the RS Limited, it featured a lightened flywheel, 4.3:1 final-drive, BBS alloys and Potenza tires, but this time had a wooden three-spoke Nardi steering wheel and gearknob, as well as wood trim on the handbrake lever.

By this time, Brilliant Black

had joined the basic color line-up; it became available from January 1995. In addition, the S Special could be bought in Chaste White, thus giving three color choices on that model instead of the former two.

The UK's 1995 season
On 14 March, the 'California' Limited Edition was launched to celebrate the MX-5's fifth anniversary. Based on the 1.8i model, all cars had Sunburst Yellow paintwork, power steering, 7J x 15 five-spoke alloy wheels, and a radio/cassette unit. Only 300 of the £15,795 cars were made, all carrying a numbered plaque on the fascia and "California" badging.

On 12 April 1995, the "1.6i" was re-introduced as the entry level model to complement the £14,495 1.8i and £17,395 1.8iS. The detuned 1598cc B6 engine produced just 88bhp but, being priced at just £12,995, few complained.

Naturally, the specification was pretty basic - 5.5J x 14 steel wheels, no power steering, manual windows, no radio/cassette, and the suspension modifications and body-bracing found on the 1.8 litre models was omitted. In addition, the brake discs were reduced in diameter (the 1.6i's discs were in effect brought back down to the original dimensions), and it was initially finished in just three

The MX-5 Gleneagles relates to the world-famous golf course in Scotland.

colors - Classic Red, Brilliant Black and Chaste White. Oddly, despite a great deal of press coverage, it was not available until November, by which time it cost £500 more.

Meanwhile, in mid-1995, the 1.8iS received a restyled steering wheel (complete with airbag), and at the 1995 Earls Court Motor Show, Mazda UK launched the 1.8 litre 'Gleneagles.' Based on the 1.8i, the Gleneagles was finished in Montego Blue and, although the soft top was black, it came with a champagne-colored soft top cover to match the interior. Priced at £16,465, it had power-assisted steering, leather seats, attractive 15-inch five-spoke alloys, a Momo leather-trimmed steering wheel (with the Gleneagles emblem on the boss), a wood effect console, a CD player, Gleneagles tartan trim on the gearlever gaiter, and special "Gleneagles" badging.

By the end of the year, the changes for 1996 were already filtering through. Armrests came back in preference to the unpopular door pockets, instruments lost their chrome ring surrounds, and the 1.8iS radio/cassette unit was changed. Laguna Blue was deleted from the color charts, leaving Classic Red, British Racing Green, Silver Stone Metallic, Brilliant Black and Chaste White, although the BRG and silver shades were still not available on the 1.6i model.

Another minor change in Japan

August 1995 saw the introduction of the 133bhp Series II 1.8 litre engine. Although the BP-ZE (RS) designation was retained, the Series II version featured a 16-bit ECU and a lightweight flywheel to enable the engine to rev more freely. The 4.3:1 final-drive ratio was brought back on five-speed cars, although automatic models stayed at 4.1:1.

An airbag was now standard on all Roadsters, the original low-mounted interior lights were replaced by a single unit by the rearview mirror, the chrome dial surrounds were deleted, the sunvisors became a simple one-piece affair, door pockets were reduced in size (and not fitted at all on the basic car or those with polished speaker surround plates), trim materials were changed, and the color of the "Roadster" script found on the rear panel was changed from red to green.

The standard model remained in manual guise only, becoming even more basic (even the soft top cover was optional), but it was available in the full range of colors: Classic Red, Chaste White, Silver Stone Metallic, Brilliant Black and Neo Green.

The Special Package model remained the most popular, with prices starting at 1,930,000 Yen for the manual version or 1,980,000 Yen for the automatic. The Special Package came with alloys, power steering, a Torsen lsd (manual cars), a new stereo radio/cassette unit, electrically-adjustable door mirrors, electric windows, and a new leather-trimmed three-spoke steering wheel, complete with airbag.

In between the base model and the Special Package, there was now a 1,790,000 Yen M Package. At 100,000 Yen more than the basic Roadster, it had steel wheels and the basic three-spoke steering wheel, but featured power-assisted steering, electric windows and a decent stereo system.

The V Special grade was retained, as was the V Special Type II with its unique features. Color options were restricted to

The 1997 M Edition. Sales were still strong in the USA, despite the car having been on the market for almost a decade.

just Brilliant Black, Neo Green and Chaste White on these models, and they came with a new three-spoke wood-rimmed steering wheel from the Nardi concern.

The manual-only S Special was also continued, but there was now an S Special Type II at 190,000 Yen more. The extra money bought Potenza tires mounted on 15-inch BBS alloys (the run-of-the-mill Type I had the usual 14-inch seven-spoke rims). The S Special was available in either Montego Blue Mica, Brilliant Black, Chaste White or Classic Red.

At the end of the year, Mazda announced the VR Limited Combination A and Combination B models; sales of these interesting variations - both based on the S Special Type I - started in January of 1996. The Combination A (limited to 700 cars) was finished in wine red with a tan-colored soft-top and matching leather-trimmed interior; an aluminum alloy gearknob, shift plate and handbrake lever were used for the first time. The Combination B was the same price, but limited to 800 examples, and came in a shade known as Excellent Green Mica. This model had a dark green soft-top, a black leather interior, and the same aluminum alloy gearknob, shift plate and handbrake. Although based on the Type I, both cars had five-spoke 6J x 15 alloys instead of the familiar seven-spoke items.

America's 1996 MY

The 1996 Model Year line-up was announced in October 1995. Engine power increased to 133bhp, but the main changes centred on meeting new regulations - namely, the 1997 Federal side-impact requirements and OBD-II emissions. Other, more minor changes, included the relocation of the interior lights and the addition of a small light in the boot.

While the base model came in at $18,750, the three option packages from 1995 were made available again (the $2090 Popular Equipment Package, the $2985 Leather Package and the $1500 R Package), but there was now also a "Power Steering Package" that added just PAS and wheel trim rings to the basic car; it was priced at a very reasonable $300.

As for individual options, air conditioning was listed at $900, as were ABS brakes, the hardtop was $1500, and an automatic gearbox cost $850. The $875 MSSS was now augmented by the Mazda Premium Sound System which, at $675, boasted a CD player and uprated speakers. Floormats rounded off the options list, priced at $80.

Only four colors were listed as standard: Classic Red, Brilliant Black, White and Montego Blue Mica. These colors were available across the range, with the exception of the blue shade, which couldn't be specified with the R Package.

Midway through 1996, the $24,760 "M Edition" appeared in Starlight Mica. Trimmed in tan leather with a matching tan-colored soft top and soft top cover, the package included such niceties as 15-inch five-spoke alloys, an lsd, ABS brakes, air conditioning, a top stereo unit with CD player, headrest speakers and an electric aerial, cruise control, a Nardi wooden gearknob and handbrake handle, a leather-trimmed steering wheel, power windows and mirrors, a remote keyless entry system, and an alarm. The only options were automatic transmission and a hardtop.

The B2 & R2

At the end of 1996, all home market models adopted a new Momo four-spoke steering wheel (with airbag), and two more limited edition Eunos Roadsters came along: the 1,898,000 Yen "B2 Limited" (or 1,993,000 with automatic transmission) and the manual-only "R2 Limited", priced at 2,098,000 Yen.

Based on the M Package, B2 apparently stood for "Blue & Bright." although the Twilight Blue Mica shade chosen for the vehicle was hardly the brightest in the Mazda range and the black interior was rather austere. Limited to 1000 examples, the main features included a dark

blue soft-top, highly-polished seven-spoke alloys, chrome door mirrors, moquette-trimmed bucket seats, chrome dial surrounds, and a combined CD/cassette/radio unit. Air conditioning was available as an option.

The 500-off R2 Limited (based on the S Special Type I) came in Chaste White, despite the R2 appellation standing for "Racy & Red"! It was actually a reference to the red and black interior, which included red leather seats. Bridgestone Potenza tires came on 6J x 15 five-spoke alloys, while the aluminum alloy gearknob, shift plate and handbrake lever were revived, along with the chrome dial surrounds found on the B2 version.

Attacking MG in Britain
On 12 June 1996, Mazda UK announced two new limited edition models - the MX-5 1.6 "Monaco" and the MX-5 1.8 "Merlot." From the press release, it was obvious that these latest additions were aimed squarely at a certain Rover Group product: "The Mazda MX-5 Monaco costs £13,750 - which is £2645 below the price of the cheapest MGF - while the high specification MX-5 Merlot costs nearly £2500 less than the MGF VVC, at £16,350.

"Finished in British Racing Green and fitted with a tan hood, the Monaco is mechanically identical to the MX-5 1.6i. Special features of this limited edition roadster include alloy wheels and a radio/cassette player. The MX-5 Monaco has a top speed of 109mph [174kph].

"The luxurious Merlot - which has a special deep lustrous red body colour called Vin Rouge - has [light gray] leather upholstery, quality wood trim, a CD sound system, alloy wheels and power-assisted steering, [along with a Momo leather-trimmed steering wheel]. The 1.8-litre [car has] a top speed of 123mph [197kph]."

Although Australian sales picked up very slightly (a 75-off Neo Green 1.8 Limited Edition boosted the annual figure), Europe was the only market to show a notable improvement. In Britain, MX-5 sales continued to strengthen, with 1996 being a bumper year ...

An American finale
In 1997, the MX-5 Miata was included in the American *Automobile* magazine's "All Stars" listing for the seventh consecutive year, although the $19,675 price was a far cry from that advertised at the start of the decade. 1997's color schemes remained the same as the 1996 Model Year, but the options were revised once again.

The Power Steering Package included power-assisted steering and wheel trim rings, while the new Touring Package listed power steering, a leather-wrapped steering wheel, electric windows, electrically-adjustable door mirrors, alloy wheels and door pockets. The latest Popular Equipment Package had everything in the Touring Package, plus a Torsen lsd (for manual cars), the rear subframe performance rods, speakers in the headrests, cruise control and an electric aerial. The Leather Package built on the Popular Equipment Package with a tan leather interior and tan vinyl top. The R Package (for manual cars only) incorporated an uprated suspension with Bilstein shock absorbers, rear subframe performance rods, a Torsen lsd, front and rear spoilers, a rear skirt, and alloy wheels with locking wheelnuts.

Separate options included a detachable hardtop, air conditioning, four-sensor, three-channel ABS brakes, the Mazda Premium Sound System, and a four-speed automatic transmission with 'Hold' facility. Accessories, such as polished alloys, stainless treadplates, racing stripes, a boot-mounted luggage rack, rear spoiler, aero parts kit, tonneau cover, front "bra," foglights and a CD changer, were also offered by dealerships.

The M Edition for the 1997 Model Year was finished in a shade known as Marina Green Mica, set off by the contrasting tan leather trim and hood. Other features included highly-polished 15-inch

The MX-5 Dakar special edition, of which, 400 were made.

six-spoke alloy wheels, stainless treadplates, special floormats, Nardi wooden gearknob and handbrake trim, a CD player, and air conditioning.

A press release dated 1 July described the latest American special edition - the $22,520 "STO Edition", limited to 1500 examples. It read: "Highlighting the 1997.5 STO Edition is Twilight Blue Mica paint, topped off by a tan leather interior and tan vinyl top. In addition to the unique paint scheme, the STO Edition features special Enkei 15-inch wheels and low-profile 50-series tires; rear lip spoiler; STO Edition logos on the floormats; Nardi leather shift knob (manual transmission only); stainless steel scuff plates; an STO Edition sequentially numbered dash plaque, and certificate of authenticity.

"The car is also equipped with a full complement of luxury features, including headrest speakers, leather-wrapped steering wheel, power mirrors, power windows and a CD player. The only options are air conditioning and a four-speed automatic transmission."

In SCCA racing, the Miata continued on its winning ways again after a couple of lean years - Pratt Cole took the E-Production title and Michael Galati claimed Showroom Stock B honours.

Interestingly, there was no 1998 Model Year Miata in the States - the Second Generation car was classed as a 1999 model.

UK news

In January 1997, the 400-off "Dakar" Limited Edition was announced. Priced at £17,210 on the road, it was finished in Twilight Blue Metallic, with the interior coming in mid-gray leather with dark blue piping. Other features included unique 15-inch alloy wheels, burr walnut trim, a chrome rear brace bar, chrome treadplates, a Momo leather-trimmed steering wheel, Dakar floormats in gray with dark blue edging, a radio/ cassette unit, and power-assisted steering. Each vehicle had a numbered plaque and 'Dakar' badging.

By the spring of 1997, a high-level brake light had found its way onto the bootlid; the interior light was now incorporated into a new rearview mirror, and the 1.8i now had the same boot release arrangement as that found on the 1.8iS.

In May 1997, Mazda UK announced the special edition MX-5 "Monza," finished in British Racing Green and priced at £14,595. Limited to just 800 examples, it featured five-spoke alloy wheels with locking wheelnuts, an uprated sound system and exclusive 'Monza' badging, in addition to the standard equipment of the 1.6i upon which it was based.

A fortnight later, it was followed by the MX-5 "Harvard." Based on the MX-5 1.8i in Silver Stone Metallic, it was equipped with power steering, 15-inch five-spoke alloy wheels, burgundy leather upholstery with gray piping, a CD player, immobilizer, chrome brace bar, wood trim, a Momo leather-wrapped steering wheel, high-level stop lamp, locking wheelnuts, polished treadplates, and special floormats with the Harvard logo.

The Harvard was priced at £17,495. To put this into perspective, the July price list quoted £14,410 for the 1.6i, the 1.8i was exactly £1000 more, while the 1.8iS was £18,510. Mica and metallic paint finishes cost £250 extra, leather trim added £923 to the list price, and air conditioning (available on the 1.8 liter cars only) was a hefty £1395.

In October 1997, the final changes were made to take the car into 1998 until the new model's introduction. Both the 1.6i and 1.8i received power steering as standard, and the 1.8iS wheels were changed to 6J x 15 five-spoke alloys - actually the same as those employed on the Japanese VR Limited models, but very similar to those found on the Harvard, only with dished centres.

At the same time, the 1.8i-based MX-5 "Classic" was launched. Finished in Brilliant Black, it featured black leather

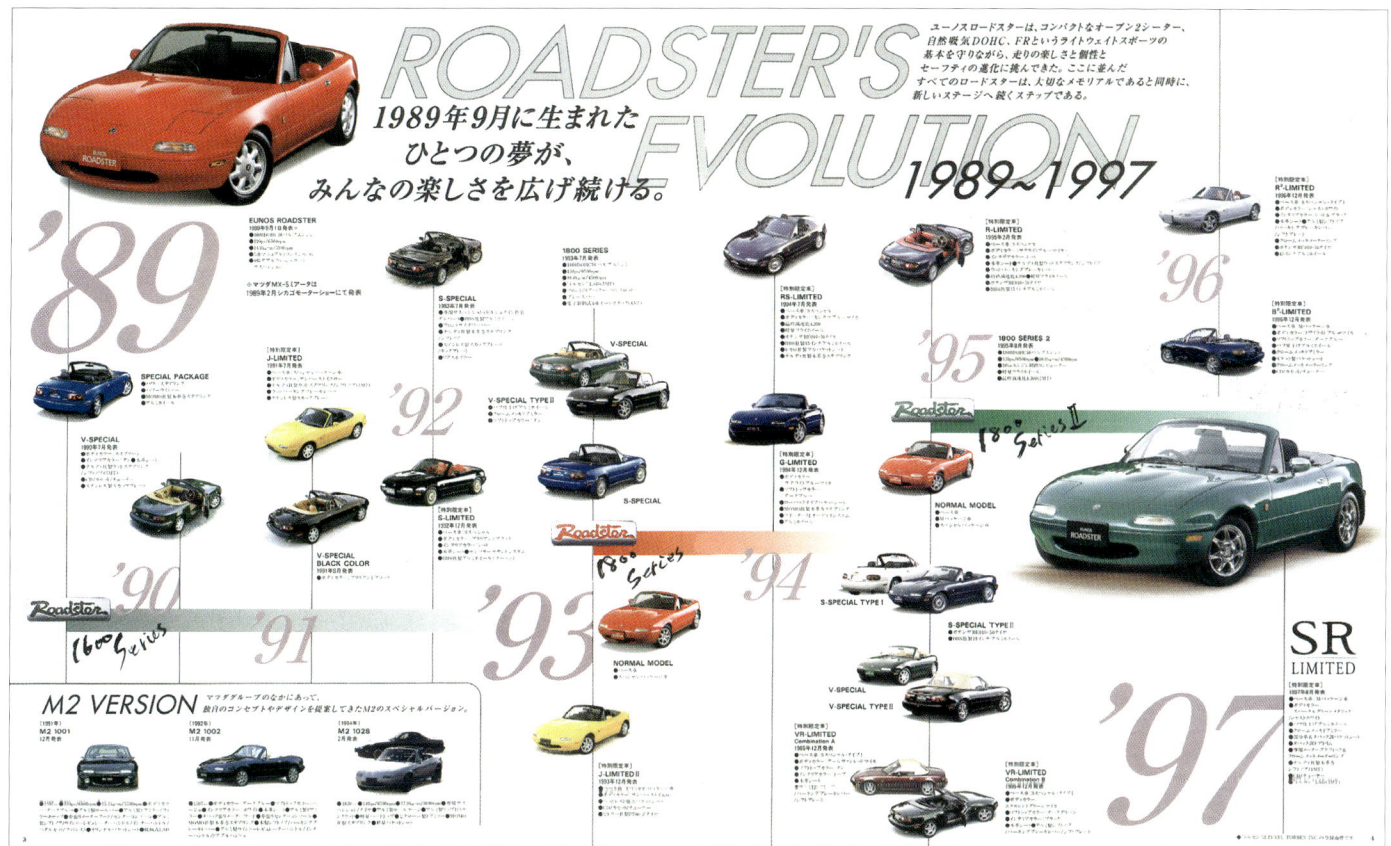

ROADSTER'S EVOLUTION 1989~1997

1989年9月に生まれた
ひとつの夢が、
みんなの楽しさを広げ続ける。

'89 '90 '91 '92 '93 '94 '95 '96 '97

M2 VERSION

SR LIMITED

seat facings with red stitching, 15-inch five-spoke alloys with locking wheelnuts, wood trim, a stainless steel rear brace bar, polished treadplates, a Momo leather-trimmed steering wheel, floormats in black with red edging, 'Classic' badging, and an RDS radio/cassette unit.

The final version of the First Generation MX-5 was announced in January 1998 - the limited edition "Berkeley," finished in Sparkle Green Metallic. Only 400 were produced, with the leading features being a black leather interior with contrasting light gray on the seat facings and door panels, 15-inch five-spoke alloy wheels with locking wheelnuts, a chrome boot rack, a stainless steel rear brace bar, stainless treadplates, dark burr wood trim, a Momo leather-wrapped steering wheel, black leather gearlever and

handbrake gaiter, a CD player, black floormats edged in gray, a numbered plaque on the centre console, and 'Berkeley' badges. It was priced at a very reasonable £17,600.

End of an era

The home market range for the 1997 Model Year was unchanged from that which resulted from the reshuffle in the latter half of 1995; standard color schemes were also unaltered. Prices had risen slightly over the last couple of years, but not by a great deal compared with those of the export markets. For instance, the basic model was 1,770,000 Yen in December 1996, while, at the other end of the scale, the V Special Type II started at 2,470,000 Yen.

In August 1997, the "SR Limited" was announced to celebrate the eighth anniversary of

the Eunos Roadster in Japan. Based on the M Package, two color options were available: Sparkle Green Metallic (the same color as that seen on the British Berkeley), and Chaste White. The standard Momo steering wheel with airbag was employed (shortly after the launch of the SR Limited, dual airbags became an option), but it had highly-polished seven-spoke alloys, black leather seats with light gray nubuck-type inserts, chrome door mirrors, chrome dial surrounds, a CD/tuner, and a Nardi leather gearknob to distinguish it from the rest of the line-up.

Mazda had a new model in the wings, however. The Second Generation MX-5 was eagerly awaited and, at the 1997 Tokyo Show, the car everyone wanted to see was finally unveiled ...

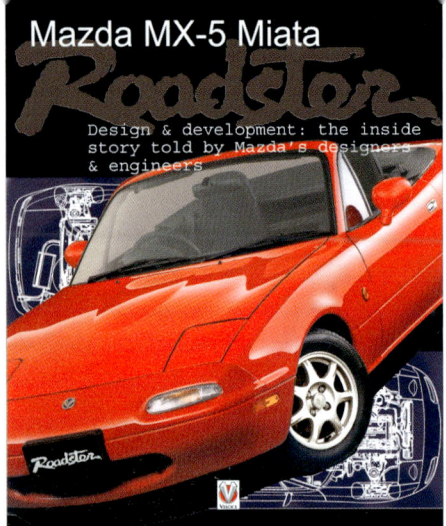

Appendix
Awards, sales & production figures

Date	Award Title	Publication	Country
1989	Most Fun, Chicago Auto Fair awards	*Autoweek*	USA
	Five Best Cars in the World (inaugural awards)	*Road & Track*	USA
	Marketing Initiative of the Year, *Autocar & Motor* Awards '89 (inaugural awards)	*Autocar & Motor*	UK
	Top Ten Import Buys '90	*Motor Trend*	USA
	Hot Products for 1990	*Life*	USA
	The Holiday Gift-giving section	*Business Week*	USA
	Coupé of the Year	*Automotive News*	USA
	Best 100 Products	*Popular Science*	USA
	Top 10 of '89	*Wheels*	Australia
	Eleven Products of the Year	*Fortune*	USA
	Best Sports Car	*Autocar & Motor*	UK
1990	Grand Prix, Exterior, Best Car Interior & Exterior	*Best Car*	USA
	(one of) Best, Best and Worst of the Year '89	*Newsweek*	USA
	(one of) Best of the Decade, Design category	*Time*	USA
	Best Products of '89	*Business Week*	USA
	Best Sports Car	*Car Australia*	Australia
	Car of Australia '89	*Car Australia*	Australia
	Best Car of 1989/90	*Modern Motor*	Australia
	Car of the Year	*Wheels*	Australia
	Automobile of the Year (inaugural award)	*Automobile Magazine*	USA
	Ten Best Cars	*Car & Driver*	USA
	Best Car '89/90 & Best Sports Car '89/90	*Modern Motor*	Australia
	First Place, Import Cabriolet category	*Readers' poll Auto Motor Sports*	Germany
	Edison Best New Products	*American Marketing Awards*	USA
	Most Fun to Drive, Cars for 1990	*Playboy*	USA
	Second place, 1990 Import Car of the Year	*Motor Trend*	USA
	Best Sports Car, Driver's Choice Awards	*Motorweek*	USA
	Best Handling Car in the World	*Autocar & Motor*	UK
	Most Trouble-Free Sports Car, Initial Quality Study	J.D. Power & Associates	USA
	Best Value Sports Car of the Year	*Buying Cars*	UK
	Sporting Car of the Year	*Middlesborough North Eastern Gazette*	UK
	Best Sports Car	*Newcastle Journal*	UK
	Top Ten Trouble-Free Cars	*Motor Trend*	USA

	Ten Best Cars in the World & Best Category Sports/GT ($13,000-21,000)	*Road & Track*	USA
	Top 10 of '90	*Wheels*	Austraila
	Car of the Year '90	New Zealand Motoring Writers Guild	NZ
	Best Sports Car	National Roads & Motorists Association	Australia
	Prize of Honor '91	*Danish Club of Motorjournalists*	Denmark
	Ten Best Cars	*Car and Driver*	USA
1991	Sexiest Car For Your Girlfriend	*Playboy*	USA
	1991 All Stars	*Automobile Magazine*	USA
	Ten Best Cars	*Car and Driver*	USA
	Best Import Cabriolet	Readers' poll, *Auto Motor und Sports*	Germany
	First Place, Fun Car Category, Auto Trophy '92	Readers' poll, *Auto Zeitung*	Germany
	Best Sports Car of the Year '91	*What Car?*	UK
	Best Sports Car, Driver's Choice Awards	*Motorweek*	USA
	Best Sports Car, Under $45,000	National Roads and Motorists Association	Australia
1992	Top 10 of '91	*Wheels*	Australia
	1992 All Stars	*Automobile Magazine*	USA
	First Place, Fun Car category, Auto Trophy '92	Readers' poll, *Auto Zeitung*	Germany
	Ten Best Cars	*Car and Driver*	USA
	Best Import Cabriolet	Readers' poll, *Auto Motor und Sports*	Germany
	Best Buys of 1992 Sports Car. Under $47,000 Category	Royal Automobile Club of Victoria	Australia
	Top 10 of '92	*Wheels*	Australia
1993	1993 All Stars	*Automobile Magazine*	USA
	Auto Trophy Best Fun Car	*Auto Zeitung*	Germany
	Best Import Cabriolet	Readers' poll, *Auto Motor und Sports*	Germany
	Top 10 of '93	*Wheels*	Australia
1994	1994 All Stars	*Automobile Magazine*	USA
	Top 10 of '94	*Wheels*	Australia
1995	1995 All Stars	*Automobile Magazine*	USA
	Most Problem-Free in Class	J.D. Power and Associates	USA
	Best Sports Car in 1995	*Auto Express*	UK
	Top 10 of '95	*Wheels*	Australia
1996	1996 All Stars	*Automobile Magazine*	USA
	Best Value in the Base Sports Car category	*IntelliChoice*	USA
	Perfect Ten	*Automobile Magazine*	USA
	Second Place, 1996 Cars Reliability	*Consumer Reports*	USA
	MY96 Most Fun to Drive Car	*Consumer Reports*	USA
	Best Buy in Sports Coupé/Sedan Category	*Consumer Digest*	USA
	Top 10 of '96	*Wheels*	Australia
1997	1997 All Stars	*Automobile Magazine*	USA
	Ten Best Cars (New MX-5)	*Car & Driver*	USA
	Top 10 of '97	*Wheels*	Australia
1998	1998 Ten Best Cars	*Car & Driver*	USA
	Best Buy in Sport Coupé/sedan Category	*Consumer Digest*	USA
	1998 Best Sports Car	*Autocar*	NZ
	1998 Best Convertible car	*Auto Express*	UK
	IBCAM Auto Design Award	The Institute for Vehicle Technology, sponsored by British Steel	UK
	Sports Car of the Year	Scottish Car of the Year	Scotland
	Best Buy	*Consumer Digest*	USA
	Top 10 of '98	*Wheels*	Australia
1999	Used Car winner Sports Car	*Auto Express*	UK
	1999 Ten Best Car	*Car & Driver*	USA
	1999 All Star	*Automobile Magazine*	USA
	Best Buy	*Consumer Report*	USA
	Sports & Coupé winner	*Good Housekeeping*	UK
	Sports winner under £10,000	*Used Car Buyer*	UK
	Eight Great Rides	*Sports Compact Car*	USA
2000	Best Convertible	*Motor Week*	USA
	IntelliChoice 2000 Best Overall of the Year Award, A Best Base Sport	*Intllichoice*	USA
	Eight Great Rides	*Sports Compact Car*	USA
	Top Picks for 2000 in driving fun category	*Consumer Reports*	USA
	All Star	*Automobile Magazine*	USA
	Guinness World Records	Guinness World Records Ltd.	UK

Sales figures in major export markets

	USA	Canada	Germany	United Kingdom	Other EEC Sales
1989	23,052	2827	0	0	0
1990	35,944	3906	3198	2168	3901
1991	31,240	2956	6131	2112	5807
1992	24,964	2277	3194	1001	2436
1993	21,588	1501	2377	891	1556
1994	21,400	1173	2791	1250	978
1995	20,174	934	2910	2910	1356
1996	18,408	558	2924	3855	2806
1997	17,218	594	2571	4942	2953
1998	19,843	1047	6390	6307	4129
Total	**233,831**	**17,773**	**32,486**	**25,436**	**25,922**

Export figures

	North America	Europe	Oceania	South America	Middle East	S.E. Asia	Africa	Others	Total
1989	32,022	508	995	452	1	18	0	25	34,021
1990	48,367	15,380	2194	788	1	11	207	452	67,400
1991	31,013	8026	549	609	3	241	129	159	40,729
1992	26,028	6492	466	466	0	402	24	218	34,096
1993	22,371	4067	736	418	0	187	7	123	27,909
1994	23,170	5408	211	72	3	191	2	22	29,079
1995	18,485	8533	336	60	44	60	119	11	27,648
1996	18,943	9556	251	21	17	409	20	14	29,231
1997	12,568	9836	129	140	26	127	26	4	22,856
1998	25,332	21,232	1673	74	0	14	19	8	48,352
Total	**258,299**	**89,038**	**7540**	**3100**	**95**	**1660**	**553**	**1036**	**361,321**

Production figures & domestic sales

	Total Production	Domestic Sales
1989	45,278	9307
1990	95,640	25,226
1991	63,434	22,594
1992	52,712	18,657
1993	44,743	16,789
1994	39,623	10,830
1995	31,886	7178
1996	33,610	4413
1997	27,037	3537
1998	58,682	10,172
Total	**492,645**	**128,703**

Certificate issued by the Guinness Book of Records.

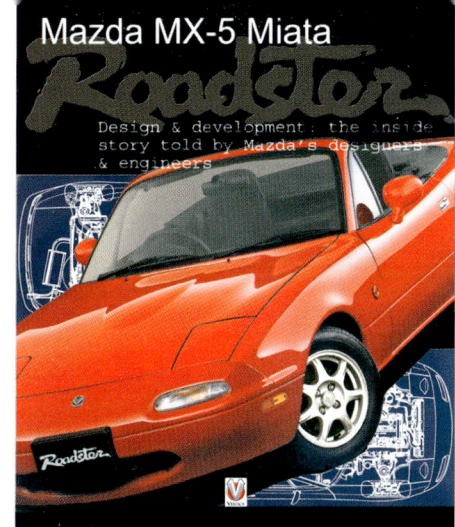

Index

Mazda and its products are mentioned throughout this book.